New Suburban Stories

Bloomsbury Studies in the City

Series Editors: Lawrence Phillips, Head of Regent's American College and Professor of English and Cultural Criticism, Regents University London, UK. Matthew Beaumont, Senior Lecturer in English, University College London, UK.

Editorial Board:

Professor Rachel Bowlby (University College London, UK); Brycchan Carey, Reader in English Literature (Kingston University London, UK); Professor Susan Alice Fischer (City University of New York, USA); Professor Pamela Gilbert (University of Florida, USA); Professor Richard Lehan (University of California, USA); Professor John McLeod (University of Leeds, UK); Alex Murray, Lecturer (University of Exeter, UK); Professor Deborah Epstein Nord (Princeton University, USA); Professor Douglas Tallack (University of Leicester, UK); Professor Philip Tew (Brunel University, UK); Professor David Trotter (University of Cambridge, UK); Professor Judith Walkowitz (Johns Hopkins University, USA); Professor Julian Wolfreys (Loughborough University, UK).

The history of literature is tied to the city. From Aeschylus to Addison, Baudelaire to Balzac, Conrad to Coetzee and Dickens to Dostoevsky, writers make sense of the city and shape modern understandings through their reflections and depictions. The urban is a fundamental aspect of a substantial part of the literary canon that is frequently not considered in and of it self because it is so prevalent.

Bloomsbury Studies in the City captures the best contemporary criticism on urban literature. Reading literature, drama and poetry in their historical and social context and alongside urban and spatial theory, this series explores the impact of the city on writers and their work.

Titles in the Series:

G.K. Chesterton, London and Modernity
Edited by Matthew Beaumont and Matthew Ingleby
Irish Writing London: Volumes 1 and 2
Edited by Tom Herron
London in Contemporary British Literature
Edited by Nick Hubble, Philip Tew and Lynn Wells
Salman Rushdie's Cities
Vassilena Parashkevova

New Suburban Stories

Edited by

Martin Dines
and
Timotheus Vermeulen

BLOOMSBURY

LONDON · NEW DELHI · NEW YORK · SYDNEY

Bloomsbury Academic
An imprint of Bloomsbury Publishing Plc

50 Bedford Square	1385 Broadway
London	New York
WC1B 3DP	NY 10018
UK	USA

www.bloomsbury.com

Bloomsbury is a registered trade mark of Bloomsbury Publishing Plc

First published 2013

British Library Cataloguing-in-Publication Data
A catalogue record for this book is available from the British Library.

ISBN: HB: 978-1-4725-1093-8
ePub: 978-1-4725-1488-2
ePDF: 978-1-4725-1032-7

Library of Congress Cataloging-in-Publication Data
New Suburban Stories / Edited by Martin Dines and Timotheus Vermeulen.
pages cm. – (Bloomsbury Studies in the City)
Summary: "An international team of scholars explore representations of the suburbs in
contemporary literature, film and culture"– Provided by publisher.
Includes bibliographical references and index.
ISBN 978-1-4725-1093-8 (Hardcover) – ISBN 978-1-4725-1488-2 (eBook (ePub)) –
ISBN 978-1-4725-1032-7 (eBook (PDF))   1. Suburbs in mass media.   2. Suburbs in
literature.   3. Suburbs in motion pictures.   4. Suburbs in art.   I. Dines, Martin, 1976–
II. Vermeulen, Timotheus.
P96.S9N49   2013
307.74–dc23
2013024850

Typeset by Newgen Imaging Systems Pvt Ltd, Chennai, India
Printed and bound in Great Britain

Contents

Illustrations

Acknowledgements

We would like to thank first and foremost our contributors for their commitment and enthusiasm. We are also extremely grateful for the support of Kingston University's Faculty of Arts and Social Sciences, which in June 2011 hosted the two-day conference 'Peripheral Visions: Suburbs, Representation and Innovation', which brought together the book's contributors and initiated much productive dialogue. Particular thanks to the various but equally vital contributions go out to the conference made by David Rogers, Vesna Goldsworthy, Rob Shields, Justine Embury and Simone Knox. Thanks also to Jo Gill for her considered observations on a draft of the anthology's introduction, and to Duncan White for pointing us toward the work of suburban artists. Last but not least, we would like to thank our partners Ines and Sergio for their constant support, good humour and love.

Introduction: New Suburban Stories

Martin Dines and Timotheus Vermeulen

In almost every large city, the space of truth is its suburbs [. . .] It's in the suburbs that there is vitality, deception, depression, energy, utopia, autonomy, craziness, creativity, destruction, ideas, young people, hope, fights to be fought, audaciousness, disagreements, problems, and dreams. It's in the suburbs that today's big issues are written on the building facades. It's in the suburbs that today's reality can be grasped, and it's in the suburbs that the pulse of vitality hurts. It's in the suburbs that there is necessity and urgency. It's the suburbs that will save the city center from a most certain death!
(Thomas Hirschhorn in Cruzvillegas, 2010)

'Each space', the literary theorist Franco Moretti writes, 'determines, or at least encourages, its own kind of story' (2007, p. 70). The Paris of Balzac encourages another kind of story to the London of Dickens; the Helsinki of Aki Kaurismaki lends itself to tales for which the Rome of Fellini is much less suited. In a similar vein, the frontier spaces of South American gaucho literature and of North American westerns help produce particular narratives quite distinct from those focused on ocean wastes, desert islands, or indeed pastoral locales. Stories of the city, the countryside and all kinds of wilderness have come under sustained, intensive scrutiny. Their generic parameters have been mapped extensively, their political and cultural import debated at length. But what of the suburbs? These are environments in which an ever increasing proportion of the world's population resides; many countries may now justifiably be described as having become 'suburban nations', since a plurality or even a majority of their citizens now live in suburbs. Undoubtedly suburbs too produce stories. Yet unlike the stories of other spaces, suburban stories are frequently maligned, misrecognized or simply ignored. This anthology is about suburban stories. It examines all kinds of representation that have emerged from and in response to these proliferating places. It explores stories of longing and community, of travelling and being at home, of growing up and growing old. To be sure, these stories, just like the locales and people they represent, are hugely varied. But, this book will convey, there remains something about these narratives which is still distinctly, and interestingly, *suburban*.

The title of *New Suburban Stories* is in part inspired by the recent and perhaps single most important development in the study of suburban environments: that which has come to be known as the 'New Suburban History'. Largely North American in its focus, this revisionist historiography has sought to demonstrate how suburban habitats have always been much more socially complex than is usually appreciated. The likes of Becky Nicolaides (2002), Mark Clapson (2003) and Andrew Wiese (2005), for instance, have challenged the assumptions of earlier writers who held that racial and class difference played no significant role in these supposedly uniformly white, bourgeois enclaves; Sylvie Murray (2003) meanwhile has contested the long-established and widely held belief that post-war American society, and suburban femininity in particular, was entirely family oriented and politically passive. Two of the limitations of much of the New Suburban History, though, are that the focus is almost exclusively on the United States, and that cultural representations of suburbs tend to be regarded as having helped establish a narrow set of preconceptions about suburban life. As we show below, such depictions are typically conceived as reproducing the suburbs as socially uniform and conventional, or as the unpromising or indeed dysfunctional fringe of the economically and culturally dynamic city. Yet, as suburbs have developed and diversified, new forms of creative production have arisen from and in response to them. Much of this cultural material has challenged rather than confirmed conventional understandings of what it means to live in and belong to these places.

Thus the anthology's title is also inspired by the nature of the cultural material in question. These suburban stories are 'new' inasmuch as they employ innovative techniques to engage with newly emerging environments and lifestyles and those undergoing change, not just in the United States or the United Kingdom, but across the globe. These stories are also all relatively recent, spanning the 1950s to the present. It is our contention, though, that throughout their history suburbs have rarely been static; on the contrary, they have been particularly responsive to multiple social and economic valances. Partly because of this, many suburban stories which have attained near-canonical status deserve reevaluation. The contributors to this volume then are themselves telling new suburban stories. Some are focused on new suburbs, new kinds of suburb, or indeed new ways of conceiving suburban space. Many examine imaginative responses to suburbs; others reappraise the work of cultural producers strongly associated with the suburbs, identifying in their stories a special understanding or appreciation of these lives and places that has previously gone unnoticed.

Some of the subject matter examined by the contributors to this book would be easily recognized by most readers as 'stories': published fiction – mainly novels – and film. But perhaps other material included seems less obviously to constitute narrative as such: lyric poetry and public performances, photography and maps, and memorials and community initiatives. Our broad conception of 'story' is purposeful. Hitherto film and television, but most of all literary fiction, has dominated the study of suburban culture (Jurca, 2001; Beuka, 2004; Hapgood, 2005; O'Reilly, 2012). Probably this is because such material is so widely available, and understood to be especially influential; it also has to do with the relative salience of the study of literature and cinema in the academy. But such assumptions and attention marginalize many rich sources of suburban culture which, our contributors demonstrate, are able to convey acutely social and physical change, as well as the experience of such transformations. Further, these texts are situated – often in a contestatory manner – within wider narratives about suburban representation. They indicate that established paradigms for narrating and conceptualizing suburban space are outmoded or limiting.

The central word of this book's title, 'suburban', is perhaps the most expansive term of all, and the hardest to define. Just what makes a story, or indeed a place, 'suburban' and not, say, urban or rural? One might perhaps think that a suburban story is simply a story about the suburbs. But must it also be set there? Reciprocally, must all stories set in suburbs be about their location? Another important question is to what extent it is sensible to talk about stories arising from Australian commuter belts, Brazilian favelas or French banlieues as suburban? Just where does the suburban story begin and end?

The difficulty of determining the remit and extent of the suburban story is demonstrated by the numerous attempts of scholars to locate it. Typically, the suburban story is rendered intelligible only through binary pairs; it either adheres to one clichéd co-ordinate or its opposite, or else exists – somewhere – between the two. This is especially true for the more widely discussed Anglo-Saxon variant. The social historian Mark Clapson, for instance, writes that the American suburban story 'has tended to view suburbia as either a heaven or a hell, within a fairly limited range of conventions' (2003, p. 11). The architectural historian John Archer, in slightly more worldly terms, argues that the suburban story should be located somewhere between the 'ideological strands [. . .] property, pastoralism, and fragmentation' (2009, p. 14). And television scholar David Marc observes that suburban television 'romanticized the suburb as an idyllic small town that was located not merely miles from the modern city but the better part of a century as well' (1989, p. 53). While these sketches each describe the suburban story in slightly different terms, interestingly, they all use the same method. Each of them describes the suburban story and its subject matter, the suburb, by way of a negative analogy. Clapson's compares the suburb to heaven and hell, Archer's sees the resemblances in premodern pastoralism and postmodern fragmentation, while Marc's evokes the figures of the small town and the city. The suburban story has things in common with these metaphors, genres and spaces, but it not reducible to any of them. According to these authors, in other words, the suburb lacks a story of its own; its story is always already another's flawed story.

The closest anyone has come to defining the suburban narrative in its own terms is to suggest it is an in-between, a middle. As Roger Silverstone puts it in his introduction to *Visions of Suburbia*: the suburban story creates 'middle cultures in middle spaces in middle America, Britain and Australia' (1997, p. i). But the definition of the suburban story as a middle is no less dependent on external entities than the method of the analogy. For to say something is a middle is to beg the question: the middle of what? It still describes the tradition in terms of what it is not.

We may call this process of othering the production of a 'second' space, a space that is defined by what it is not. The phrase 'second space' echoes, of course, Simone de Beauvoir's 1949 study *The Second Sex*. In this foundational feminist text de Beauvoir contends that women are defined uniquely and exclusively in a negative relationship to men. One is a woman, in other words, because she is not a man. 'Man', she famously writes,

> represents both the positive and the neutral, as is indicated by the common use of man to designate human beings in general; whereas woman represents only the negative, defined by limiting criteria, without reciprocity. [. . .] She is defined and differentiated with reference to man and not he with reference to her; she is the incidental, the inessential as opposed to the essential. He is the Subject, he is the Absolute – she is the Other. (1997, pp. 15–16)

More has been written about this particular fragment than we can possibly reiterate here. For our purposes, the second sentence is the most interesting. Women are defined, de Beauvoir writes, by 'limiting criteria, without reciprocity'. What she says here, in other words, is that woman's negative definition produces an uneven division of power between men and women. Women compete in a game whose rules are set by men, i.e. where men are the standard. Women might do well, but they can never win. In de Beauvoir's view, then, the idea of emancipation is pointless as long as the aim is to be more like men. What is needed, she asserts, is an equality based on the mutual acknowledgement of difference.

There is a similar mechanism at work in the above-cited approaches to the suburb. Indeed, it is remarkable how many of de Beauvoir's assertions about women's apparent lack applies also to popular perceptions of the suburbs and suburbanites: 'they have no past', she writes, 'no history, no religion of their own'; they lack solidarity, and 'live dispersed' (ibid., p. 19). One could easily exchange this for Beuka's indictment of the fictional suburb as 'homogenized, soulless, plastic landscape of tepid conformity, an alienating "noplace"' (Beuka, 2004, p. 4). Just as women are defined by the restrictive principles of men, the suburban text tends to be defined by the limiting criteria of other genres. The analogy is further reinforced when one considers how suburbs have long been treated as the feminine counterpart to cities.

Taking inspiration from de Beauvoir, the aim of this volume is twofold. First, *New Suburban Stories* seeks to develop a new linguistic game, a new discourse, in which equality is based not on illusions of sameness but on the mutual acknowledgment of difference. Paying close attention to matters of composition and style, rhythm and tone, spatial practice and cultural geography, the essays in this anthology describe suburban stories from across the globe not in terms of analogy but in terms of distinction. Secondly, this volume seeks to emancipate suburban stories according to the logic of this new discourse. What is important here is that suburban stories be considered a tradition – or perhaps a practice – that is worthy of study in its own right. Far from a second space, the suburb and the stories that emerge in response to it simply denote another kind of space existing alongside (though often interacting with) the spaces and temporalities of the twentieth- and twenty-first-century wasteland, countryside, small town and the city. The suburb does not lack stories of its own, it merely encourages other kinds of story, of which we need to still learn the language.

It is perhaps no wonder that the parameters of the suburban story are hard to delineate, given that no one seems to agree even on what constitutes a suburb. As Ann

Forsyth (2012) has shown in her very useful survey of the field, while many scholars writing about suburbs comment on the difficulty of defining their subject, few offer an explicit definition. Partly this frustration is has to do with the different associations the term suburb has in different national and local contexts. To be sure, there is no monolithic 'Anglo-Saxon' conception; for historical reasons suburbs are conceived in distinct ways in the United States, the United Kingdom and Australia.[1] Such difficulties are also a consequence of divergent interests that different academic disciplines bring to the study of suburbs. Urban studies and planning, geography, social history, sociology and, we would add, literary and cultural studies all tend to advance different criteria. Many studies, though by no means all, begin by describing *physical* characteristics. These are typically locational or morphological: indeed, the very word 'suburb' implies a spatial relationship (denoting a place at or beyond the limits of a city, or at least beyond its centre); or otherwise relates differences in scale (for instance, suburbs are characteristically less dense and low rise compared to the city). Some studies emphasize *function*: for example, by defining suburbs as primarily residential spaces (Dunham-Jones and Williamson, 2009), or as being economically dependent on the urban centre (Clapson, 2003, p. 2). More historically focused studies emphasize *process*: the mechanisms which bring suburbs into being such as property speculation and the development of transport infrastructures (Hayden, 2003); or the ways in which suburbs subsequently transition into other kinds of spaces, for instance, by taking on attributes that are more obviously urban (Tuan, 1979, pp. 225–40); the assumption here is that suburbs are essentially recent. Yet other studies stress the importance of *social* aspects. The historian Robert Fishman (1987) insists that suburbia ought to be understood as a specifically middle-class utopia; others articulate an identifiably suburban 'way of life', involving, for instance, owner occupation, the nuclear family and commuting (Teaford, 2008).

It is probable that no single criterion detailed above is sufficient alone to define suburbanity. For instance, if we define a suburb as being beyond the city centre, it still may be impossible to determine where the city ends and the suburb begins, or for that matter what constitutes the outer limits of the suburb. On the other hand, it is easy to see how several of these criteria, either individually or cumulatively, might exclude

---

[1] In the United States, suburbs tend to be understood as places which lie beyond the city limits and which are self-governing; their existence owes in large part to a shared desire (which took its most notorious form as 'white flight' in the early to mid-twentieth century) to be socially, politically and fiscally independent from the central city (see Harris and Larkham, 1999). By contrast, in Australia the potential purlieu of the term 'suburb' is much broader. In part because municipal government in Australian cities has historically been fractured across numerous authorities, 'suburb' (often taking the prefix 'inner', or even 'inner-city') is readily employed to describe areas immediately beyond a city's central business district. In Britain, suburbs are not usually understood to be self-governing; spatially, suburbs correspond to a rather indistinct borderland, a consequence of the continual outward expansion of London throughout the centuries. Most neighbourhoods within the currently constituted borders of the capital once lay outside its boundaries. As well as their being a whole host of overlapping official demarcations of the city's limits, and between 'inner' and 'outer' London, all manner of borders are used informally to mark the limits of 'London proper', from the River Thames to the orbital M25 motorway or the edge of the pre-1965 County of London. Many areas fall between different sets of boundaries, resulting in disagreements over their status. (In Chapter 14, Nichola Smalley wrestles with some of these issues when locating the neighbourhood of Tottenham; indeed, she reminds us that the term 'inner city', like 'suburb', provides no straightforward indication of location.)

that which might intuitively be understood to be suburban. For example, if a suburb is conceptualized as a low-rise, residential and middle-class environment, then what of high-rise suburban estates, or industrial and working-class suburbs? If a suburb is by definition recent, does this preclude the possibility of historic suburbs? Perhaps the obvious way forward is to avoid any limiting definition comprised of necessary and sufficient conditions and simply accept that suburbs are highly varied spaces. Suburbanity, then, possesses no truly essential qualities; rather, following Wittgenstein (1953), suburbs share a family resemblance, that is, certain features are common to some suburbs but not all. Further, the significance of the suburb may be seen to be determined by its *use* within a particular linguistic or cultural context.

Alternatively, perhaps the time has come to abandon the critical concept of the suburb altogether. Indeed several observers have argued that the traditional distinction between city and suburb is no longer meaningful. The form and function of metropolitan environments, and the processes which govern their development, are so radically altered as to require whole new 'post-suburban' vocabulary: 'urban villages' (Leinberger and Lockwood, 1986) 'technoburbs' (Fishman, 1987); 'edge cities' (Garreau, 1991); 'ethnoburbs' (Li, 1998); 'edgeless cities' (Lang, 2003); and 'boomburbs' (Lang and LeFurgy, 2007). This neologizing zeal is also prompted by an understanding that what we tend to speak of as suburbs are in fact highly dynamic and diversified environments, built for different purposes and functioning according to different modi operandi. But despite this diversity the following generalities about post-suburbia may reasonably be asserted: across the globe suburbs have become more urban in function if not in form, and operate within broader polycentric metropolitan systems. Yet, whether understood as a new settlement type or as a new era, post-suburbia is by no means immune to the problems of definition that beset the suburbs (Phelps and Woo, 2011). Just as the suburb is etymologically linked to the urban, the emergent nomenclature of post-suburbia is dependent on both city and suburb, suggesting less radical transformation than gradual evolution. Indeed, Jon Teaford argues that contemporary post-suburban landscapes are 'simply suburbanization carried to the extreme, the end product of two centuries of continuous deconcentration', whether residential, industrial or commercial (2011, p. 33). Furthermore, as contributors to the New Suburban History insist, it was always misleading to focus on individual suburbs in isolation, since these environments were shaped by their social, political and economic relationships with other locations, including other suburbs (Kruse and Sugrue, 2006, pp. 5–6). In other words, the defining characteristics of post-suburbia have long inhered in suburbia.

While acknowledging the potential usefulness of post-suburban categories in accounting for recent geographical developments, we favour 'suburb' because it remains today the most widely used term to designate certain kinds of environments and lifestyles. Scholars and specialists may talk of technoburbs and edgeless cities, but politicians and advertisers still invoke suburbs and target their inhabitants (Gilbert and Preston, 2003). Even as metropolitan experience becomes more decentred, signage on roads and public transport continues to indicate 'suburban' routes and services. Descriptions of metropolitan life – whether in editorial columns, literary fiction or daily conversation – still employ the term suburban to describe places, people, even moods. Indeed, so long as there is no demonym with any currency to denote those who live, work or play in post-suburbia – or, for that matter, a term used by such people as a self-ascription – it seems sensible to continue using a more traditional vocabulary in order to make sense of the stories which narrate such places.

Such a conclusion may seem anti-climactic, and even conservative. In resuming a Wittgensteinian approach to meaning, we succeed in sidelining the frantic tail-chasing involved in scholarly attempts at definition, but we risk acquiescing to established forms of knowledge. There seems little scope for any kind of radical realignment, and, for certain, few opportunities for new suburban stories. However, we would stress the ubiquity of disagreement rather than concordance. That the suburbanity of many places is frequently contested relates to an important point that is so often elided in academic accounts of suburbs. Understandings of suburbs are so frequently subjective, contingent on particular spatial relationships and experience. Two anecdotes adumbrate this. Kingston University's Centre of Suburban Studies recently organized an evening for local residents to discuss the identity of their locality: they were invited to consider whether Kingston-upon-Thames (which lies on the southwestern edge of Greater London) was a town, a suburb, or something else. Some attendees insisted the town's heritage – a Saxon burgh boasting an ancient site of coronation – meant it could not be considered a suburb. Many who claimed for Kingston the identity of a town had lived there the longest – in some cases over half a century. Others who worked in central London declared that they had always considered Kingston a dormitory suburb; those who commuted to Kingston from elsewhere said they rarely felt it to be part of London. Several declared neighbouring Surbiton to be truly suburban. It was after all, the setting for the 1970s situation comedy *The Good Life*, which satirizes middle-class pretension. (But then, as one participant insisted, unlike Kingston, Surbiton has no theatre.)

When one of the authors of this introduction spent time in a small university town on the west coast of the United States, he received very different responses upon declaring an interest in suburbs. Several – all hailing from larger American cities – suggested that the town was an ideal place to visit, since it was suburban in its entirety. However, one academic, a long-time resident of the town, implied quite the opposite when he suggested that in order to get any fieldwork done, the author would need to take a flight to San Francisco. Notably, one of the first interlocutors also described the town as idyllic – but then was startled when the author linked her two descriptions of the locality in a single expression, 'suburban idyll'; she declared that the conjunction had never occurred to her.

It is precisely this kind of short circuit which demonstrates the limitations of the kind of technical discourse which insists on definitions. In ordinary language, talk of suburbs, which so often resolves itself into stories, continually foregrounds contingency and contradiction. This does not mean that its significance is simply inchoate. Rather, it is a reminder of how any study of the suburbs must be responsive to the fluid ways in which the term is employed, both within and across national cultures; the above anecdotes after all show people demonstrating, variously, physical, processual, functional and social conceptualizations, each of which are steered by their own relationships with such places. These different criteria coalesce to produce blind spots and aporia which are indicative of the powerful and conflicting currents that suburbs produce within culture; repeatedly, the suburbs are simultaneously desired and disavowed. It is a transdisciplinary, transnational suburban study which will be best able to make sense of these currents. Moreover, it will need to look to the stories people produce, consume, reorganize and recycle in order to assess the reasons for and consequences of these prolific, diverse assemblages.

Thus we continue to employ the term suburban while being wary that its referents are contested and mutable. We are conscious too that understandings of suburbs are often culturally specific, and further, that by being written in English, this anthology may be seen to privilege distinctly Anglophone perspectives even while it explores contexts from other cultures and territories. The problems of translation are as manifold as those of definition, and these may often be witnessed during the transmission of cultural productions across national frontiers. For instance, the French action film *Banlieue 13*, which is discussed briefly by Carrie Tarr in Chapter 2, was retitled 'District 13' for English audiences; its suburban location is thus transmuted into an urban one, presumably because 'Suburb 13' fails to resonate with the film's violent and disorderly milieu. On the other hand, the Swedish film *Patrik 1.5*, which depicts a gay couple attempting to adopt an unruly teenager, takes place in a suburb which appears startlingly American, replete with white picket fences, cocktails on the lawn, a block party and even a 1950s Buick. Such overtly American imagery may be part of a conscious attempt to render a local story more legible – with the American scenery approximating 'universality' – and therefore more appealing to other national audiences. (It would not be the first gay suburban narrative to adopt this strategy; see Blues, 2010, pp. 96–7.) Alternatively, these distinctly foreign accoutrements may be understood to serve as a kind of warning to the gay couple seeking to assimilate to this heterosexist environment.

We certainly welcome further research into the ways audiences interpret and reproduce suburban representations from other cultures. The current anthology serves to contrast cultural material arising from diverse suburban locations, from the emergency developments built to house shanty dwellers on the fringe of Buenos Aires to the verdant parks of suburban Melbourne, and from the sprawl of New Jersey on the United States' east coast to the government-built flats that crowd beyond Singapore's Central Business District. The individual chapters pay close attention to the physical and social particularities of their various locales, but overall the anthology identifies new patterns in the ways suburbs have their stories told. *New Suburban Stories* identifies four distinct though related innovations across recent cultural material arising from and responding to suburban environments, and is correspondingly organized into four parts.

The first, 'Delineating the Margins', extends the above discussion of locating and defining suburban space. In particular, the chapters in this part explore changing social and spatial relations between urban centres and their peripheries following the economic and demographic transformation of cities. Such change, the authors indicate, often escapes official recognition but also confounds various orthodoxies about these places and their populations. Part I focuses especially on suburban spaces which historically have been socially or economically marginalized, and the ways such marginalization is both perpetuated and challenged through representation.

Fittingly, Adriana Massidda's chapter opens proceeding with an examination of the ways such suburbs are literally mapped. Her study focuses on cartographic representations of three neighbourhoods of social housing built in the south-western periphery of Buenos Aires by the Argentinean government as part of a plan to eradicate the informal settlements of internal migrants. Massidda shows how official and commercial maps produced over the last six decades have often been startlingly incomplete; she argues that such limited representation was not only a measure of the social and political neglect of these suburbs, but also of how the informal practices of residents continually eluded formal representation. In Chapter 2, Carrie Tarr focuses on another socially marginalized suburb – the Parisian *banlieue*. Tarr's account of the *banlieue* film, however, indicates the extent to which the genre's parameters have been dramatically altered in recent years. If earlier films focused on troubled, postcolonial masculinity and the absence of opportunities for social mobility, subsequent work by women filmmakers – exemplified by the 2010 box-office hit *Tout ce qui brille/ 'All that Glitters'* – have provided a more female-centred articulation of space, gender and ethnicity, and indeed have demonstrated the potential social porosity between city and suburb. Caroline Merkel's chapter outlines the as-yet unrecognized genre of suburban fiction in German literature. The environments described in novels like Georg Klein's *Roman unserer Kindheit* (2010) or Feridun Zaimoglu's *Kanak Sprak* (1995) might at first glance affirm ideas of the suburbs as empty and excluded places. However, Merkel's close reading of the protagonists' spatial and linguistic practices discloses the suburbs' potential as a productive contact zone. Following Yuri Lotman's semiotic concept of the peripheries as 'hot spots' of culture and Michel de Certeau's focus on the everyday practices which form space, Merkel's chapter explores the ways in which suburban stories might challenge – and expand – the social, affective and aesthetic composition of the German literary canon. In Chapter 4, Jarrad Keyes examines the radical reappraisal of the relationships between urban and suburban space to be found in the work of the British writer J. G. Ballard. While dictionary definitions of 'Ballardian' prioritize the author's dystopian vision, Keyes argues that what is truly distinctive about Ballard's oeuvre is its perspective on emergent spaces which defy interpretation via traditional binaries such as city/suburb or urban/rural. Such a revisioning is evidence of Ballard's responsiveness to what Henri Lefebvre has termed the 'urban revolution', the subsumation of all rural space to a capitalist centre, and the corresponding homogenization of all local functions according to the universal logic of the market.

Part II, 'The Past in Its Place', examines the production of history in suburban representation. Suburbs are so often seen as places outside of time, and as lacking history, having 'no archaeology to exhume' (Webster, 2000, p. 2). The presumption that newness is an essential quality of the suburb undergirds commonplace rhetoric of suburbs as frontier territories, or as landscapes of modernity, or indeed postmodernity. History is forever ceded to other environments – the city in particular; indeed, the suburb's acquisition of a past is sometimes taken as a measure of its having become some other type of place altogether. We would argue that such assumptions ignore the possibility of social and physical change of the kinds sketched by the contributors to the previous part – and the ways these changes are perceived and acted upon by suburbanites. Further, it ignores how suburban environments have increasingly become embedded in national histories. The chapters in Part II examine practices of history-making located in suburban space, and the ways these local strategies interact – sometimes conflictingly – with national narratives. Hannah Lewi and Caroline Jordan's chapter addresses the role of commemoration in suburban communities by looking at the function and use of memorials and public art works in the Melbourne suburb of Alphington Park. The authors examine a range of contested commemorative gestures built between the aftermath of the First World War and the present day. Lewi and Jordan argue that because broader national concerns tend to be referenced in suburban contexts, the inhabitants of Alphington Park are heavily invested in the creation and maintenance of memorials. Their study demonstrates that multiple traces of contested commemoration can coexist, often uneasily rubbing together in contemporary suburbia, constituting a layering rather than a replacing of narratives. Alan Mace's chapter describes how many of the London suburbs built in the early twentieth century once embodied the future – Underground posters and stations commissioned by Frank Pick both played heavily on the imagery of the electric-powered future; the future was bright. These suburbs are now 80 years old; their future has come and gone. While community formation in newly established suburbs has been the subject of a number of studies, it is less common to trace how residents manage change over time. Mace focuses on how residents employ nostalgia as a way of managing change and maintaining a sense of belonging within present-day places. Drawing on interviews with over 60 residents in three parts of outer London, many of whom spent considerable periods of time in their area, Mace argues that London suburbia is neither weighed down by its own ghosts nor the nostalgia of individuals; rather, it is a place of accommodation and of possibilities. Gaik Khoo's chapter deals with the recent attempts by filmmakers and communities to represent suburban housing estates in Singapore. Many of these projects deal with place, history and memory; several focus on estates undergoing redevelopment and their fast-disappearing landmarks. Khoo demonstrates the ways in which filmmakers make the seemingly sterile Housing Development Board flats more interesting by representing the environment as places of sensuous and affective memory that generate, authenticate and anchor a personal yet collectively shared Singapore identity. However, Khoo warns that the affective civic life created on film is not entirely independent of the state's goals for urban development; indeed, in the last 15 years the Singaporean state has set out on an agenda to use affective memory in combination with economics to develop a stronger sense of civic nationalism.

Part III, 'Aesthetics of Affect', stands as a challenge to the overwhelming tendency in all kinds of cultural criticism to see suburban stories first and foremost as vehicles for social commentary. Critics read the suburban text variously as an indictment of embourgeoisement, a metaphor for multiculturalism, or a critique of gender relations or consumerism. But they rarely take into account the stories' particular poetic and aesthetic qualities. As Catherine Jurca has noted, in reviews and popular accounts, the significance of American suburban stories 'has been cast in terms of the truth and utility of their insights into assessments of American Society rather more often than in terms of aesthetics' (Jurca, 2001, p. 15). Cain's *Mildred Pierce*, for instance, is praised for its 'anthropologist's tenacity and 'invaluable gloss on Middletown' (ibid.), while *Babbitt* is described as a 'portrait of an American Citizen', 'fiction only by a sort of courtesy' (ibid., p. 48). However, Jurca herself does little to redress this critical imbalance. In this anthology we engage with suburban stories from the perspective of the curator as much as from the perspective of the sociologist. We are concerned with how stylistic choices are influenced by particular qualities of the suburban environment, and how the suburban story as an aesthetic tradition interacts with other cultural projects. Following on from Khoo, the contributors to Part III also seek to relate how cultural producers have sought to develop a poetics, visual language or voice to better articulate to the distinctive sensual qualities of life in the suburbs. These suburban affects, however, are never ends in themselves, but always also relate to wider political and ethical concerns. Jo Gill's chapter examines the often-overlooked place of poetry in the establishment and maintenance of what we might call the suburban imaginary. The poetry of the post-war American suburbs, Gill proposes, works in thematic and formal ways to evoke and to question the conditions of the suburban everyday. A close reading of a number of poems from the 1950s and 1960s reveals traces of an emergent anxiety about the environment, a tentative testing of the relationship between centre and margin, an exaggerated vision of the burdens of contemporary manhood, and an acute sensitivity to the significance of suburban space on the construction and mediation of subjectivity. Bridget Gilman's chapter examines photographer Bill Owens's 1973 publication *Suburbia*, in order to reassess the cultural contents and impact of the American suburban image. Though many have viewed Owens's photo book as the quintessential embodiment of an all-too-quaint period of domestic aspirations, Gilman argues that *Suburbia* is neither a paean to such mainstream domesticity nor an ironic indictment of white middle-class values. Instead, the work challenges viewers to reconsider standard categories associated with the place of suburbia. Yet in spite of the richness of this project and its substantial publishing success, Owens's place in the twentieth-century photographic canon is often one of omission. His practice, perched between the rise of the 'New Documentary' movement and conceptual and postmodernist developments, raises the thorny issue of how to evaluate works that rest on the boundary of multiple image-making strategies and thus have eluded substantial art historical attention. Gilman fills this gap by placing *Suburbia* in the larger context of contemporaneous aesthetic practices and evolving sociopolitical mandates for documentary photography. Tim Foster's contribution argues that Richard Ford's Frank Bascombe trilogy – *The Sportswriter* (1986), *Independence Day* (1995), and *The Lay of the Land* (2006) – represents the suburban landscape as an environment that is constantly changed by the process of the social production of space. At the same time, through his use of first-person narration, Ford suggests the importance of language and imagination to the evolution of Frank's New Jersey setting. Using close textual analysis, Foster seeks to position Frank not as a victim of his environment but as – to use his term – its 'citizen scientist': someone who, through experience, understands that 'place means nothing' in and of itself and that it can be rearranged if its inhabitants put their minds to it. To show this Foster draws on the work of Henri Lefebvre and his notion of a spatial dialectic, both to suggest Frank as someone who is actively engaged in, and able to influence, this process, and to show how Ford sees Frank as a man apart from those Americans who seem more content to affirm the commercialized spaces of suburban sprawl. In Part III's final chapter, Neil Campbell identifies a growing appreciation that even the most generic spaces of suburbia are enlivened by the embodied knowledge and sensuous geographies experienced by the people who actually live there. Increasingly, visual and literary representations focus on how people work out 'habits of being' within their own lives and daily interactions with space and place. Campbell examines these haptic or affective landscapes, with particular reference to the 'cultural poesis' of Kathleen Stewart (such as in her *Ordinary Affects*) and the 'suburban memoirs' of D. J. Waldie in his *Holy Land* (1996). Stewart states that 'my work is an experiment that writes from the intensities in things. It asks what potential modes of knowing, relating or attending to things are already being lived in ordinary rhythms, labors, and the sensory materiality of forms of attunement to worlds' (Stewart, 2009). Campbell tracks some of these 'attunements' in Waldie's work and, in so doing, suggest some ways one might rethink contemporary notions of suburbia as an affective landscape.

The anthology's fourth and final part, 'Suburban Communities and Cultural Production', explores how suburbanites have conceived of themselves as distinct peoples with clearly defined territories. Suburbs and their inhabitants have often been the target of condescension by urban cultural elites. Increasingly, though, suburbanites have evinced a new confidence by taking matters into their own hands. The contributors to Part IV examine how suburbanites have developed cultural material and practices which help bolster community identity. At the same time, these innovations indicate how suburbanites have become critically reflective of their own situation and their relationships with wider world. Hugh Bartling's chapter examines how, as discourses of sustainability and the awareness of the environmental and health impacts of factory farming have become more widespread in recent years, many residents of suburban communities have become interested in producing their own food. While much of this activity is allowable (and encouraged) by local governments, some suburban agricultural activity falls outside the limits of permissibility in local zoning codes and land use ordinances. On the basis of case studies, interviews and discursive analysis, Bartling analyses the conflict around the specific issue of the introduction of backyard chicken-keeping in suburban communities. Looking at a variety of locales, Bartling concludes that efforts to promote chicken-keeping are reflective of a larger social ambiguity relating to the meaning of consumption, production and suburban space. Dalibor Prančević's chapter focuses on the recent activities of KVART, a collective of artists operating in Trstenik, a suburban district (or 'kvart') of Split, Croatia's second city. KVART was founded in 2006 in response to the challenges faced by the local community. On the one hand, settlements like Trstenik have been marginalized by an institutionalized vision of art and culture that locates both in the central city. On the other, since the 'liberalization' of Croatian economy, the area has been exploited by profiteering developers keen to capitalize on the privatization of public space. KVART's art activism not only draws attention to current conflicts taking place over urban and suburban spaces, but also seeks to challenge the presumption of dependence of the periphery on the centre. Prančević evaluates the group's attempts to foster more critically minded responses to suburban development as well as more active participation on the part of the local community. Nichola Smalley's chapter discusses the role played by rappers in disseminating to the wider world emerging language practices from the social and geographical contexts in which they have developed. Smalley focuses on language practices which have emerged on the peripheries of major Swedish cities and in areas of London. These practices have developed over the last 30 years among young people in areas of high ethnic and linguistic diversity. Smalley examines what she identifies to be an interplay between location and linguistic innovation. She demonstrates how hip-hop and grime artists are among the most visible practitioners of these linguistic phenomena: through their construction and performance of identities, these artists emphasize their connection with the places they live. Well-known and appreciated, these musicians fulfil a key role in the dissemination of re-appropriated language features to a wider context. Yet, this dissemination confirms the fluid, adaptable and adoptable nature of these language varieties. Not fixed to a given social or geographical environment, they are liable to flow into other receptive environments. Smalley demonstrates how this flow occurs through numerous matrices, including friendship links, online interactions and music culture. In the anthology's final chapter, Helen Wickstead explores the activities which perpetuate the legend of the 'goat boy' Lefi Ganderson as (part-spoof) heritage in the London suburb of Surbiton. She suggests that this heritage both appropriates and perpetuates largely negative representations of Surbiton. In literature and television comedy, Surbiton is defined by its ordinariness – it is the quintessential un-historic, faceless, suburb. For the self-proclaimed 'Villagers of Seething', Surbiton supplies an all-purpose suburban backdrop against which improbable scenarios play out. Reclaiming the absurd as their inheritance, the 'Villagers' celebrate the notion that suburbia is the natural home of the improbable, and that, therefore, it surely deserves an epic past. Thus, the perception of suburbs as places without an authentic connection to the past fosters creation of unauthorized heritage. The idea that suburbs lack authentic communities makes community-building, rather than authoritative factual discourse, the focus of archaeological activities. From the 'rootlessness' of suburbs spring mythical times and places that re-enchant such unprepossessing terrain.

The anthology's trajectory thus parallels our argument in this introduction: both move from matters of mapping and definition, and towards a consideration of spatial practice. If *New Suburban Stories* begins by foregrounding the changing nature of the spaces in which suburbanites reside, it concludes with an examination of suburbanites' agency in contesting and transforming their lived environments. In his encomium to the suburbs which we quoted at the beginning of the introduction, Paris-based artist Thomas Hirschhorn finds a tumult of inspiration in such struggles. While we and many of the contributors to this book would question Hirschhorn's insistence that the suburbs are seared with an authenticity that is no longer possessed by urban centres, we concur that the suburbs are frequently sites of creativity, and that such creativity is often borne of conflict. In an increasingly suburbanized world it becomes ever more important to register and respond to suburban stories – interventions which not only trace the shifting contours of suburban environments, but which also articulate competing visions of what such places might yet become.

Part I

Delineating the Margins

1

Mapping the Suburbs: Cartographic Representations of Villa Celina, Buenos Aires (1956–2011)

Adriana Massidda

This chapter examines cartographic representations of Villa Celina, an area located in the south-western suburbs of Buenos Aires, Argentina, and in particular the mapping of three neighbourhoods of social housing built in 1958–62: Barrio Vicente López y Planes, Barrio Urquiza and Barrio Sarmiento. From the time these neighbourhoods were first built, their representation in maps has often been partial or incomplete, becoming more exhaustive only in recent mappings. While all maps are inherently limited in terms of the detail which they can reproduce, in the case of the maps of the south-western suburbs the lack of detail appears particularly acute. In this chapter, the role that Barrio Vicente López y Planes, Barrio Urquiza and Barrio Sarmiento (BVLP/U/S from now on) and their inhabitants occupied in twentieth-century Argentine society are explored in relation to the mapping of Villa Celina in order to help explain the limitations of these cartographic representations.

The way in which urban maps represented BVLP/U/S has varied over time, often involving telling omissions. The same can be said about areas that have been developed more recently in Villa Celina: these places have not been portrayed fully – if at all – in the urban charts published during the last ten years. As argued through an analysis of official and commercial maps, the zones that were only partially shown were areas which did not comply with urban or legal regulations, or areas whose place in the collective imagery was to some degree controversial. There are of course technical reasons why maps are limited in the information they are able to include: each square inch of paper or screen, for example, can only support a finite amount of readable data. Distortions related to the representation of a tri-dimensional object in two dimensions inevitably occur too. However, the decisions made in order to overcome these difficulties are structured by the perspective of the cartographers, and embody a codification of their views; they are specialists empowered to decide on issues regarding urban representation. Further, there are instances in which the exclusion of information can no longer be attributed to the technical difficulties

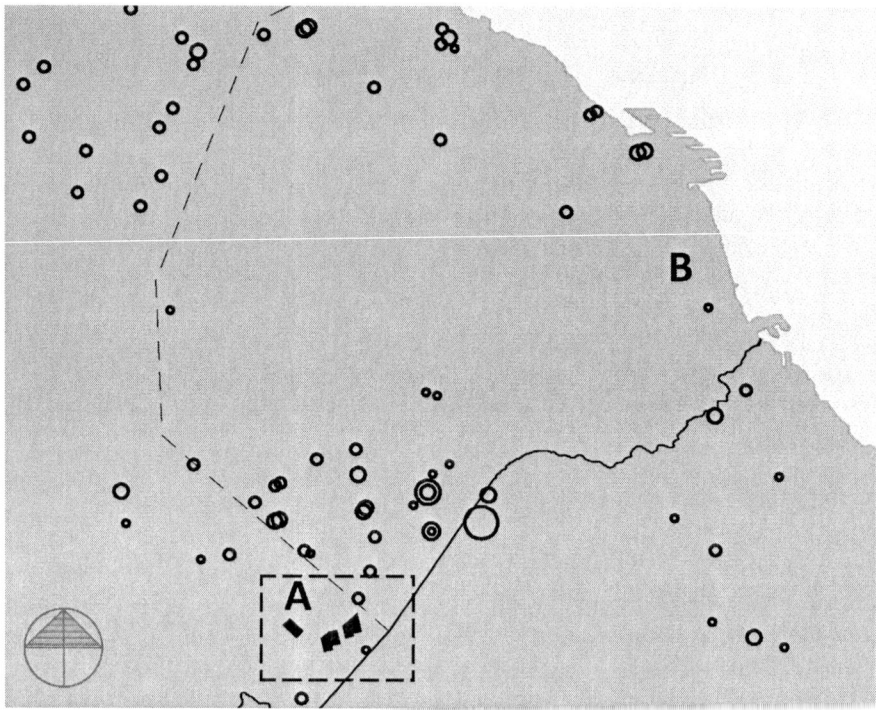

Figure 1.1 Barrio Vicente López y Planes, Barrio Urquiza y Barrio Sarmiento in context: (A) corresponds to Villa Celina, (B) to the city centre, and the lines designate the river Riachuelo and city district boundary respectively. The circles point to the shantytowns reported by the *Plan de Emergencia* (CNV, 1956). The polygons outline the neighbourhoods
Drawn by A. Massidda

of representation, such as the cases where maps represent shantytowns or black-market fairs as blank spaces, parks or water (d'Angiolillo et al., 2010, pp. 187–93). Such transfigurations rather suggest that the irregular status of these places hampers their cartographic representation. Considering the complex history of villa Celina, an area that was already fragmented by the time internal migrants were forced into BVLP/U/S, technical limitations are insufficient to explain the omissions from the maps.

A selection of maps of Villa Celina will be analysed in relation with the social and political context in which they were produced. Thus, a brief account of the political situation of the south-western suburbs will be outlined, including a summary of the genealogy of BVLP/U/S in their historical context. The analysis will draw on concepts traced by the French philosopher Michel Foucault to shed some light upon the way in which a modality of knowledge – maps – is embedded in, and at the same time reproduces, relations of power present in society. The five urban maps under scrutiny span six decades, and include two official charts (1956, 2011) and three commercial urban guides (c. 1965, 1986, 2008).

Urban conceptions in the Plan de Emergencia

BVLP/U/S were built as part of a wider plan to eradicate informal settlements. The plan was implemented between 1956 and 1964, a period during which both the physical fabric of the settlements and their residents – mostly internal migrants and workers – were at the centre of political debates and discussions about the city. In the 1940s, numerous internal migrants moved to large cities in Argentina, but finding them already overcrowded many settled in shanty towns (Germani, n.d., p. 40). Some groups of shanties already existed in Buenos Aires, and these expanded as a result of this influx, while many new settlements emerged. Although shanty towns existed all around the city, most were located in the northern and southern suburbs, and in particular along the lowlands of the river Riachuelo (Figure 1.1). The coalition that took over the government after the coup d'état of 1955, Revolución Libertadora (RL), was backed by a wide spectrum of political actors, including conservatives, liberals and socialists, most of whom felt uneasy about the presence of internal migrants in the city. Furthermore, they were especially troubled by the emergence of the shanty towns. Once in power, the RL called for a commission of specialists to issue a plan to remove the settlements and relocate their inhabitants to purpose-built neighbourhoods of social housing: the Plan de Emergencia (Massidda, 2012).

This unease was rooted in earlier decades of Argentine history. During the government of Juan Domingo Perón (1945–55), the groups that supported the RL had been disgusted with the social and political ascendancy of workers and migrants and with what they felt to be an invasion of the city (Podalsky, 2004, pp. 1–21).[1] Metaphors of intrusion, for example, abound in literary works written by anti-Peronists, while the rhetoric of the political opposition animalized the working classes through phrases like 'zoological barrage' (i.e. the Peronist demonstrations) or 'the paws in the fountain' (which referred to the Peronist supporters stepping into the fountains of the central square in one of these demonstrations).[2] This discourse became official during the administration of the RL, and initiatives like the Plan de Emergencia stressed the difference between 'us', the inhabitants of the formal, established city, which included members of the government and the commission writing the plan, and 'them', the settlers.

Six neighbourhoods of social housing were built under the Plan de Emergencia, BVLP/U/S being three of them (BHN, 1958). The design of these neighbourhoods consisted of the repetition of three housing typologies forming continuous rows of houses, and a communal centre which included shops and facilities. The neighbourhoods built in Villa Celina were composed on average of 950 houses each. The housing rows were paired back-to-back creating blocks 27 metres wide and typically 81- or 102-metres long.[3] Edge blocks varied in length, in some cases, in order to follow the

---

[1] The political actors backing the Revolución Libertadora and their perspectives regarding the shanty towns were varied. I refer here to the prevailing position.

[2] 'Aluvión zoológico' and 'las patas en la fuente' were frequently spoken expressions but can also be found in written form, for example, in CARL, 1985, p. 11.

[3] Although the original plans of the neighbourhoods are lost, the disposition of the buildings can be traced back using the satellite photos of the time and the plans provided by the BHN in its construction report (BHN, 1958). I have also used cadastral documents issued in the 1980s for the reconstruction of another PE neighbourhood, Barrio Rivadavia, to estimate the block sizes presented here. I am following Oscar Yunovsky for what refers to the dates of completion (Yunovsky, 1984, p. 100).

borders of each plot. This layout differed substantially from the urban grain of the existing city, which consisted on a continuous grid of blocks of approximately 100 × 100 metres. In the context of Buenos Aires, where the urban fabric had traditionally been homogeneous, the layout of the neighbourhoods appeared as an interruption and contributed to their isolation.

In addition to accommodating former shanty town residents, the neighbourhoods were presented by the Plan de Emergencia as 'adaptation dwellings': by inhabiting them, the dwellers would be forced into a specific lifestyle (CNV, 1956, pp. 151–3). Ignoring the results of surveys of shanty town populations taken previously, which had reported the presence of a wide variety of households, the houses were designed exclusively for nuclear families of five to ten members. Residents were not allowed to host more people than the houses were designed for or to build extensions. Moreover, each room was supposed to be used only as prescribed: to this aim, concrete tables and benches and steel-framed beds were incorporated in living areas (BHN, 1958, p. 5).

The Plan de Emergencia did not explicitly articulate a strategy for segregating the former shanty towns' residents from the rest of the city. Segregation, however, was implied in the design of the neighbourhoods, the lack of concern about their social and urban integration, and the Plan's hostile discourse towards the informal settlements' inhabitants. The neighbourhoods were not conceived of as part of the existing urban fabric but rather as self-functioning communities inserted into the city's gaps. Furthermore, the very idea of their educative function was also a form of segregation, since it implied that the residents were not yet in a condition to join the existing city and should not reside in it until their re-education was complete. They were a burden to society and it was the mission of the government to educate them in the ways of civilization in order that they may become citizens. The neighbourhoods built by the Plan de Emergencia remained thus in a hybrid condition between what might be called the 'formal' and the 'informal' city: although planned and built in the context of a State-funded programme, they suffered stigmatization and isolation as is often the case with shanty towns (Massidda, 2012).

Official mappings of Villa Celina, 1956

The map shown in Figure 1.2 is a detail of the chart *Lanús*, published in 1956 by the then Instituto Geográfico Militar (IGM, Military Geographic Institute; now Instituto Geográfico Nacional). This map combines consecutive surveys of Buenos Aires and its surroundings taken from 1907 to 1910, which were updated in 1949 and 1956. Over this background I have marked the silhouettes of BVLP/U/S, built a few years after the publication of the chart. It is interesting to note that the blocks of the old core of Villa Celina (marked C), which were already built and consolidated by 1956, are represented in the same way as the empty land where Barrio Vicente López y Planes and Barrio Sarmiento would be built. The proximity of this low-lying area to the River Matanza made of it subject to frequent floods, and its grounds had in fact never been developed until the Plan de Emergencia. The 1958 report on the construction of BVLP/U/S

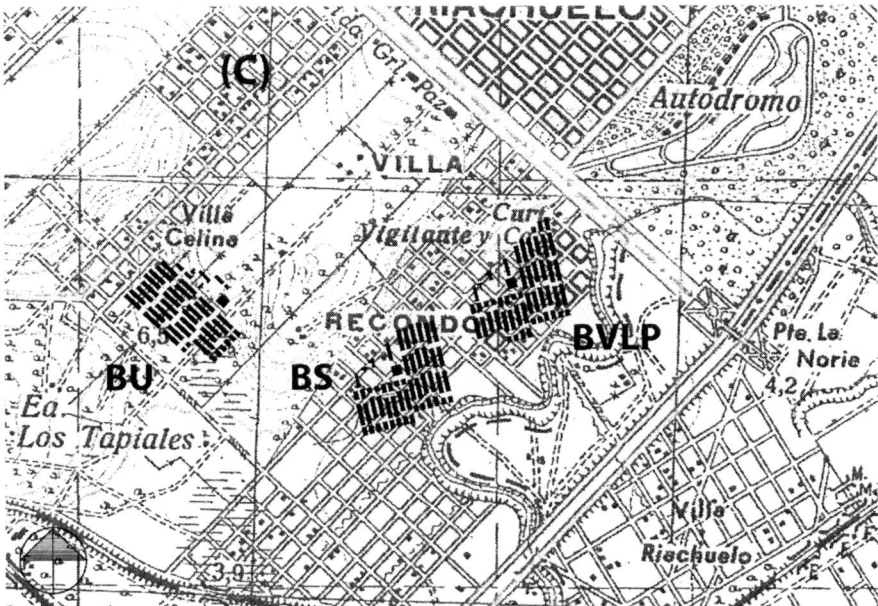

Figure 1.2 Background map: Detail of *Lanús* (Instituto Geográfico Nacional, 1956). Courtesy IGN. The black silhouettes drawn over indicate the future outline of BVLP/BU/ BS and the mark (C) indicates the old core of Villa Celina

Silhouettes, marks and compass traced over background by A. Massidda

corroborates this fact, since it does not mention any demolition of pre-existing blocks but rather stresses the costs of in-filling the land (BHN, 1958, pp. 2, 6). The photos published in this report and the information collected through interviews of long-time residents of the area also depict this land as undeveloped.[4]

The grid pattern drawn where Barrio Vicente López y Planes and Barrio Sarmiento would be built might have referred to a planned extension of the city fabric, which was never realized. The drawing of the traditional grid of Buenos Aires in areas that were not yet part of the built environment is noted by Adrián Gorelik in relation to a map published in 1904 by the Municipalidad de Buenos Aires, which traces the boundary of the city and its grid both in areas where the blocks already existed and in what was then open countryside (Gorelik, 1998, p. 27). In this sense these official maps are performing as planning documents rather than records of the existing city.

Also of interest is the way in which the chart omits the housing complex Barrio 17 de Octubre (now General Paz), built in Villa Celina in 1948–54 under the government of Juan Domingo Perón (Ballent, 2005, pp. 85–6). Were the map less accurate and complete than it is, the omission of Barrio 17 de Octubre could be attributed to poor production. However, the overall map is exhaustive and well-detailed, which makes

[4] In particular I would like to acknowledge José and Norma Furnari for their descriptions of 1950s Villa Celina.

such an omission even more compelling. One possible explanation relates to the political context: the missing complex had been built by the administration that the RL had overthrown just one year before the publication of the map.

The information presented in this map can be read through a foucauldian lens of power–knowledge relations. In Foucault's approach, knowledge is not something given but constructed artificially, and usually inscribed in specific fields of power relations (Foucault, 1979, pp. 27–35). As part of the construction of knowledge, maps propose a reality in which power can perpetuate and reflect itself: in the case of *Lanús*, for example, by ignoring specific public works and taking as granted a subdivision that had been only planned. Beyond its task of reporting the existing city, the IGM invested itself with the right to produce new information. It should be borne in mind that the chart was not presented as a planning document but as the result of the collection of geographical data. The map, in short, appears to be closer to an idealized version of Villa Celina, planned by public agencies, than to Villa Celina's material reality – in other words, it did not represent Villa Celina as it was but as specific State agencies would have liked it to be.

Commercial maps in the 1960s and 1980s

The map *Buenos Aires y Alrededores*, published by the Automóvil Club Argentino (Argentine Automobile Club) circa 1965, presents an austere outline of BVLP/U/S (Figure 1.3). It shows only the internal roads, and ignores pedestrian corridors, common services and the perimeter routes (ACA, [1965]). The internal roads have been drawn as distributed evenly, in positions that differ from what contemporary satellite photos show.[5] More than two decades later, the map of Villa Celina included in the *Guía Filcar* (Filcar, 1986) displays only car lanes too, but following a different pattern: only the perimeter and a selection of internal roads, this time in their actual positions, appear (Figure 1.4).

Given that both the ACA and Filcar maps were designed mainly for car drivers, it is not surprising that they do not represent all of the communal features but only roads for automobiles. However, had this been the only reason behind their incomplete representation of the neighbourhoods, both would have traced similar outlines – for example, showing all the streets open to cars. Furthermore, the missing information in the maps also calls into question their effectiveness: the pedestrian corridors were necessary to reach the houses, and information about the locations of blocks and communal buildings would have helped readers to find their way around the neighbourhoods too. The omission of key information about BVLP/U/S, necessary for occasional visitors to get their bearings in the area, suggests that the publishing companies did not expect their readers to be particularly interested in these neighbourhoods.

While the map published by the IGM reflects the vision of a public institution, *Buenos Aires y Alrededores* and *Guía Filcar* offer a hint about the interest (or lack of)

---

[5] See, for example, the 1965 satellite photo in http://mapa.buenosaires.gob.ar/ [last accessed 12 September 2012].

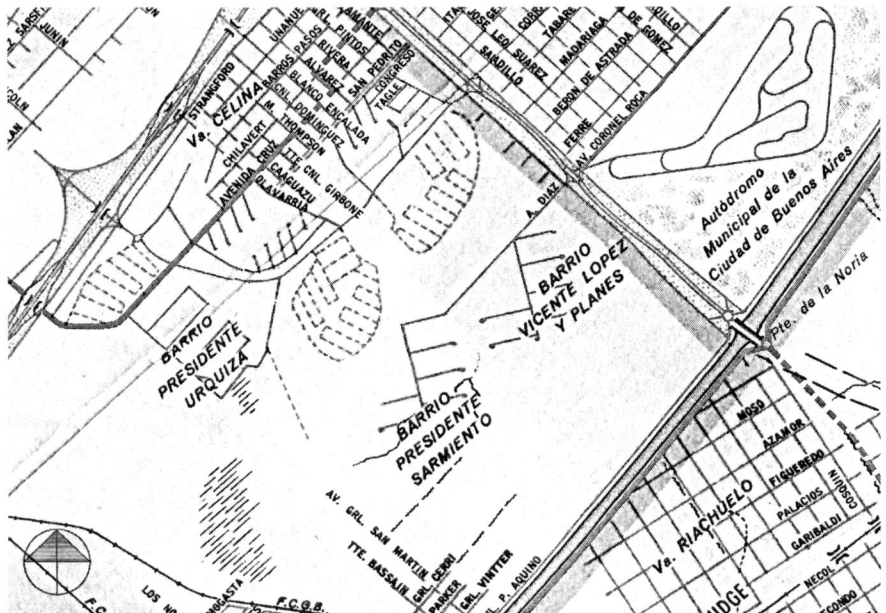

Figure 1.3 *Buenos Aires y Alrededores* (Automóvil Club Argentino, [1965])
Courtesy ACA

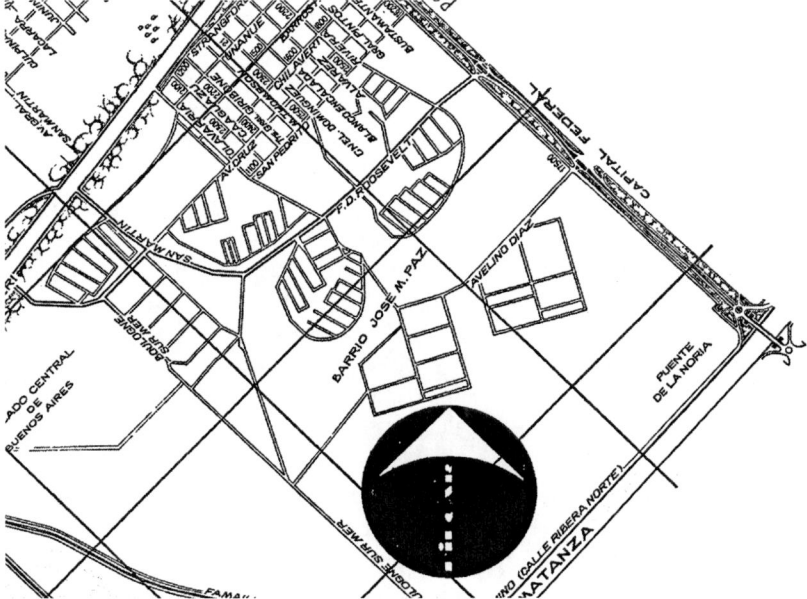

Figure 1.4 *Guía Filcar* (Filcar, 1986)
Courtesy Editorial Filcar

that BVLP/U/S generated among the city's population. Commercial maps are limited, as are official charts, since they select information according to what they anticipate the readers will need or will look for; it might be said that they work within the boundaries of a collective consensus about an area. The map of the IGM was, as has been argued, embedded in a field of power relations – creating and reproducing information that responded to specific interests. Commercial maps generate a specialized type of knowledge as well, mainly because they are working for a theoretical, idealized reader. The success in the longer term of Filcar and ACA as cartographic companies suggests that their production was effective. It could be thus inferred that the actual users were not too far from the abstract reader that the companies foresaw.

This mechanism is thus not a top-down imposition of power – at least not only. The power relations shown by these maps are present and reiterated throughout society. I have in mind a foucauldian concept of 'power' here, where power is not something coming 'from above' but something reproduced by each member of society, and enforced through each relationship. Says Foucault:

> Power is not exercised simply as an obligation or a prohibition on those who 'do not have it'; it invests them, is transmitted by them and through them; it exerts pressure upon them, just as they themselves, in their struggle against it, resist the grip it has on them. This means that these relations go right down into the depths of society. (Foucault, 1979, p. 27)

Power relations are thus embedded into society and multiplied by each of its members, who are at the same time subject to it – and this is how commercial maps, as a reflection of the users' interest, are also a tool to multiply these relations.

By employing this perspective, it can be argued that the under-representation of BVLP/U/S reveals the way in which part of Argentine society neglected these neighbourhoods. The contempt towards the shanty towns expressed by some social groups, such as the ones who wrote the Plan de Emergencia, was passed on to the neighbourhoods built to accommodate their residents. I am thus arguing that consequently there was a lack of interest, from these sectors of the society, in mapping BVLP/U/S in depth. In addition, it has been already mentioned that the south-western suburbs of Buenos Aires had traditionally had a marginal role in the representations of the city for being poor, working-class areas – except during Peronism, which was precisely the political tendency that the RL wished to attack. For all these reasons it is not surprising to see that neighbourhoods built for former informal settlers in the south-western suburbs were not mapped with as much attention as other areas until more recent decades.

The notion of social production of space proposed by the French sociologist Henri Lefebvre can also help to shed some light on the assumptions about the urban that underlay commercial maps. Lefebvre proposes a way of understanding how the collective construction of places, and their images, functions. For him, space is the result of the interaction of forces applied by society onto territory: social practice, representation, inhabitation or representational space. Space is a product, while at the same time a medium of production: it is in space that processes of production are located, and for this reason it conditions them (Lefebvre, 1998, pp. 26–46). From this perspective, BVLP/U/S can be read as a collectively constructed apparatus and not exclusively as the outcome of the designs of planners, architects and governments.

Furthermore, if space is socially produced, it is possible to argue that its representations express the social conception of each specific area. In line with Foucault's observations, Lefebvre thinks that representations of space are a particular kind of top-down knowledge, informed by reasoning rather than by inhabitation and experience, which as such helps to perpetuate the dominant system of production (Lefebvre, 1998, p. 36). Representation – in cartographic terms – is not the main focus of Lefebvre's work, but it is one of his interests, not least because he finds it to be a key mechanism for the collective construction of space. In the case of the maps analysed, the anti-Peronists' contempt for the masses of internal migrants and their alarm about the emergence of the informal settlements led to specific ways of perceiving and conceiving the spaces related to settlers: in this sense, these tensions and conceptions produced the spaces. Places like the south-western suburbs, the settlements, the neighbourhoods built under the Plan de Emergencia, and even the centre of Buenos Aires, were loaded with new meanings throughout these social transformations, and they were thus collectively produced. It must be noted that the conceptions found in the maps analysed here are not the only ones that emerged from the cited processes, which not all social actors experienced in the same way. Opinions did vary, and works like *Villa Miseria también es América* (Verbitsky, 1957), Antonio Berni's Juanito Laguna series (Berni, 1999), or the short *Buenos Aires* (Kohon, 1958) are good examples of views about the shanty towns that did not concur with the official one. But the social tension around migrants and shanty towns was pressing enough at that time to leave a key mark on the social construction of space.

Recent mapping

Recent commercial maps have provided a more thorough representation of BVLP/U/S than their earlier counterparts. The *Guía Filcar* 2006 (Filcar, 2006), for example, includes and labels all the pedestrian corridors built in 1957–64 (Figure 1.5). However, the recent extensions south of Barrio Vicente López y Planes and Barrio Sarmiento (D) are only partially taken into account. These extensions consist of housing built following the old street pattern. In response to what is referred to as the Barrio Las Achiras (E), south of Barrio Urquiza, and the developments marked F, a trace of streets has been outlined, but no further information is provided. In addition, other recent transformations in Villa Celina, such as the 'Barrio boliviano' (the land marked G, where a large Bolivian community settled in the early 1990s; Figure 1.6), are not represented at all.[6]

---

[6] The map of Villa Celina included in the Guía Filcar 2006 is nevertheless more detailed than many of its contemporaries. Other examples are *Lumi* (2002), *Guía Lumi: Transportes Capital Federal y Gran Buenos Aires*. Buenos Aires; Editorial Betina (2008), *Guía T: Capital Federal, Gran Buenos Aires y aledaños*. Buenos Aires; and even Filcar (2004), *Guía Filcar*. Buenos Aires.

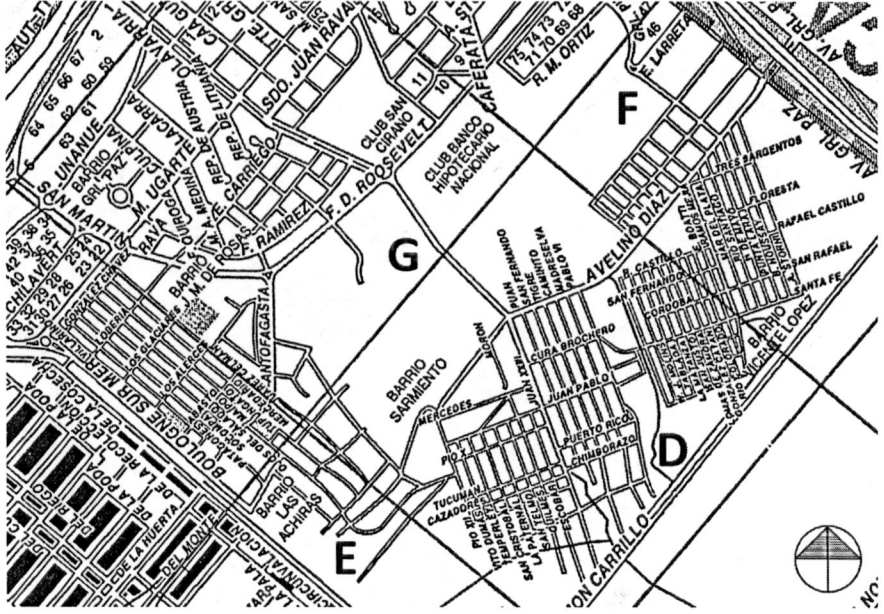

Figure 1.5 *Guía Filcar* (Filcar, 2006)
Courtesy Editorial Filcar

Figure 1.6 'Barrio Boliviano', Villa Celina. Despite what the maps suggest, the place is far from empty. January 2011
Photo by Adriana Massidda

Documents provided recently by public agencies, in turn, present more succinct information than commercial maps: a complete outline of the original neighbourhoods, but no sign of the recent settlements – and in this case no trace either. A cadastral plan issued in 2011 by the Municipality of La Matanza, for example, includes BVLP/U/S with their street names and complete layouts, but overlooks newer developments such as the areas marked E–G (Figure 1.7). Indeed the cadastral plans do not aim to portray the everyday life of Villa Celina but to provide a scheme of land ownership. The absence of the newer developments could be due to their administrative status being to a greater or lesser extent unresolved.[7]

As I have observed throughout the text, maps belong to a network of power relations which underpin decisions about what is represented and how. They are part of an artificial construction of knowledge which serves, and at the same time is generated by, power. This conception of power is not limited to official agencies, such as the ones who produced the maps I have presented, but also extends to and is deeply embedded in the whole body of society. Power is thus borne, and at the same time multiplied, by each individual. It is to control this multiplicity of micro-powers that documents emerge as tools of vigilance: 'The examination that places individuals in a field of surveillance also [. . .] engages them in a mass of documents that capture and fix them' (Foucault, 1979, p. 189).

Territory, Foucault argues, provides a physical support for the circulation of individuals. Therefore space and territory stand as key objects of control:

> I think we have here one of the axes, one of the fundamental elements in this deployment of mechanisms of security, that is to say, not yet the appearance of a notion of milieu, but the appearance of a project, a political technique that will be addressed to the milieu. (Foucault, 2007, p. 27)

At the same time, writers like David Shane have related Foucault's concept of heterotopias – places of exception that redefine the rest of the spaces they are related to (Foucault, 1967) – to the informal, to the lack of representation of the informal, to what escapes this control performed by maps: 'The invisibility of these [informal] settlements on official maps, and yet their obvious presence adding to the city, conforms to the "hidden in plain sight" characteristic of the medieval almhouses' (Shane, 2011, p. 66). Finally, it is worth mentioning that the under-representation of the informal has also been stressed by David Harvey in the context of a critique of property speculation and the commodification of urban land (Harvey, 2012, p. 18).

Thus, even though the representation of BVLP/U/S is more exhaustive in more recent commercial maps, important transformations of Villa Celina have been overlooked; the information has been enriched but the problem has been updated. It could be argued that this process is embedded in the very nature of maps, since

---

[7] Note that, apart from the cadastre, I rely only on oral sources for what regards the property status of this land.

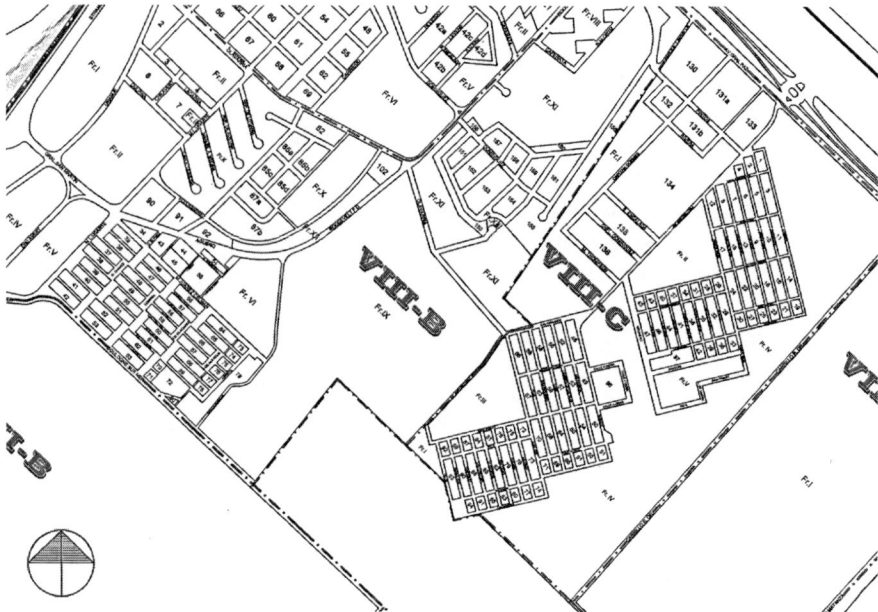

Figure 1.7 Cadastral map of the district La Matanza by the Municipality. Printed on demand. January 2011

Courtesy Municipalidad de La Matanza

they aim to show a fixed image about territories that are continuously becoming. The fact that the places which are incompletely represented are the newest sectors of Villa Celina seems to support this interpretation. However, the construction of these spaces was well advanced by the time the maps were published. Their under-representation could be also read in terms of their relationship with other groups within society; until being collectively acknowledged, it is unlikely that the public will expect to find information about them in the maps, and in this case the cartographic companies might not find surveying or collecting data about them worthwhile.

The importance of the most recent developments, that is the areas marked E–G, for the economy and atmosphere of Villa Celina becomes self-evident when visiting the site, both through conversation with residents and in the face of their hectic, lively activity. The differences between any of these recent maps and the actual built environment can be easily seen in satellite photos of Villa Celina such as the ones that are available online.[8] The spaces that are emerging but which are not fully acknowledged by official departments or civil groups offer, in many cases, a hint of unattended needs and potentialities of the populations residing in them. Thus, even today the way in which urban cartography deals with informal areas – whether they

---

[8] http://maps.google.com.ar/ or other satellite maps.

are mapped or not, and, if they are, in what ways – says something about the positions of different social and government actors towards these spaces.

Concluding remarks: Representing the under-represented

Many of the problems outlined throughout this chapter appear more frequently in the suburbs than in the consolidated neighbourhoods of the city – at least in the context of Buenos Aires. The emerging, fragmented, hybrid areas are characteristic of the southern, western and south-western suburbs, and consequently the controversies around representation are perhaps to be expected. Urban maps reflect the interests of different parties, and for this reason they are documents which help one to grasp not only the spatial transformations of the city, but more importantly the way in which each space is perceived.

During the decades following their construction BVLP/U/S offered cartographers a challenge, for they necessitated the introduction of a new set of criteria with which to outline their fabric that was quite different from the traditional grid of Buenos Aires. The matter of representation was further complicated by political tensions around the shanty towns and their inhabitants, some of whom were transferred to BVLP/U/S. These tensions contributed to the partiality of the cartographic representations of BVLP/U/S. Later on, after tensions subsided and the neighbourhoods came to be part of the collective imagination about the city, it became natural for cartographic companies to represent them more fully. The challenge for cartographers then became whether and how to take into account non-official, emerging phenomena. There is currently some degree of variety in the way cartographic companies represent the under-represented, but it could be said that in general terms urban informality tends to remain incompletely portrayed.

The nature of this work is that of a preliminary exploration of places which have received little attention before. I have shown how the tense position occupied by a geographical area of Buenos Aires – the south-western suburbs – in the collective imaginary affected not only its material but also the way in which both the area and the interventions were represented in various types of maps. I have also proposed a politicized interpretation of these maps: the omission of information involves issues related to society and power. As with other types of representations, maps perpetuate power relationships and consolidate the way in which spaces are collectively produced. Finally, I think that the nature of the suburban areas of Buenos Aires renders cartographic representation even more challenging, since conditions of inhabitation are not yet settled and spaces are difficult to classify. Many dichotomies such as formal/ informal, ownership/invasion or ongoing/complete, for example, need to be suspended in order to apprehend the changing nature of the area. Questions of the political and the social underlay the discussion of urban mapping, and it is through an analysis which incorporates these matters that the complexity of the suburbs can be grasped.

*   *   *

I would like to acknowledge Felipe Hernández for his attentive reading and suggestions, as well as Liliana Weisert, Rosalinda Ortale and Rubén Albanese, from the Instituto Geográfico Nacional, Marcela Vega from the Automóvil Club Argentino, Reinaldo Rebella from Editorial Filcar and Patricia from Municipalidad de La Matanza for their permission regarding the use of images, and for their kindness and help.

2

From Riots to Designer Shoes: *Tout ce qui brille/All that Glitters* (2010) and Changing Representations of the Banlieue in French Cinema

Carrie Tarr

Since the publication of *Reframing Difference: Beur and Banlieue Filmmaking in France* (Tarr, 2005), which appeared the same year as riots originating in the multi-ethnic suburbs outside Paris spread throughout the nation, the banlieue has continued to feature prominently in French cinema.[1] It has attracted not just ethnic minority filmmakers, but also majority French auteur filmmakers, filmmakers seeking to profit from the commercial success certain types of banlieue films can offer, and, increasingly, in the latter half of the 2000s, women filmmakers whose foregrounding of female banlieue characters offers a certain feminization of a cinematic space which has hitherto been considered primarily a space for the expression of young, troubled, postcolonial masculine identities. The most celebrated of the male-centred banlieue films is undoubtedly Mathieu Kassovitz's *La Haine/Hate* (1,978,328 spectators in France), an international hit dating back to 1995, a year which saw the emergence of at least four other French films with contemporary banlieue settings, and which gave rise to debates as to whether this signalled the birth of a new cinematic genre (see Tarr, 2005, pp. 73–85). At the time of writing, however, the latest banlieue film to achieve box office success by gaining over a million spectators (the industry benchmark for popular success in France) is *Tout ce qui brille/All that Glitters* (2010, 1,439,624 spectators in France), a first film by Géraldine Nakache and Hervé Mimran, which is also the first 'millionaire' banlieue film to foreground young women from the banlieue and to have been (co-)written and directed by a woman. This article focuses on the innovative ways in which *All that Glitters* addresses questions of gender, space and identity, and in the process not only challenges the male bias of previous banlieue films but also works to break down perceived divisions between banlieue and city centre.

[1] The word 'beur' derives from French 'verlan' (backslang) for 'arabe' (Arab), and has been used to refer to second-generation migrants from the Maghreb (now more commonly referred to as being 'of Maghrebi heritage'). The word 'banlieue', meaning suburbs in general, has come to refer more specifically to those suburbs associated with large populations of working-class ethnic minorities, social disadvantage and criminality. See Echchaïbi (2007) for an analysis of the 2005 riots.

Banlieue cinema in context

In order to place *All That Glitters* in context, it is necessary first to consider in more detail how the banlieue has been represented in recent French cinema. For most international observers, the most dominant cinematic images of the banlieue to have reached the screen since *La Haine* will be those featured in either the hyper-masculinized, fantasy manifestations of the genre like Pierre Morel's *Banlieue 13/ District 13* (2004) and Patrick Alessandrin's *D13: Ultimatum* (2009), or occasional auteur films like Claire Denis' *35 Rhums/35 Shots of Rum* (2008) and André Téchiné's *La Fille du RER/The Girl on the Train* (2009), films which address family life in the banlieue in the context of wider, social issues: the integration and settlement of former migrants from the French Caribbean in *35 Shots of Rum*, white alienation and contemporary anti-Semitism in *The Girl on the Train*. The differences between these two types of film – action films geared towards a mass youth audience and small-scale, socially concerned auteur films aimed at an arthouse audience – point to the dangers of generalizing about banlieue films and their impact. And in fact the diversity of forms taken by the banlieue film in the past five years or so is even more striking than these few titles would suggest, ranging as they do from social realism and action thriller to comedy and even horror, and from settings in the most disadvantaged suburbs to those that are far more affluent.

Clearly it is important to note that, historically, the suburbs of French cities which provide locations for these films are indeed quite diverse. In the case of outer Paris, they range from the remnants of the Communist-run, working-class, 'red belt' towns that surrounded Paris in the 1930s to the longstanding well-established, affluent suburbs, like Neuilly-sur-Seine, notably in the West. However, the suburbs that have given rise to the contemporary usage of the word banlieue, and provide the *mise en scène* of the majority of banlieue films, are those areas of lowest income that are dominated architecturally by the rundown, high rise, concrete estates built in the post-war period to house France's poor whites and immigrant workers and their families, mainly of North African, but also sub-Saharan African and Caribbean origin. These are to be found particularly to the north of Paris, situated literally beyond the 'périphérique', the ring road which demarcates central Paris from its suburbs and which divides city centre and periphery in ways which have symbolic as well as spatial significance. Long neglected by politicians and the state, they are characterized by low educational achievement, high levels of unemployment, poor-quality housing and social unrest. The periodic riots adopted as a form of protest by some of their inhabitants have, perhaps not surprisingly, led to dominant media imagery of the banlieue as a problematic, demonized space of ethnic difference, criminality and violence, a place where the police may fear to tread.[2] Often experienced by its disenfranchised inhabitants as a nowhere space, a site of exclusion from life in the metropolis, or indeed, the nation as a whole, the multi-ethnic banlieue has nevertheless, since the late 1970s, with the coming of age of the 'beur' generation, that is, the sons and daughters of first-generation Arab/Berber-Muslim immigrants from the Maghreb, given rise to a variety of forms of alternative

---

[2] See Hargreaves (2007) for an analysis of the prejudices and misconceptions faced by ethnic minorities living in France's banlieues.

cultural expression, most notably in the field of hip-hop culture. But cinema, too, has proved a dynamic space for filmmakers drawing inspiration from the banlieue to make visible the multilayered lives of individuals and communities otherwise excluded from, marginalized by or stereotyped in dominant media representations, and – particularly on the part of 'beur' filmmakers themselves – to give them a human face.

That human face has, for the most part, been embodied by young males, as exemplified in the first films of the 1980s to feature the working-class, multi-ethnic banlieue, that is Serge Le Péron's *Laisse béton* (1984), the title an example of the new banlieue slang, meaning 'Drop it!', Mehdi Charef's *Le Thé au harem d'Archimède/Tea in the Harem* (1985), the first feature film by a 'beur' filmmaker, and Jean-Claude Brisseau's *De bruit et de fureur/Of Sound and Fury* (1988).[3] These three films focus on the identity problems of white déclassé youths and/or youths of Maghrebi origin torn between two cultures, and on the banlieue itself as a place not only of alienation, oppression and social exclusion, but also (unlike American 'hood' movies) of intercultural male friendship. Claire Denis' first banlieue film, *S'en fout la mort/No Fear No Die* (1990), a sensual, meditative examination of the exploitation of black immigrants involved in illegal cockfighting, similarly focuses on the issue of male identity and violence (see Beugnet, 2004, pp. 66–81). It was only in 1993 that Anne Fontaine's *Les Histoires d'amour finissent mal en général/Love Stories Usually End Badly* became the first feature film to centre on a young banlieue woman of Maghrebi origin, whose problematic identity is exemplified by her inability to choose between her dull but steady boyfriend from the banlieue and the more exciting lover she meets in the city, and who eventually loses them both (see Tarr, 2005, pp. 86–96), a trope taken up and reworked in *All That Glitters*. A more feminized view of the banlieue was also expressed in Malik Chibane's first films, *Hexagone/Hexagon* (1994) and *Douce France/Sweet France* (1995) (see Swamy, 2011). However, it was the trope of problematic banlieue masculinity that was taken up and re-worked in *La Haine*, the film which established the multi-ethnic banlieue as an exciting cinematic space, with its edgy characters, confrontations with the police, and exhilarating, stylized cinematography (see Vincendeau, 2005). Indeed, as Ginette Vincendeau points out in the aftermath of the 2005 riots, *La Haine*'s lack of a female presence was considered necessary for the film to be taken seriously:

> When Kassovitz was questioned in 1995 about the absence of women from his film, he replied that they would have detracted from the seriousness of its purpose: 'I did not want to soften the topic. What would love have to do with this story?' – as if women could only signify love and did not have a social identity too. The plight of women as victims of male violence, and their frequent opposition to violence in real life (e.g. black and *beur* women staged demonstrations against the rioters in several locations), are ignored. (Vincendeau, 2007)

In the years between 1995 and 2005, other banlieue films such as Jean-François Richet's *Etat des lieux/Inner City* (1995), Thomas Gilou's *Raï* (1995), Yolande Zimmerman's

---

[3] 'Laisse béton' is backslang for 'laisse tomber' ('drop it!'), but the slang expression also introduces a poetic allusion to the concrete (béton) image of the banlieue.

Clubbed to Death (1996), Richet's *Ma 6-T va craqu-er* (1997), Fabrice Génestal's *La Squale* (2000) and Rabah Ameur-Zaïmèche's *Wesh wesh, qu'est-ce qui se passe?* (2002), even if they involved significant female roles (as in *Clubbed to Death* and *La Squale*), also emphasized the banlieue as the site of ethnic difference and male violence and criminality, and highlighted social problems such as unemployment, drug abuse, gang rapes, deportation and police violence. The period also saw new takes on the banlieue, on the one hand in comedies such as in Mahmoud Zemmouri's *100% Arabica* (1997) and Djamel Bensalah's *Le Ciel, les oiseaux . . . et ta mère/Boyz on the Beach* (1999, 1,264,964 spectators in France), the first film by a filmmaker of Maghrebi origin to achieve over a million spectators, on the other, in spectacular action films such as *Yamakasi – Les samouraïs des temps modernes* (Ariel Zeitoun, Julien Seri 2001) and *District 13* (2004); all of which also foreground male subjectivities and identities. Only three low-budget banlieue films of this period offer alternative female-centred narratives: Zaïda Ghorab-Volta's *Souviens-toi de moi/Remember Me* (1997), a medium-length film in which the central protagonist of Maghrebi origin is eventually able to accept her hybridity and reconcile the constrictions of her home life in the banlieue with her warm relations with her family in Algeria and her intercultural friendships in central Paris; Philippe Faucon's *Samia* (2001), which focuses on a rebellious young teenager of Maghrebi origin living with her family in the banlieue of Marseille; and Ghorab-Volta's *Jeunesse dorée/Gilded Youth* (2002), which centres on two white French banlieue girls who set out to photograph banlieue-type housing estates throughout provincial France, thereby morphing the banlieue film into a lowkey road movie (see Tarr, 2005, pp. 92–6, 111–16 and 183–5). Ghorab-Volta's reflections on gender and place, which emphasize the successful mobility of their female banlieue protagonists, make a strong (if commercially insignificant) contrast with the less successful attempts at female (and male) mobility represented in most other social realist banlieue films (see Geesey, 2011).

However, the most important take on the banlieue film in the early 2000s, and one which offers a new, subtly feminized perspective on the banlieue, is the award-winning *L'Esquive/Games of Love and Chance* (2004), the second feature film to be written and directed by Abdellatif Kechiche, an actor and filmmaker of Tunisian heritage.[4] Winner of four Césars, France's equivalent of the Oscars, *Games of Love and Chance* achieved over 470,000 spectators in France, and, arguably, revolutionized the image of the banlieue (see Tarr, 2007). The film focuses on the everyday lives and loves of a group of banlieue adolescents of various ethnic backgrounds, some of whom take on and perform a play by Marivaux as part of their school programme, and creatively juxtaposes their dynamic use of banlieue slang with the play's elegant but outmoded eighteenth-century language. It thus reworks the space of the banlieue, not as a site of criminality and violence, but rather as a site of performance, self-expression and desire, and one which privileges the roles of girls. In the end, the film is ambivalent as to whether or not it is possible for young people such as these, however creative and dynamic, to transcend the limitations of their life in the banlieue: in one key scene,

---

[4] The first was *La Faute à Voltaire/Blame it on Voltaire* (2001), which is mostly set in central Paris, viewed from the perspective of an illegal immigrant (see Tarr, 2005, pp. 195–8).

their teacher uncritically explains the meaning of the Marivaux play, namely, that people remain trapped by their origins; in another the youngsters find themselves at the periphery of the banlieue, where they get stopped and searched by the police, a violent and forcible reminder of the reality of those limitations. However, if the future of Kechiche's fictional banlieue protagonists is uncertain, the young actresses who embodied them in such a lively fashion, notably Sarah Forestier and Sabrina Ouazani, have since found themselves a permanent place in the French film industry.

Banlieue cinema after L'Esquive

What then of representations of the banlieue in French cinema after *L'Esquive*? In addition to action thriller *D13: Ultimatum* and Chibane's low-budget comedy *Voisins voisines/Neighbours* (2005), notable auteur films include Ameur-Zaïmèche's *Dernier maquis* (2008), an exploration of the negative consequences of a man of North African origin setting up a mosque for his workers in their banlieue workplace, and Andre Téchiné's *The Girl on the Train* (2009), based on a *fait divers* in which a young white woman from the banlieue (falsely) claimed to have been mugged by Arab-Muslim youths who thought she was Jewish, both films which explore tensions arising in a multicultural, multi-faith society. But the two key phenomena of the last five years have been on the one hand, the increasing number of banlieue films by women filmmakers, and on the other the unexpected box office success of the banlieue as a site of mainstream comedy.

Since 2005, at least five films by women privilege the role of young women who have grown up in the banlieue (six if we include Claire Denis' *35 Shots of Rum*, which focuses on the relationship between a black Caribbean railway worker and his mixed-race daughter). Four do so by foregrounding the potential limitations of the class and/ or ethnic identities of their protagonists and their difficulties in finding a space of belonging: an oppressive, diasporic, Sephardic Jewish heritage in the case of Karin Albou's *La Petite Jérusalem/Little Jerusalem* (2005) (see Tarr, 2009); a poor white, post-Communist, working-class background in Isabelle Cjazka's *L'Année suivante/The Year After* (2006); white, black and 'beur' sexism and the difficulty of male–female relations in Audrey Estraougo's *Regarde-moi (ain't scared)* (2006); and an oppressive Maghrebi family heritage in Nora Hamdi's *Des poupées et des anges/Dolls and Angels* (2008). These films typically construct the banlieue as a site of female oppression, particularly in relation to the family and male peer groups, in opposition to the city centre as the longed-for site of integration and/or independence, which can only be achieved, if at all, at the cost of separation from the family and the cultural traditions that it represents. The heroine of *Little Jerusalem* (the name of the Jewish district in Sarcelles) finally looks set to find freedom in Paris only once her family has decided to emigrate to Israel; only one of the two sisters in *Dolls and Angels* eventually manages to escape her oppressive banlieue family, and does so by finding a modelling job in Paris, thanks to her rich, white boyfriend. In contrast the heroine of *The Year After* has to resign herself to a dreary, monotonous life in the banlieue with her unloving, widowed mother, while the young women whose tears and fears inform *Ain't scared* (which uses the device of relating the events of the film first from a male, then from a female point of view) are similarly unable to move on, the only person able to do so being the young male footballer in their midst.

However, the fifth film, *All That Glitters*, takes the form of a light-hearted comedy in which the relation between Paris and the banlieue is constructed in a rather different way. In this film Paris is not simply an impossible dream or a place which results in rejection and exclusion, but rather a porous space that enables its banlieue heroines not only to go shopping, but also to work through and re-evaluate the strength of their relationships with each other and with their families. It comes hot on the heels of another comedy set in the banlieue and an even bigger box office hit, Gabriel Julien-Laferrière's *Neuilly sa mère!/ Neuilly Yo Mama!* (2009, 2,517,140 spectators in France), set in the affluent Parisian banlieue of Neuilly-sur-Seine where former President Nicolas Sarkozy began his career, and which also features in *All That Glitters*. *Neuilly Yo Mama!* takes up the trope of the banlieue kid being parachuted into a social setting in which he does not belong, first used successfully in *Boyz on the Beach*, where a group of banlieue youths find themselves winning a holiday in the posh seaside resort of Biarritz, and subsequently reworked in Jean-Paul Sinapi's *Camping à la ferme* (2004), where a group of delinquent teenagers from the banlieue have the chance to work for a month in a small country village instead of serving a prison sentence, and in Lucien-Jean Baptiste's hit comedy *Première étoile/First Snow* (2009, 1,647,563 spectators in France), where a black Caribbean father and his mixed-race children from the banlieue find themselves the only black holidaymakers in a French ski-ing resort. In *Neuilly Yo Mama!*, bright 14-year-old Sami, who is of Maghrebi origin, finds himself wrenched from his beloved but 'difficult' housing estate in Chalon-sur-Saône, and forced to stay in Neuilly with his elegant aunt Djamila who has married a divorced, white French businessman with two children. The film plays with and unmasks stereotypes and prejudices arising from both disadvantaged and affluent banlieue backgrounds, but eventually allows Sami to overcome all obstacles and bring together friends and family from and in both spaces, pacifying his neurotic adoptive family and also cementing his romance in the city with the object of his desire, the beautiful white, blonde girl-next-door. The film thus offers a cheeky, albeit utopian vision of the interpenetration of city and suburbs, in which, even in Sarkozy's former fiefdom, both class and ethnic difference are overcome.

All That Glitters

All That Glitters, another feelgood film, centres on the relationship between two young women, Ely (Géraldine Nakache) and Lila (Leïla Bekti), one of Jewish, the other of Arab-Muslim heritage, who have grown up together in a housing estate in the Parisian banlieue of Puteaux (where Nakache herself grew up), the other – wrong – side of the river from Neuilly. However, if Puteaux is less affluent than Neuilly, it nevertheless houses part of the La Défense business and shopping complex, built as a prolongation of the axis which follows the Champs-Elysées past the Arc de Triomphe to the Grande Arche, which celebrated the fiftieth anniversary of its inception in 2008. As a choice of setting, it is therefore less distinct from the metropolitan centre than the banlieues which feature in films like *La Haine* or *Wesh wesh,* even if, for the film's protagonists, the ten-minute taxi ride from the capital, and the distant view of the Eiffel Tower, still make Paris seem like a far-off dream.

The film begins with Lila and Ely aimlessly hanging out in Puteaux, in the open space outside a block of high-rise flats, passing the time by miming pop stars, making faces, trading insults and occasionally breaking into song and dance (in a performance which earned Leïla Bekhti the 2011 César for Most Promising Actress). But the real, or imagined, antidote that they seize on to relieve the perceived boredom of the banlieue is the prospect of a night out in Paris, in particular at the latest trendy nightclub, an address they get from the pages of a woman's magazine. Getting refused entry to a Parisian nightclub is a familiar trope of the male-oriented banlieue film with its stress on the exclusion of ethnic minority males from the city centre. However Lila and Ely manage to gain access by the back door, and as a result, Lila meets and subsequently starts an affair with rich, handsome Maxx (Simon Buret), while Ely gets them invited to a party at the home of exotic lesbian couple Agathe (Virginie Ledoyen) and Franco-Vietnamese model Joan (Linh Dan Pham), after headbutting a man who is trying to mug Agathe. These three characters represent the glittering fantasies offered by Paris: on the one hand sex and romance with a man who drives a sports car and offers his girlfriend weekends away and designer shoes; on the other access to a glamorous lifestyle in a flat with views over Paris, exotic meals and a huge walk-in wardrobe of designer clothes, jewellery, sunglasses and, once more, a symbol of their aspiration to a different lifestyle, designer shoes. Thus when Agathe (and later Maxx) asks where Ely and Lila live, in order to drive them home, Ely says Puteaux but Lila overrides her, saying Neuilly, setting in train a pretence that might enable the two friends momentarily to live out their dreams, but which also threatens to come between them (as well as forcing them to walk home from Neuilly over the bridge to Puteaux).

The film contrasts the excitement of Paris night life with the more mundane reality of life in Puteaux, establishing the banlieue as a space of everyday banality rather than of violence and criminality. Lila sells popcorn at the cinema in the local shopping mall, while Ely works in a sandwich shop run by Lila's boyfriend, Eric (Manu Payet), and the duo regularly meet for a sandwich in the mall with their sports trainer friend Carole (Audrey Lamy), who lives in Paris but comes to Puteaux to visit her ancient, ailing aunt, a reminder of what awaits the young women if they don't manage to get out. Ely is desperate to move to Paris, and feels oppressed by having to live at home in a crowded flat with a noisy little sister with whom she shares a bedroom, while Lila is not committed to Eric and feels remote from her immigrant mother, who is still pining for the return of her former husband from Morocco after 16 years' absence (and spends her spare time singing nostalgic French songs at a local karaoke bar). But the film minimizes the significance of the parents' ethnic origins, providing only the most cursory of references to signs of ethnic difference (Jewish artefacts in Ely's parents' flat, Lila's letters from her Moroccan father). Instead, the assonance of the names, Ely and Lila, and the fact that they share aspirations, exchange clothes and often get taken for sisters, constructs the two young women not as victimized, marginalized, ethnic outsiders, but rather as typical, contemporary wannabes, 'elles', whose aspirations supposedly reflect those of every young woman in France. This is reflected, too, in the film's music track, which, though punctuated with music by British rap act *The Streets*, is dominated by the duo's reworking of a catchy French pop song, 'Chanson sur ma drôle de vie' ('Song About My Funny Life') by Véronique Sanson, which dates back to 1976, a time which predates the contemporary multicultural banlieue and confirms the film's integrationist, mainstreaming ambitions. The song as Ely and Lila perform it not only underlines the two young women's desire to live life the way they want to, but also highlights the affectionate bond between them, rather than being directed at an imagined masculine object of desire.

Given their dead-end jobs and rather dull, ordinary existence, it is not surprising that Lila and Ely get their kicks from minor transgressions, notably spending the money they ostensibly collect for charity outside the shopping mall in Puteaux on a shared pair of expensive designer shoes in central Paris. But their attempt to disguise their banlieue origins and their lack of money and social know-how from their new Parisian friends proves to be their greatest transgression, since it leads to various forms of betrayal. Ely betrays her taxi driver father, when she claims not to know him in front of Agathe and Joan; Lila betrays Eric by starting an affair with Maxx; both Lila and Ely betray Carole, because they are ashamed of her working-class accent and loudness (Lila even accuses Carole of theft when it was she who stole a ring from Agathe, which Ely has replaced); and Lila turns on Ely when Ely eventually tells Maxx the truth of where they live, just as Ely turns on Lila because she fails to acknowledge it. However, the truth purveyed by the film is that however charming the Parisians may appear, they are all ultimately affably vacuous and fickle: Maxx already has a girlfriend and eventually dumps Lila, while Agathe and Joan simply use Ely to baby-sit their son. In other words, as *Variety* reviewer Jordan Mintzner puts it, their Parisian dream world turns out to welcome them as 'accessories at best' (Lila), 'servants at worst' (Ely) (Mintzner, 2010). In contrast, the bond between the two feisty young banlieue women is constructed as heart-warming and authentic, as is Ely's relationship with her family, particularly once she is reconciled with her father, and, ultimately, Lila's relationship with her unhappy mother. Thus when Ely discovers that Lila's father has written to her telling her to forget him because he will never come back, she is able better to understand Lila's neediness and make the peace. The film's final scene celebrates the two young women's shared, high-spirited attitude to the world by reworking a trick they have deployed at various moments within the film, that is, taking a taxi into the city and then at the magic words 'Djobi! Djoba!' (translated as 'Tweedledum! Tweedledee!'), jumping out without paying and running off hand-in-hand through the streets of Paris! This transgressive act, which in the case of banlieue males might be cast as criminal activity, here unproblematically serves to underline the young women's shared mobility, agency and refusal of victimhood.

Indeed, this trope, and the frequency of the car and taxi trips the young women take between Paris, Puteaux and Neuilly, make this film different from other banlieue films, where travel between the centre and the periphery is usually problematic, and visits to the city centre end in disaster (as in *La Haine*). Here, if the young women's travel possibilities break down, it is because of their various betrayals rather than through any lack of agency; and though their wearing of the coveted but crippling designer shoes might be expected to impede their mobility, they simply remove them if the need arises. Furthermore, the blurring of the boundaries between Paris and the banlieue, evident in the film's views of and from La Défence, is evident, too, in the protagonists' changing occupation of space at the end of the narrative. Ely ends up swapping flats with Carole, with Carole moving to the flat in Puteaux acquired for Ely by her father, while Ely moves to Carole's flat in the 20e arrondissement of Paris, the location of which strangely resembles that of the banlieue with its surrounding blocks of high-rise flats. Meanwhile, Lila blags her way into a job in Paris selling designer shoes, a step up from selling popcorn in Puteaux, perhaps, but one that still bears some resemblance to it (while also giving her the occasion to show Maxx she is over him when he comes to buy shoes for the girlfriend she momentarily displaced). If, as Ely says in the middle of her row with Lila, no one cares about the difference between Neuilly and Puteaux any more, the distinction between Paris and Puteaux seems equally blurred, if only to demonstrate that life in Paris is not all that it is cracked up to be. At the same time, this blurring of borders and occupation of city space is clearly related to both gender and class. For if Lila, Ely and Carole can cross relatively easily between Puteaux and Paris, as can their wealthy Parisian friends, the same is less true of Eric, Lila's over-possessive, unimaginative, working-class boyfriend. Eric does not share Lila's aspirations, and his one trip to Paris, to drag Lila away from a party, leads directly to Lila deciding to leave him. The success of this film, then, is to some extent predicated on the continued marginalization of the young banlieue male, who is represented here, not as a stereotypical unemployed delinquent, but rather as someone whose old-fashioned values make him incapable of giving his girlfriend the excitement she craves.[5]

The primary feature of this film, then, and the new, and newly acceptable face of the banlieue that it presents, lies in its cheerful foregrounding of female performances, feminine desires and female friendship, which used to be something of a rarity in mainstream French cinema but has recently become established as a feature of numerous popular non-banlieue films by women directors, notably Lisa Azuelos's *LOL (Laughing Out Loud)* (2009, 3,649,758 spectators in France). No doubt, it could be argued that the feminization of the banlieue to be found in *All That Glitters* not only marginalizes young banlieue men and brushes aside ethnic differences, but also wishes away the very real social problems which beset the banlieue, and deprives it of the edginess that it has contributed to filmic representations elsewhere. However, the film's lack of sociopolitical edge cannot simply be elided with its focus on femininity; it may rather be that the cinematic site of disaffected otherness and social rebelliousness in France is now to be found elsewhere, as in Isild Le Besco's *Bas Fonds/Lower Depths* (2010), whose shocking vision of murderous, feral, underclass femininity in the provinces is far removed from the witty but well-groomed and ultimately unthreatening performance of designer shod femininity from the banlieue in *All That Glitters*.[6]

---

[5] However, the latest smash hit comedy in France, *Intouchables/The Intouchables* (2011, 15,698,471 spectators in France), written and directed by Nakache's older brother, Olivier Nakache, and Eric Toledano, allows a black banlieue youth (temporary) access to the city centre and the experience of wealth that Ely and Lila merely dream of, as he is first employed then befriended by a disabled white French aristocrat.

[6] For a discussion of *Bas-Fonds*, see Knipp (2011).

3

Entering No-Go Areas: Suburbs in Contemporary German Literature

Caroline Merkel

Introduction: Looking down on the suburbs

Ganz oben war eine Plattform, von der ich auf das Märkische Viertel hinunterschaute: ab und zu kreuzten einander Autobusse, Autos fuhren kaum, da die Männer drinnen in der Stadt arbeiteten und nur wenige Frauen hier Zweitwagen hatten. Außer ein paar Betrunkenen neben einem fahrbaren Würstchenstand sah ich weit und breit keine lebende Seele.

(At the very top was a platform from which I looked down on the Märkisches district: every now and then buses crossed paths; hardly any cars drove by, because the men would be working in the city and only a few women living here owned a second car. Apart from a bunch of drunks standing beside a hotdog stand, there was not a soul to be seen as far as the eye could see.) (Handke, 1974, 32f.)[1]

Looking down on the newly built suburbs of West Berlin in 1974, the narrator of Peter Handke's essay 'Die offenen Geheimnisse der Technokratie' is not able to see very much – except maybe the lack of urban life; he peruses monotonous, vast and deserted spaces. Ironically, however, watching and reading the suburbs from above, he also reminds us of de Certeau's critical vantage point from the World Trade Center over the epitome of urbanity – Manhattan – in the beginning of *Walking in the City* (de Certeau, 1980, p. 91). De Certeau states that seeing a city from above, immobilized, transformed into a text, does not tell us all that there is to know about a place: 'The panorama-city is a "theoretical" (that is, visual) simulacrum, in short a picture, whose condition of possibility is an oblivion and a misunderstanding of practices' (de Certeau, 1980, p. 93). However, urban planners, architects – as well as literary scholars – often do the very same thing when talking about the suburbs' problems or potential: a distant and abstract perspective is necessary in order to make more general statements. While this chapter cannot dispense with a more or less overarching analysis of suburban environments

---

[1] This and all subsequent translations by the author.

in contemporary literature, I would like to modify such an analysis, complementing it with what de Certeau would describe as a 'ground level' view (de Certeau, 1980, p. 97). It is my first working thesis that *literary* texts are more able to approach suburban space by focusing on the protagonists' paths and their 'microbe-like' practices (de Certeau, 1980, p. 96), that is, how they use and re-appropriate such space by exploring, avoiding or simply moving through it, making it 'their own'. Thus, the texts draw a mental map by tracing their protagonists' paths through their neighbourhood.[2]

Handke's text though is at first glance a typical example of criticism of the mostly suburban housing estates established in West Germany in the 1970s, which viewed the suburbs as not urban; they are seen as quite exotic or deserted places, almost inhumane environments. The people actually living there (at least by day) are housewives, children and unemployed drunks. Of course, suburbs in Germany are quite heterogeneous: you may find idyllic single-family housing in dormitory towns for the middle classes as well as the already mentioned housing estates that were built after World War II to symbolize West Germany's modernity and democratic development. Nowadays these estates have unfortunately often become places of social or ethnic segregation and marginalization, separated from the centre by poverty, language or levels of education.[3] However, both types of suburb share some characteristics that correlate with their peripheral position: they are mostly considered only in terms of how they contrast urbanity's sophistication and tradition (Halsall 2004); they are characterized by their apparent lack of distinguished buildings or sights and are presumed to be barely worth a visit. In urban planning discourse, both have also been problematized as a threat to urbanism and in particular to historic European cities because of their lack of architectural variety.[4] Since the 1990s, though, several attempts have been made not only to reinvent the suburbs but to acknowledge their importance and innovative potential. Thomas Sieverts (2003), for example, initiated a new approach to describe and plan today's urban landscape with his concept of the *Zwischenstadt* (the 'in-between-city').

Still, it is safe to say that the marginal status of the suburbs is not only a geographical matter: texts about the suburbs always seem to range on the fringes of urban and/or literary discourse. Taking a closer look at two literary examples, I shall argue nonetheless that the suburbs in contemporary literature are places of innovative potential, not least in a poetological sense. I would therefore like to turn to a conception of cultural theory that not only offers a spatial model of languages and cultures but even focuses on the very margins of those semiotic systems: Yuri Lotman's 'semiosphere'.

Hot spots at the borders: Lotman's semiosphere

In the 1980s Yuri Lotman, initially a formalist of the Tartu-Moscow Semiotic School, developed the concept of the semiosphere, describing it as 'the semiotic space, outside

[2] The analyses presented in this chapter are part of a larger PhD project at the German Department at the University of Tübingen.
[3] On German architectural history after World War II see, for example, Spliid Høgsbro and Wischmann (2010), Kuchenbuch (2010) and Ingeborg (1999).
[4] An early and typical example for the harsh criticism on urban development is Mitscherlich (1965).

of which semiosis cannot exist' (Lotman, 2005, p. 205). The semiosphere contains the total of the semiotic codes of a language or a culture. Its internal structure falls into centre and periphery. Especially interesting for my purposes is the fact that from the beginning Lotman emphasizes the possible correlation of semiotic and territorial space:

> When the semiosphere involves real territorial features as well, the boundary is spatial in the literal sense. [. . .] Hence the appeal of the centre for the most important cultic and administrative buildings. Less valued social groups are settled on the periphery. Those who are below any social value are settled on the frontier of the outskirts [. . .], by the city gate, in the suburbs. [. . .] And these are the spaces which marginalized social groups make 'their own'. (Lotman, 2001, p. 140)

Lotman uses this concept to describe the cultural innovation taking place in those cultural borderlands. If de Certeau is critical of vertically organized perspectival hierarchies, Lotman draws attention to certain horizontal structures. For him, it is not the 'centre' of a culture or a language that develops and innovates a semiotic system, it is rather its borders. Seen from the centre, the peripheries of sign- or cultural systems may appear to be mute or empty, because the language or code of the periphery does not coincide with the hegemonic central one. But at the margins of a semiotic system – that sometimes coincide with its spatial borders like in Lotman's example of the expanding cultural area of Ancient Rome – influences and innovative impulses from other systems can be selected, translated and integrated, thus not only making the marginal position 'one's own' but even conquering and innovating the system from its borders. (Lotman, 2005, p. 212) According to Lotman, the periphery is therefore the most important structural position of a culture, which slowly develops into a new centre: 'The hottest spots for semioticizing processes are the boundaries of the semiosphere' (Lotman, 2001, p. 136).

Entering the suburbs: Georg Klein and Feridun Zaimoglu

As I stated above, literary texts often do not confine themselves to the point of view of looking from the rooftop down on the suburbs. Instead they follow de Certeau in his request to approach the streets and focus on everyday practices, which form and appropriate suburban space. I would like to show that the practice of storytelling in particular not only catalyses the creation and innovation of language but also the appropriation of suburban space. Therefore I also assume that suburbs in literature can form those productive marginal spaces where borders of cultural systems or literary genres can be negotiated, with the potential even to influence the system's centre, as Lotman suggests.

The following two examples of contemporary German literature are very different texts, and take place in very different suburban settings, but they are both able to negotiate as well as integrate new elements from the outside with regard to their content and their genre.

Georg Klein: Roman unserer Kindheit (2010) [Our childhood's novel]

'To practice space is thus to repeat the joyful and silent experience of childhood; it is, in a place, to be other and to move toward the other.' (de Certeau, 1980, p. 110)

German author Georg Klein has been critically acclaimed since the publication of his first novel *Libidissi* in 1998. In 2000 he received the Ingeborg Bachmann Prize for his unique style and his ability to write texts which form rich puzzles that elude easy solution (Sternburg, 2010; Hartwig, 2010). In Klein's latest novel, *Roman unserer Kindheit,* we enter the suburbs by way of childhood memories: the reader follows the paths of a group of children through a post-war housing estate in the early 1960s; narration is provided by a fairy-like unborn child of one of the families. It is the last summer holiday in elementary school for at least one of the mentioned children:

> Das ganze ungeheure Imperium der Sommerferien liegt vor ihnen. Sie ahnen alle, nur noch einmal, ein letztes und deshalb besonderes Mal darf sich die Grenze dieses Reichs hinter einem Horizont aus weißgolden gleißendem Sonnenlicht verlieren. Danach, im Herbst, wird einer der großen Gelenk-Omnibusse [. . .] den Älteren Bruder jeden Schultag, [. . .] aus der Siedlung hinein in die Stadt, ins Gymnasium verschleppen.
>
> (The whole enormous empire of summer holidays lies before them. They all sense that for only one more time, one last and therefore outstanding time, the border of this realm is going to lose itself beyond a horizon of white golden glittering sunlight. After that, in the autumn, one of those big articulated buses [. . .] will take the Older Brother away, out of the neighbourhood, into the city and to secondary school, every school day.) (Klein, 2010, p. 25)

Both the location and the time frame of the novel seem to form a threshold to something new and indicate the children's coming adventures to be some kind of rite of passage. Of course, many recent novels located in the suburbs deal with aspects of coming of age and seem to reflect the adolescent's feeling of standing outside of society, waiting at the threshold of adulthood.[5] In this particular case, however, the protagonists' youth seems to correlate with yet another aspect of their surroundings: both the suburbs and the children, all of them born after 1945, seem to represent a new beginning after the war, a clean slate, an example of the Republic's modernity, rationality and *Wirtschaftswunder*:

> Von Herzen willkommen in der Neuen Siedlung! Die Sonne ist blank wie Konservendosenblech, der wolkenlose Himmel prunkt mit klassisch reinem Blau. Der letzte Sommermonat wirft ein präzises Licht in den Kreuztöterweg . . .
>
> (A warm welcome to the New Housing Estate! The sun is as shiny as a canning tin, the cloudless sky flaunts his classical pure blue. The last month of summer casts a precise light on Kreuztöterweg . . .) (Klein, 2010, p. 441)

---

[5] A prominent example from English Literature is Hanif Kureishi's 1990 novel *The Buddha of Suburbia.*

Nevertheless, the lack of history, the seeming total absence of the terrors of the recent war, turn the housing estate into a place as uncanny as it is idyllic, a place de Certeau would call '. . . [n]othing "special"', possessing 'nothing that is marked, opened up by a memory or a story, signed by something or someone else' (de Certeau, 1980, p. 106). The ordinariness of the suburbs has often caused problems in defining them. They often appear to be void spaces lacking specific functions, signs and maybe most of all history and therefore an identity of their own. As Roger Webster states, 'suburbia has no "history": its archives are empty' (Webster, 2001, p. 2), which can even be seen as an allusion to Marc Augé's concept of 'non-place', which is among other things characterized by an absence of history.[6]

However, the novel begins with the Older Brother's bike accident, a significant first scratch on the idyllic surface. And with the help of a group of odd, almost alien veterans – sole reminders of the recent war – the children discover the history lying beneath their homes: a medieval underground system of tunnels accommodating monsters that breed irrationality and fear, and which are apparently out to get one of the children.

The trope of the underground labyrinth serves to evoke certain metaphors relating to memory and also oblivion: buried, repressed memories that need to be discovered or excavated; the journey through the underworld as an encounter with the dead or as an image of the subconscious.[7] In addition, Renate Lachmann states that one of the cultural functions of the fantastic is to compensate for what is forgotten, repressed or forbidden within a culture (Lachmann, 2002).[8] In this context, the children's adventures in *Roman unserer Kindheit* can be read as acts of recovering repressed parts of a collective identity and history.

If we take a closer look at the practices that not only contribute to the novel's plot-development but also produce its suburban setting, it is remarkable how the children are constantly making the surrounding space 'their own'. For example, they do not only roam the usual everyday places, but also the margins of the suburb – the woods, a private dumping ground, an unfinished and abandoned construction site – thus expanding their suburban world and exploring its hidden secrets on foot or by bike:

> Das Eingangstor der Kolonie steht offen. [. . .] Eigentlich wäre dahinten Schluss. Selbst bei Tag ist es dort mit dem Weiterfahren vorbei. Seit sie zusammen losziehen, kennen sie die Grenze, die dort ihrem Vorstoßen Richtung Norden gesetzt ist. Hinter ihr wartet zwar noch ein weiteres Stück der Welt, sie wissen sogar seinen Namen, aber als Kind geht man besser nicht hin.

> (The gate to the allotment gardens stands open. [. . .] Normally, over there would be the end. Even in daylight, there would be no going further. Ever since they started strolling around together, they have known that their exploring of the northern area has had to stop here. There is yet another bit of world beyond that border,

---

[6] 'A place which cannot be defined as relational, or historical, or concerned with identity will be a non-place' (Augé, 1995, pp. 77–8).

[7] Excavation is a prominent image that Sigmund Freud (1937) uses to describe the work of the psycho-analyst.

[8] For a discussion of the way Lachmann's thoughts on the fantastic connect with ideas of collective and cultural memory, see Feld (2006).

they even know its name, but you had better not go there as a child.) (Klein, 2010, p. 197)

They 'actualize' the suburban space, extending their territory, taking shortcuts, climbing walls, discovering hidden doors, thereby renewing some locations and abandoning others; as de Certeau puts it: 'In that way, he [the walker] makes them exist as well as emerge. But he also moves them about and he invents others, since the crossing, drifting away, or improvisation of walking privilege, transform, or abandon spatial elements' (de Certeau, 1980, p. 98).[9] Besides the appropriation of space by moving around, it is often the storytelling, mainly by the Older Brother, that enables and encourages these adventures, allowing the real and the imaginative to merge:

> Die Eschen ragen am höchsten. Wie die Spitzen von Masten piksen sie ins weiche, noch nicht von der kommenden Hitze ausgehärtete Blau, und damit ist unserem Älteren Bruder offenbar, dass er für seine Freunde heute als Erstes eine Piratengeschichte erfinden wird.

> (The ash trees rise highest. Like the tops of masts they pierce into the soft azure, not yet cured by the heat that will follow; and just like that it becomes obvious to our Older Brother that he is first of all going to make up a pirate story.) (Klein, 2010, p. 29)

His stories, rooted in their surroundings, evolve into a fantastic narrative that even merges with the book's storyline itself, when, for example, the children discover the magical key of a fairy tale told before, opening not one but three closed doors on their way (ibid., p. 378).

The possibility of the fantastic thus broadens the suburban world of the children on another level. Integrating the fantastic into their everyday life, the children are able to find words and images for the unspeakable that still dominates their apparently rational, modern post-war environment. It furthermore becomes clear that the seemingly ahistorical place is filled with stories and history of its own. The children tell stories and legends; their own adventure turns out to be a piece of suburban myth and identity – maybe the beginning of a suburban archive. The two practices of exploring and storytelling can therefore be seen as two components of developing a suburban myth and as such, are an essential element of a local suburban identity. The novel itself turns out to be a contribution to suburban legend following Renate Lachmann's thesis that literary texts 'construct [. . .] architectures of memory, in which they deposit mnemonic images, as in the processes of the *ars memoriae*' (Lachmann, 1997, p. 11).

Feridun Zaimoglu: Kanak Sprak (1995) [Kanak Talk]

Storytelling plays an important part in my second example as well: Feridun Zaimoglu's debut *Kanak Sprak* (1995) and its sequels *Abschaum* (1997) and *Koppstoff* (1998) examine the suburbs of Kiel by means of fictional interviews. The interviewees are

---

[9] Tim Ingold (2007) categorizes the children's journey as typical 'wayfaring' along the paths of an unknown prey.

residents of Gaarden, a troubled suburb of Kiel, segregated from the rest of the city mainly by ethnicity and their own argot:

> Wir sind wüchsige aus gaarden, hier, wo man das olle gras halm für halm wachsen hört, wo nix außer gebell steckt, hier in jeder toten gasse, hierhin hat man uns wie'n faden popel geschnickt [. . .] Gaarden is knochenbrecher, `n sperrbezirk, das is hier das olle ostufer und dort der reiche westen, und dazwischen reckt sich wie'n langer arm die gablenzbrücke, doch du denkst, die vermaledeite brücke is tag wie nacht und ewig hochgeklappt, so is es in gaarden, wo ja prall unzählige kümmel hausen . . .

> (We're Gaarden born and bred, here, where you can hear the old grass growing blade by blade, where there's nothing but dogs barking, here in every dead-end street, here is where we were flicked like a bogy [. . .] Gaarden is a bonecrusher, an off-limits area, it's the worn-out eastern banks over here and the rich west over there, and in between, stretching like a long arm, the Gablenz-bridge, but you're thinking, that accursed bridge is folded up day and night and forever, that's what it's like in Gaarden, where there are countless numbers of caraway-eating Turks . . .)

(Zaimoglu, 1995, p. 91)

In the 1990s, Zaimoglu became an important representative of Turkish-German youth culture. By turning the derogatory term 'Kanak' into a label of self-designation, and combining codes of German hip-hop and literary prose, he built a platform not only for himself but also for many other young writers and performers.[10]

The suburbs in this context are at first mainly referred to as non-urban, as divided and excluded from the 'real' city. The texts create their spatial structure mainly by constructing a collective subject of 'we, on this side of the river' juxtaposed with the city's hegemonic other. Their inhabitants seem restricted to the area, unable to make their way into society, mirroring the limitations and restrictions of the label 'migrants'. Throughout the text, however, the suburbs gain the status of a cultural and ethnic contact-zone, their language undermining not only the literary *Leitkultur* but also mobilizing its protagonists' fixed position in their peripheral 'ghetto'. As I want to show in the following, counter-strategies can be found in the text's choice of words as well as its use of spatial metaphors, again combining language and space to illustrate cultural dynamics.

In terms of language use, it is mainly Zaimoglu's handling of the term 'Kanake' that has received attention (Günter, 1999; Cheesman, 2004). Indeed, Zaimoglu's preface to the novel already suggests his intention to actively resignify the derogatory term 'Kanake' in the Butlerian sense, citing it 'against its originary purposes, [to] perform a reversal of effects' (Butler, 1997, p. 14):

> Kanake, ein Etikett, das nach mehr als 30 Jahren Immigrationsgeschichte von Türken nicht nur Schimpfwort ist, sondern auch ein Name, den 'Gastarbeiterkinder' der zweiten und vor allem der dritten Generation mit stolzem Trotz führen.

---

[10] On Zaimloglu's reception, his effect on German literary culture and on his use of language, see Adelson (2003) and Moraldo (2007).

('Kanake', a label, which after more than 30 years of Turkish immigration history is not only a term of abuse, but also a name, borne in proud defiance by the children, and especially grandchildren, of guest workers.) (Zaimoglu, 1995, p. 9)

The hate-speech term 'Kanake' had earlier been appropriated and resignified by German-Turkish hip-hop culture as a term of self-identification. As Tom Cheesman points out, 'This combative usage goes back to the late 1980s in urban hip hop circles, where it is compared with US rappers' "niggah", though closer connotative equivalents are "spick" or, in the UK, "Paki"' (Cheesman, 2004, p. 85).

Such re-appropriation becomes a subversive practice when taking the form of aggressive speech, accentuating rather than negating the marginal position (Günter, 1999, p. 20). The novels deliberately play with mainstream culture's fears and prejudices, stating that 'We're the Kanaks you Germans have always warned against. Now we're real, exactly as you feared and imagined us' (Zaimoglu, 1997, p. 183). Zaimoglu's strategy is to invent a 'pseudo-ethnicity' (Cheesman, 2004, p. 83) with its own stylized language. Reiterating and exaggerating common labels can become a subversive practice, undermining the stereotypical polarization by challenging not only the concept of 'Kanaks' but of German 'Alemans' as well. Conflicts and discrepancies between both groups may be increased rather than neutralized. Yet the concept of ethnic or cultural identity in itself can be exposed as a product of ascriptive iteration, and thereby its implied hierarchies might be destabilized. Regarding Lotman's concept of the semiosphere, resignification might be one example of how borders of semiotic systems turn the centre's imposed language into something productive.

The suburbs, in this context, are a spatial representation of both the exclusion from a seemingly homogeneous and hegemonic cultural identity as well as of the limitations of stereotypes. 'Kanaks', as 'the others', are not only banished from the well-restored historic centres, they are fixed in certain positions in society and categorized in 'reservations'. As Zaimoglu puts it:

> Der einheimische hat für'n kümmel ja zwei reservate frei: entweder bist du'n lieb-
> alilein [. . .] dann gibt's noch'n zweites reservat, in dem der fremdländer den part
> des verwegenen desperados übernimmt . . .

> (The native finds only two reservations suitable for the 'caraway eaters': you're
> either a good-little-Ali [or] there is a second reservation, in which the foreigner
> takes on the part of the bold desperado . . .) (Zaimoglu, 1995, p. 31)

Similar to the re-appropriation of terms like 'Kanake' or 'Kümmel' (which means something like 'caraway eater') and related clichés, Zaimoglu's interviewees develop spatial strategies to make the assigned space at the margins – like the suburb Gaarden – their own 'hood':

> Also in der gegend wohn ich schon seit meinem ganzen leben, [. . .] daß ich fragen
> kann: hier hängt ihr rum, das geht klar, weil's meine verdammte gegend is. [. . .]
> weil der wert, den gibt's nicht im kaufhaus, den hast du, weil die leute sagen: er ist
> die gegend.

(So, I've lived in this neighbourhood all my life, [. . .] that's why I have the right to ask: you're hanging around here, that's ok, 'cause it's my fucking neighbourhood. [. . .] because that value [to 'own' my district] cannot be bought at the department store, you got it because people say: he is the neighbourhood.) (Zaimoglu, 1995, p. 92f.)

In this paragraph, it becomes clear that the 'neighbourhood', even if mostly described as a restrictive 'ghetto', at the same time presents an essential part of one's self-staging, enhancing a person's standing as a status symbol would. Conquering the limited suburban area compares to constructing one's own identity within the limitations of prejudice even if the appropriated space still remains foreign territory, or 'Pseudoterritorium' – 'is ja gar nicht deins, es gehört ja den Deutschen' ['pseudo territory' – 'it's not yours actually, it belongs to the Germans'] (Zaimoglu, 1997, p. 65). The city's margins remain a place where ethnic identities as well as questions of belonging and territorial claims have to be negotiated constantly.

It is striking that the interviewees in 'Kanak Sprak' mention the experience of provoking fear among the rest of society when occupying a space of their own. The appropriation of the space that was allotted to them seems to suggest that the margins may expand and threaten to enter the centre itself: 'Da kommt er, er muß doch kommen, wir hören schon seine Schritte, morgen rennt der Kanak unsere Zäune ein . . .' ['There he comes, he just has to come, we can hear his footsteps already, tomorrow the Kanak will be knocking down our fences . . .'] (Zaimoglu, 1998, p. 27).

The collapsing of borders and penetration of boundaries are in many contexts associated with violence. Indeed the fear of riots in troubled neighbourhoods of the kind that occurred in Paris in 2005 and 2010 or London in 2011 has been widely discussed in the German media (e.g. Klingst, 2005; Kröncke, 2010; Kerstan, 2011). Zaimoglu confirms this dread in a way. One whole interview focuses on 'attacking' the Germans – who are barricading themselves behind high fences – and on trying to penetrate the invisible walls of cultural segregation.[11] Though he also states: 'Attacking is something completely different from intending a massacre' (Zaimoglu, 1998, p. 131). Still, claiming your own territory is already a form of attack, since you defy those wishing to make the same claim.

Zaimoglu's Kanaks do not even express the desire to reach the core of city or society for that matter. Even if *Kanak Sprak* is in many ways comparable to Kureishi's earlier novel *The Buddha of Suburbia* (Kureishi, 1990) (in terms of negotiation of identity and ethnic stereotypes), unlike Kureishi's Karim, Zaimoglu's protagonists do not yearn to be part of the inner city's culture or to climb the social ladder, they definitely are not 'going somewhere' (Kureishi, 1990, p. 3). Actually, the centre's culture in Zaimoglu's texts does not make a desirable impression overall:

. . . denn biste mal inner Deutschsiedlung [. . .] siehst du, was wirklich Sache is: Alemania is n Nepplokal, und nix wie weg vom Scheißtrödel.

---

[11] 'Und Aleman hat sich ja auf seine lausigen Güter zurückgezogen, und er wird rübenrot, weil da hat sich so n Kümmelkeil aufn Weg gemacht. Die Schneise is echt ordentlich, die so nen Keil da man treibt innen Alemangrundstück.' ['And the Aleman has retreated into his own lousy properties, and he turns as red as a beetroot, because there's a caraway-wedge on its way. It's a really decent swath, well driven into Aleman's lot.'] (Zaimoglu, 1998, p. 134).

(. . . cause if you've been to a German estate [. . .], you see what really is going on: Alemania is a rip-off joint, let's get away from that rummage.)

(Zaimoglu, 1998, p. 135)

Even while 'attacking' mainstream culture, the Kanaks do not really wish for a place in it; they want their own space that at the same time belongs to someone else, because that is what might enable them to create an identity independent from concepts of territorial heritage and belonging.

It is therefore only appropriate that Zaimoglu also gives his interviewees a language that is not easily tied to only one culture or ethnicity. He plays with the concepts of authenticity and identity, lending the people on the margins of the city not one but many different voices, pretending to simply write down an authentic street language while in fact creating a highly stylized language that combines German, Arabic and hip-hop style: Kanak Sprak ('Kanak Talk').[12] Intentionally or not, one might even say that by neither assimilating to conventional literary style nor lapsing into a niche of 'ethnic authenticity', with *Kanak Sprak,* Zaimoglu has managed to integrate subculture into main literary culture by creating a new kind of literary language.

Making contact: Suburbs as creative spaces

In summary, this chapter has shown that it is important to take a closer look both at the city's margins and at the practices that form suburban space. Both novels at first seem to affirm established images of the suburbs as represented in Handke's essay from the 1970s: in Klein's novel, the housing estate seems like a cold and vacant non-place due to its lack of history and stories to tell; in *Kanak Sprak* Zaimoglu accentuates the suburbs as the antipode of the city, which is characterized only by its otherness. However, through close reading, both assumptions turn out to be short-sighted, because the protagonists' spatial and linguistic practices disclose the suburbs' potential as a contact zone – between the real and the fantastic, the visible and the unspeakable and society's insiders and outsiders. Suburbs can also be seen as contact zones in the sense of Mary Louise Pratt's definition, as 'social spaces where cultures meet, clash, and grapple with each other' (Pratt, 1991, p. 33). Texts like *Kanak Sprak* and *Roman unserer Kindheit* trace the creative potential of these outer limits of the city: the suburbs as a border and contact zone do not necessarily marginalize their residents, but sometimes allow them to 'own' their district and turn the housing estates into a culturally creative place that influences the core of both culture and city.

[12] For a detailed analysis of Zaimoglu's literary language, see Skiba (2004).

4

J. G. Ballard: The 'Seer of Shepperton' as the Seer of Suburbia

Jarrad Keyes

The suburbs are the last great mystery.

(Ballard, 2007, p. 49)

The *Collins English Dictionary* defines 'Ballardian' as 'resembling or suggestive of the conditions' depicted in Ballard's works, including 'dystopian modernity' and 'bleak man-made landscapes'. While it contains an element of truth with respect to earlier novels like *The Drowned World* (1962), *The Drought* (1965), *The Crystal World* (1966) and the short stories of *Vermillion Sands* (1973), this definition illustrates a wider misconception of Ballard's oeuvre. In emphasizing the 'dystopian' elements of 'bleak man-made landscapes', such an approach overlooks the importance of suburbia as an archetypal Ballardian concern. For where dystopia, in temporal terms, denotes the degradation of an ideal form, and the adjective bleak conveys a negative order of representation, neither term sufficiently captures the complexity of Ballard's spatial thought.

As early short stories such as 'The Concentration City' (1957), 'Chronopolis' (1960) and 'Billennium' (1961) demonstrate, Ballard's fictional imagination was long exercised by questions of space. In a 1989 interview, Ballard described his novels from the 1970s as being concerned with 'the effects on human psychology of the changes brought by science and technology, the modern urban landscape, the freeways and motorways, [and] the peculiar psychology of life in vast high-rise condominiums' (Dibbell, 1989, p. 51). The 'irony' of this emphasis on psychological space, Will Self notes, is that Ballard's works have proved 'far more accurate predictions of the character of evolving modern life' (Self, 2000, p. 14). Amid the context of profound social, economic and technological changes throughout the latter half of the twentieth century, not least with respect to England's changing physical and social geographies during this time, Ballard's works help us to reappraise the growing significance of suburbia as a literary concern and as a figurative response to historical change. With reference to several lesser-known newspaper articles and essays, this chapter argues that Ballard's corpus constitutes a lifelong reappraisal of suburbia which is significant because it rethinks the conventional terms of its relationship with the city. No longer to be viewed against the city, whether as a monstrosity or as insipid and repetitious outgrowths, Ballard's suburbia provokes an important re-examination of the language of space in light of what he calls the 'virtual city'.

*   *   *

Suburbia was long recognized by Ballard as an important aspect of the emergent character of modern British life. 'Something about the word "suburb"', Ballard wrote in 1973, 'convinces me that I was on the right track in my pursuit of the day after tomorrow'. This 'pursuit' raises the relationship between the city and suburbia: 'As the countryside vanishes under a top-dressing of chemicals, and as cities provide little more than an urban context for traffic intersections, the suburbs are at last coming into their own. The skies are larger, the air more generous, the clock less urgent' (Ballard, 1985, p. 7). The languid time of suburbia contrasts temporally with the country and the city alike. Consider the diminishing significance attached to the countryside, cloaked by a 'top-dressing of chemicals'. Ballard's suggestive metaphor connotes the need to reappraise ideas of the 'natural' realm in light of twentieth-century scientific and technological developments.[1] Accordingly, there is a conspicuous absence of natural space in Ballard's novels. Note also the dwindling value attributed to cities. As 'little more' than 'traffic intersections', such metropolitan centres are for Ballard notably devoid of experiential value. The suburbs come 'into their own' as traditional ideas of the city are brought into question.

Ballard's rising interest in suburbia contrasts with what he identifies as a dominant nostalgia among responses to the city. In a 1974 interview, Ballard argues that: 'We tend to assume that people want to be together in a kind of renaissance city if you like, imaginatively speaking, strolling in the evening across a crowded piazza [. . .] One is not [however] living in something like an 18th-to-19th-century city' (Ballard, 1973). The 'renaissance city', a form of public open space associated with the Italian concept of the piazza, is for Ballard incompatible with the contemporaneous form of metropolitan space. Consistent with the sense of cities being 'urban contexts for traffic intersections', it follows that the very idea of strolling around the metropolis is a misnomer. As *Crash* and *Concrete Island* demonstrate, to congregate with others is not something that occurs on foot but within the automobile. Ballard accordingly recognizes that the automobile is fundamental to understanding the changing social and physical landscape of the twentieth century.[2]

Contemporaneous changes in Britain's social geography provide another significant dimension to Ballard's interest in suburbia. Combined with the settings of his novels, the fact that Ballard's protagonists are almost exclusively white men employed within the tertiary sector is an important indicator of socio-economic change. Take, for example, Ballard's 'concrete and steel' trilogy (1973–5). In *Crash* (1973), James Ballard's employment as a television commercial director at Shepperton Studios conveys the

---

[1]   Ballard here pre-empts the sociological reconceptualization of 'risk' and reconceptualization of the 'natural' world. See Beck, 1992, p. 10; Giddens, 1991, p. 4.

[2]   See Urry, 2004.

growing importance of the media. Robert Maitland is an architect who crashes on the eponymous *Concrete Island* (1974), whose location – adjacent to television studios (ibid., p. 11) and a derelict scrapyard (ibid., p. 39) – figuratively portends the eclipse of British industry within an increasingly post-industrial economy. Meanwhile in *High-Rise* (1975), Richard Wilder is a director, Nicholas Royle is an architect and Robert Laing is a doctor. The latter novel is especially important because it connects demographic and geographic change. Housing 2,000 'virtually homogeneous professional[s]' and set within an area of 'abandoned dockland and warehousing along the north bank of the river [. . .] already zoned for reclamation' (Ballard, 2005, pp. 10, 8), the eponymous *High-Rise* anticipates the social and physical consequences of gentrification enshrined by Docklands.[3]

Amid these twin forces of deindustrialization and gentrification, Ballard's subsequent works chiefly focus on non-metropolitan spaces. The 1979 novel *The Unlimited Dream Company* marks a turning point in Ballard's conceptualization of suburbia. In the 'quiet suburban town' (Ballard, 1981, p. 9) of Shepperton, narrator Blake recounts several conventional tropes of suburbia. Shepperton is variously described as a 'deserted riverside town', a 'suffocating town' and the medium for 'sterile lives' (ibid., pp. 7, 46, 35). Blake's Shepperton thus appears distinctly 'Ballardian' insofar as it resembles 'bleak, man-made landscapes'. As Blake's allusions to Plato's cave (ibid., pp. 90, 100, 106) suggest, however, appearances are deceptive.

In a remarkable passage, Blake describes Shepperton as 'the everywhere of suburbia, the paradigm of nowhere' (ibid., p. 35). Contrary to commonplace 'images of sprawling and homogeneous residential areas away from the town and city centres' (Clapson, 1998, p. 2), Blake's 'paradigm of nowhere' heralds an important break with orthodox accounts of suburbia defined in terms of its relationship with the city. It is paradigmatic inasmuch as it is not defined through or against the city; it is neither a 'peripheral' space nor homogeneous. Put differently, Blake's Shepperton is not a space that occupies the margins of the city, nor does its place-ness rely on a contrast with the city. Anticipating the discussion of the virtual city which concludes this chapter, Blake's Shepperton – as a figurative social and physical geography – impels a reappraisal of the category of the real. Blake's allusions to Plato's cave, a foundational work in Western philosophy, are useful here. 'That real world which I was slowly unfolding as I drew back the curtains that muffled Shepperton and the rest of this substitute realm', Blake notes, amounts to 'a re-ordering of reality in the service of a greater and more truthful design' (Ballard, 1981, pp. 90, 106). Such references prompt Andrzej Gasiorek to conclude that Blake's Shepperton is merely 'a pale copy of the world, an empty simulacrum of the real' (2005, p. 136). Such a reading fundamentally misunderstands the underlying logic of spatial representation. 'The simulacrum is not a degraded copy', Gilles Deleuze writes. 'It harbours a positive power [. . .] The copy is an image endowed with resemblance, the simulacrum is an image without resemblance' (1989, pp. 299, 295). Unlike Gasiorek's 'empty simulacrum of the real', Blake's Shepperton is an image that is, in Deleuzian terms, 'without resemblance'. That is to say, its image of suburbia is not a

---

[3] See 'Thatcher's London' in Porter, 1994, pp. 445–70, esp. 464–7.

'pale copy' (Gasiorek) of the world; it is not a degraded spatial form consistent with the dystopian dimension of the adjective Ballardian. Contrary to being a 'parody of a genuine "place"' (Gasiorek, 2005, p. 136), Blake's 're-ordering of reality' begins a process of redefining space and conventional definitions of the real that concludes with the concept of the virtual city.

Ballard's 1989 novella *Running Wild* provides an excursus on the subject of gated communities. Comprising 32 acres of land 'ringed by a steel mesh fence fitted with electrical alarms' and 'regularly patrolled by guard-dogs and radio-equipped handlers' (Ballard, 2002, p. 13), Pangbourne Village is located in Berkshire, approximately 40 miles west of London. Such defensive spaces, the novel points out, are designed to maintain socio-economic privilege. 'Secure behind their high walls and surveillance cameras', narrator Dr Greville observes that: 'These estates in effect constitute a chain of closed communities whose lifelines run directly along the M4 to the offices and consulting rooms, restaurants, and private clinics of central London. They remain completely apart from their local communities' (ibid., p. 12). Central London is never simply the absent centre of Ballard's works. Rather, its plight is inextricably linked to that of Pangbourne Village, which houses the senior management of the service sector synonymous here with central London. That the capital presently represents little more than a space for consumption and the accumulation of wealth represents a shift in Ballard's spatial thought. Since the publication of *High-Rise* (1975), the gentrification process associated with the docklands has spread out from central London, along the M4 and into these insular estates. *Running Wild* is thus notable because it associates the gentrification of city centres with the creation of outlying defensive spaces. The creation of such defensive spaces, the novel suggests, is inextricably linked to the commodification of city centres.

Though Ballard's recurring Alcatraz metaphor (Ballard, 2000, p. 110; 2002, p. 40; 2005, p. 52) suggests that insularity and disconnection are important features of the new spatial paradigm, and so help explain his earlier repudiation of the piazza, the processes of change his works illustrate do not simply homogenize space. Estates such as Pangbourne Village accentuate difference. Despite the dubious 'success' of the village, which resulted in 'plans for the construction of similar estates nearby' (Ballard, 2002, p. 85), such developments rely on an 'outside' against which to define themselves. 'All walls are boundaries', architectural critic Peter Marcuse notes, 'but not all boundaries are walls' (Marcuse, 1997, p. 101). Boundaries can be as much psychological as physical; the exclusivity of Pangbourne Village is largely attributable to maintaining physical and psychological differentiation. Where the village 'is remarkable only for having advanced these general trends [of defensive space] towards almost total self-sufficiency' (Ballard, 2002, p. 13), such 'trends' cannot efface all vestiges of spatial difference and maintain claims of exclusivity. The reluctance to collapse the tension between processes of gentrification and spatial difference is characteristic of Ballard's geographical imagination.

Ballard's 1996 novel *Cocaine Nights* provides a wider narrative of spatial change in western Europe. Consistent with Ballard's later fiction, narrator Charles Prentice departs from central London, leaving behind his 'Barbican flat' (Ballard, 1996, p. 14) for Spain. Upon arriving in the Costa del Sol, Prentice discovers a coastal strip – 'a nondescript plain of market gardens, tractor depots, and villa projects' – that amounts to:

> A zone as depthless as a property developer's brochure [. . .] lack[ing] even the rudiments of scenic or architectural charm [while] Sotogrande [a large resort and privately owned residential development] was a town without either centre or suburbs, and seemed to be little more than a dispersal ground for golf courses and swimming pools. (ibid., pp. 15–16)

Lacking the 'rudiments' of 'scenic' contemplation, Sotogrande recalls Ballard's earlier contention that the countryside had disappeared 'under a top-dressing of chemicals'. The resemblance to a 'property developer's brochure' suggests that the financial interests of the residential complex have supplanted the aesthetic function of the landscape as a scene of contemplation. Ballard's analogy raises the subject of the restructuring of Western capitalism in the 1970s, which broadly placed a greater emphasis on real estate speculation at the expense of industrial production.[4] This 'urban revolution', to use Henri Lefebvre's phrase, structurally transformed capitalism and the production of space. Sotogrande figuratively captures this twofold process, illustrating the growth of the tertiary sector and being a 'town without either centre or suburbs'. It is, in other words, a place whose identity cannot be measured in a conventional language which understands space in binary terms.

Anticipating the discussion of the virtual city, the importance of Ballard's conceptual overhaul of suburbia concerns its relationship to the city. Suburbia is not, Ballard suggests, merely an adjunct to the city. A byword for the gentrification of city centres which is for Ballard illustrative of contemporary spatial trends, 'heritage London' (Ballard, 2007, p. 101) here attests to the paucity of conventional hermeneutic approaches to space. Contrary to Raymond Williams, for whom 'there is a wide range of settlements between the traditional poles of country and city' – including 'suburb' – to describe 'our own world' (1973, p. 1), Ballard does not take the growing significance of suburbia to validate the binary approach to space encompassed within the 'traditional poles' of city and country. Amid the context of structural transformations within capitalism in the 1970s, the heightened status Ballard accords suburbia presages the end of the city as it is conventionally figured. Where 'each city receives its form from the desert it opposes' (Calvino, 1979, p. 18), the emergence of the virtual city refracts the image of the city by disrupting that 'desert' – be it country or suburb – against which its 'form' depends.

To return to *Cocaine Nights*, Prentice later weds economic with sociospatial transformation while appraising a neighbouring resort. 'Purpose-built in the 1970s by a consortium of Anglo-Dutch developers', Estrella de Mar was:

> A residential retreat for the professional classes of northern Europe. The resort had turned its back on mass tourism, and there were none of the skyscraper blocks that rose from the water's edge at Benalmadena and Torremolinos. The old town by the

---

[4] See, for example, Lefebvre, 2003, pp. 159–60; Harvey, 1989.

harbour had been pleasantly bijouized, the fishermen's cottages converted to wine
bars and antique shops. (Ballard, 1996, pp. 35–6)

In converting fisherman's cottages into wine bars and antiques shops, and so transforming a space of production into a site of consumption, the process of gentrification
signals the figurative eclipse of industrial production. As a brief history of the region
reveals, a number of significant developments postdate the construction of the resort.
According to Prentice's confidante Bobby Crawford, Estrella de Mar was:

> Built in the 1970s – open access, street festivals, tourists welcome. The Residencia
> Costasol is pure 1990s. Security rules. Everything is designed around an obsession
> with crime [. . .] defensible space raised to an almost planetary intensity – security
> guards, tele-surveillance, no entrance except through the main gates, the whole
> complex closed to outsiders. (ibid., pp. 212, 211)

Although designed to be a private development for a social elite, Estrella de Mar (c.
1970s) theoretically retained 'open access' to those with the requisite income levels.
By contrast, the Residencia Costasol complex (c. 1990s) is 'closed to outsiders'. Read
alongside *Running Wild*, Pangbourne Village (c. 1980s), by virtue of postdating Estrella
de Mar and predating the Costasol development, provides a comparative timeline
of spatial change. Associated with 'open access', Estrella de Mar – and by extension
the 1970s – emerge as a turning point. It follows that the 'general trends' for which
Pangbourne Village was 'remarkable only for having advanced' (Ballard, 2002, p. 13)
are international in origin.

Between *Running Wild* and *Cocaine Nights*, the following spatiotemporal narrative
emerges. The 1970s appear as a breaking point, with an economic and geographic
shift of emphasis away from traditional concepts of cities. By the mid-1980s, this
shift becomes associated with a decline in civic society and the maintenance of
defensive space. An important qualification nevertheless applies. Though they discern
important trends in gentrification and the creation of defensive space, Ballard's works
do not frame a teleological narrative around the privatization of space. Alongside
discerning important trends in defensive space, they illustrate the changing nature of
the suburbs.

One problem with viewing Ballard's works through a 'Ballardian' lens is the potential
for interpreting them as merely dystopian. Crawford's following extrapolation implicitly
critiques such reductionism. The Costasol, he argues, 'is a prison [. . .] We're building
prisons all over the world and calling them luxury condos' (Ballard, 1996, p. 220). They
are indicative of 'the way the world is going', a nascent vision of:

> The future [. . .] The Costasols of this planet are spreading outwards. I've toured
> them in Florida and New Mexico. You should visit [the] Fontainebleau Sud
> complex outside Paris – it's a replica of this, ten times the size [. . .] Town-scapes
> are changing. The open-plan city belongs to the past – no more ramblas, no more
> left banks and Latin quarters. We're moving into an age of security grilles and
> defensible space. (ibid., pp. 218, 219)

Crawford's account universalizes a notion of the '*fourth* world [. . .] The one waiting to take over everything' (ibid., p. 216). There is an element of truth in this reading. Gentrification has structurally altered the social and physical geography of the city, as has the trend during the 1970s and 1980s of urban entrepreneurialism in local government, which led to standardizing certain spatial trends while attempting to attract investment amid increased 'intra-urban' competition.[5] Nevertheless, the comparative geography of Ballard's works belies the universality of Crawford's account. A selling point for developments like Pangbourne Village and the Costasol complex is their difference – their exclusivity – *from* the outside world. Prentice's response therefore sounds an important cautionary note: Bobby's argument is as 'an amalgam of alarmist best-sellers, *Economist* think-pieces, and his own obsessive intuitions' (ibid., p. 219).

Super-Cannes (2000) continues Ballard's longstanding interest in non-metropolitan spaces. Narrator Paul Sinclair and his wife leave their house in Maida Vale (Ballard, 2000, p. 43) for Eden-Olympia, a business park in South-East France. Again, the narrator adopts a comparative approach to consider its significance. 'The France of the 1960s, with its Routier lunches, anti-CRS slogans and Citroen DS', Sinclair reflects, had:

> been largely replaced by a new France of high-speed monorails, MacDo's [. . .] And Eden-Olympia was the newest of the new France. Ten miles to the north-east of Cannes, in the wooded hills between Valbonne and the coast, it was the latest of the development zones that had begun with the Sophia-Antipolis and would soon turn Provence into Europe's silicon valley. (ibid., p. 5)

Unlike Crawford's universalizing account of the 'fourth world', Sinclair adopts a more measured tone to suggest that that a world of high-speed travel and consumption had '*largely* replaced' the France of the 1960s. There is sociological validity to this claim. Take the Citroen DS reference. Used to analyse the dynamics of Western capitalism, the concept of Fordism takes its name from an iconic automobile brand and so recognizes the car as one of the twentieth-century's quintessential manufactured objects. In a periodizing sense, 'Europe's silicon valley' is qualitatively distinct from the heavy industry of automobile manufacture, being more readily associated with a post-Fordist economy. The science park is a metonym for Harvey's concept of urban entrepreneurialism (Harvey, 1989, p. 11), while its employees are principally high-tech research and design personnel associated with the tertiary and quarternary sectors.

With one notable exception, Ballard's literary focus after the concrete and steel trilogy does not encompass the great cities of industrialization (Manchester) or Modernism (Paris), but gated communities in Berkshire, the tourist region of the Costa del Sol, a science park among the Côte d'Azur and, in his final novel, a shopping centre in the Home Counties. The exception is *Millennium People* (2003), a novel which substantiates much of Ballard's previously implicit critique of the social,

---

[5] These include gentrification and the serial reproduction of science parks, world trade centres and shopping malls (Harvey, 1989, p. 11).

ideological, cultural and experiential relevance of central London. Set in Chelsea Marina, an exclusive estate built on 'the site of a former gasworks' within the 'vast metropolis' (Ballard, 2003, pp. 51, 5), the novel is ostensibly framed around narrator David Markham's investigation into his ex-wife's death following a bomb explosion at Heathrow Airport. Like *Cocaine Nights* and *Super-Cannes*, the narrator of *Millennium People* adopts a comparative approach to illuminate the significant spaces of the novel. Markham departs from the 'stucco silences' of South Kensington, with its 'looming museums, so many warehouses of time', and:

> Westwards along the Cromwell Road. Inner London fell behind us when we left the Hammersmith flyover and Hogarth House, joining the motorway to Heathrow. Twenty minutes later, we entered the operational zone of the airport, a terrain of air-freight offices and car-rental depots, surrounded by arrays of landing lights like magnetic fields. (ibid., p. 128)

With their 'stucco silences' and 'warehouses of time', South Kensington captures the solemnity of received history – inner London as an historical *centre*. This datedness and silence compares with the bustle and transit of the airport, where upon arrival Markham enters a wholly distinct 'territory'. The latter's 'magnetic fields' compound this difference, suitably recalibrating the directional, ontological, and thematic compass. As a prelude to considering the specifics of this recalibration in the concluding discussion of *Kingdom Come* (2006), this chapter will now detail Ballard's critique of central London.

In a largely overlooked but important article, 'Airports' (1997), Ballard repeats Markham's comparative approach to London. 'By comparison with London [Heathrow] Airport', he maintains that:

> London itself seems hopelessly antiquated. Its hundreds of miles of gentrified stucco are an aching hangover from the nineteenth century that should have been bulldozed decades ago. London may well be the only world capital – with the possible exception of Moscow – that has gone from the nineteenth century to the twenty-first without experiencing all the possibilities and excitements of the twentieth in any meaningful way. (Ballard, 1997)

Previously evoked by Kensington's 'warehouses of time', the 'hopelessly antiquated' nature of London is objectionable to Ballard in aesthetic and social terms. A 'hangover' from the nineteenth century, the 'gentrified stucco' admonishes the capital's physical and social geography. Upon visiting London, Ballard has 'the sense of a city devised as an instrument of political control'. This control manifests in the physical and social geography of London, Ballard argues, where the 'labyrinth of districts and boroughs' and the 'endless columned porticos [. . .] together make clear that London is a place where everyone knows his place' (ibid., 1997). Gentrification is a modern manifestation of such class control, as witnessed in the 'increasing middle-class recolonisation of central London' (Davidson and Lees, 2005, p. 1187). Together, the physical and social makeup underlies Ballard's hostility to London.

That said, the city is very large and so the scope of Ballard's critique needs refining. To this end, *Millennium People* provides a few pointers. During his investigation, Markham becomes embroiled in the activities of the terrorist group he initially sought to examine. Part of these clandestine operations involves bombing the Millennium Wheel and the National Film Theatre (Ballard, 2003, p. 141) on the South Bank, close to the Houses of Parliament and London Waterloo railway station. Markham's justification for these actions is that they comprise an attempt 'to build something positive' from 'break[ing] down the old categories' (ibid., p. 273). As these attacks suggest, the real target of Ballard's opprobrium is central London, which is repeatedly associated with dissimulation. Far from revealing historical authenticity, London's 'dealing rooms were a con' whose 'money was all on tick', while across the Thames are 'two more fakes' – the reproduction of Shakespeare's Globe and the Tate Modern, 'an old power station made over into a middle-class disco' (ibid., p. 180). Like the fishermen's cottages in *Cocaine Nights*, the Tate Modern represents the transformation of a site of production into a space of consumption. Such places signify for Ballard the increasingly ubiquitous commodification of city space, whereby the rubric of simulation conveys the process through which sites of cultural consumption literally and figuratively consume spaces of material production. As such, London's dealing rooms, the Tate Modern and Shakespeare's Globe are simulated spaces divested of a deeper sense of place-ness; their increasing homogenized appearance and branded identity – indeed, their very simulation – is for Ballard synonymous with central London.

The key to understanding this sense of dissimulation, and the social significance of the bombing of central London in *Millennium People*, lies in another of Ballard's underappreciated essays, 'Welcome to the Virtual City' (2000). 'The cities that tourists most enjoy', Ballard contends, are:

> those in long-term decline – Venice, Florence, Paris, London, New York. The last two are gigantic money-mills, churned by a Centurion-card elite who are retreating into gated communities in Surrey and the Upper East Side. Already their immense spending power has distorted social life in London and New York, freezing out the old blue-collar and middle classes. (Ballard, 2001, p. 33)

The 'gigantic money mills' raise the role of real estate speculation as a privileged means of accumulating surplus capital, whose net effect is the 'distorted social life' which results from 'freezing out the old blue-collar and middle classes'. Such transformations, Ballard argues, demonstrate the 'long-term decline' of these cities. Their popularity among tourists indicates a number of underlying social and physical changes within the fabric of such cities. Britain has, since the 1970s, 'come to specialize in history and heritage' within the field of tourism, and 'this affects both what overseas visitors expect to gaze upon, and what attracts UK residents to spend time holiday making within Britain' (Urry, 2002, p. 45). The underlying 'discursive battles', as David Harvey calls them, form an important part of the contemporary practice of rebranding cities. Following the physical and social reconstruction of the city, there exist a number of important 'advocates [. . .] in the media and academia' whose role, Harvey argues, is to create a popular myth of cities. By focusing on the fashionable status and desirability of cities, typically by glossing over or eliding the social costs of such transformations, these advocates fundamentally help to rebrand the city; indeed, they 'gain their audience as well as their financial support in relation to these processes'. Such 'interventions in the field of culture, history, heritage, aesthetics, and meanings' (Harvey, 2001, p. 409) are an increasingly commonplace feature of urban existence, one of the means by which capitalists maintain and maximize monopoly rents.

Harvey's account contextualizes Ballard's point concerning the validity of 'the dreams that money can buy [being] a perfectly fit topic for the young painter, novelist and film-maker' (Ballard, 2001, p. 33). Whether of cities or fashions, the theme of consumption as an end in itself is for Ballard a distortion, which, when read through the lens of Harvey's 'discursive battles', assumes an important ideological dimension. 'It's not their own ambition that corrupts today's artists', Ballard writes, 'but the subject matter facing them' (ibid., p. 33). Cities, and the powerful socio-economic influences underlying them, are a corrupting influence. This explains why central London frequently appears as a 'fake' in Ballard's later works, a hollowed out remnant associated with experiential paucity. As against 'the great dying city centre dinosaurs', Ballard finds 'a more astringent, a more challenging and a more real world' among those:

> Hundreds of virtual cities [which] [. . .] surround London, Paris, Chicago, and Tokyo, and, as it happens, I live in one of them. 'Shepperton', some of you will say, appalled by the thought. 'My God, suburbia. We went to London to get away from that'. But Shepperton [. . .] is not suburbia. If it is a suburb of anywhere, it is of London Airport, not London. And that is the clue to my dislike of cities and my admiration for what most people think of as a faceless dead-land of inter-urban sprawl. (ibid., p. 33)

The 'virtual city' is part of a 'more challenging' world for two reasons. First, it involves overcoming a number of powerful ideological interests that sustain particular ideas of the city. Those 'hurrying back from Heathrow or a West Country weekend to their ludicrously priced homes in Fulham or Muswell Hill carefully avert their gaze from this *nightmare terrain*' (ibid., p. 33) in order to protect their financial interests. The second reason revolves around the concept of the virtual.

In categorical terms, the virtual is not opposed to the real but instead 'possesses a full reality by itself' (Deleuze, 1994, p. 244). A modified concept of the virtual thus 'troubles any simple negation because it introduces multiplicity into an otherwise fixed category of the real' (Shields, 2003, pp. 2, 21; Shields' italics). Such ontological disruption is characteristic of what Roger Silverstone calls the 'suburban imaginary', a 'virtual space no longer visible either on the planner's drawing board or on the margins of cities' (1996, p. 13). Each of these definitions sheds light on Ballard's concept of the virtual. As the 'everywhere of suburbia, the paradigm of nowhere', Ballard's Shepperton is a virtual space inasmuch as it modifies the concept of the real. It cannot be conventionally defined as suburbia inasmuch as Ballard does not define this term in terms of its contrast with the city: it is 'the paradigm of nowhere' because it disrupts conventional spatial categories. It is no longer the case that beyond the city's limits resides a discernible entity called suburbia. Such distinctions, Ballard's works suggest, cannot readily be drawn. Ballard's Shepperton thereby occupies the 'suburban imaginary', and is not visible 'on the "margins of cities", precisely because it does not rely on a centre-periphery epistemology.[6] To reiterate Ballard's earlier point, 'the suburbs are at last coming into its own' (Ballard, 1985, p. 7) as conventional ideas of the city and the countryside are waning.

With respect to conceptualizing space after the urban 'revolution', Henri Lefebvre distinguishes between two 'opposing movements':

> *Regressive* (from the virtual to the actual, the actual to the past) and *progressive* (from the obsolete and completed to the movement that anticipates that completeness, that presages and brings into being something new). (Lefebvre, 2003, p. 24, Lefebvre's italics)

Read accordingly, Ballard's account identifies a regressive focus on the 'great city centre dinosaurs' and provides a progressive movement towards the virtual city. As the former are increasingly transformed into spaces of consumption, they nevertheless are part of what Lefebvre calls 'the actual'. It is the degree to which 'the actual' becomes obsolete in social terms that dictates its 'regressive' character. By this yardstick, Ballard's 'dinosaurs' articulate Lefebvre's argument that '[t]he concept of the city no longer corresponds to a social object' (ibid., p. 57). This critique of city centres as obsolete is part of that 'movement' which 'brings into being something new', as Ballard's final novel demonstrates.

Kingdom Come (2006) begins by offering a familiar sense of periodization when narrator Richard Pearson departs from 'the jittery, synapse-testing metropolis' – a modernist-inspired account of the city – for the 'Thames Valley towns – Chertsey, Weybridge, [and] Walton' (Ballard, 2007, p. 4), a 'terrain of inter-urban sprawl' and 'geography of sensory deprivation' (ibid., p. 6). Thereafter, the novel presages the emergence of a new concept of space by foregrounding disparaging tropes of suburbia. After aping derogatory descriptions of the 'Heathrow towns' as 'the suburbs of nowhere', 'this nondescript town', the 'motorway flatlands', the 'desert wastes of retail England' and 'these moribund motorway towns' (ibid., pp. 151, 137, 151, 108, 108, 171), Pearson focalizes the attendant subject position. By describing a 'prosperous Thames Valley town, a pleasant terrain of comfortable houses, stylish office buildings, and retail parks' as 'every advertising man's image of Britain in the twenty-first century' (ibid., p. 13), the narrator foregrounds the socio-economic interests underpinning what another character calls the:

> Hampstead perspective [. . .] [those who] look down from the motorway as they speed home from their West Country cottages [and discern only] faceless

---

[6] A dualist epistemology has long been the hallmark of analyses of literary representations of space: the most influential account in this respect is (Williams, 1973). Williams's city-country dichotomy has re-emerged throughout the intervening period, most clearly in Timms, 1985, p. 1; Wilson, 1992, p. 153; Wirth-Nesher, 1996, p. 7, though also reformulated in terms of the distinction between the 'static' city and the 'city of flows' (Pike, 1981) and the 'real' and 'unreal city' (Sharpe, 1990).

inter-urban sprawl, a nightmare terrain of police cameras and security dogs, an
uncentred realm devoid of civic tradition and human values. (ibid., p. 85)

This 'perspective' reworks the 'rhetorical literature of great cities', a 'distinct literary
genre' that constitutes 'a long tradition of rejection of the periphery, the conurbation,
[and] suburban sprawl' (Wilson, 1995, pp. 147, 153). Such approaches are accordingly
oblivious to Britain's changing social landscape. Part of Ballard's percipience is his
awareness that suburbia attracts disdain because it disrupts conventional social,
economic and spatial divisions. Following this logic, *Kingdom Come* interrogates
dualist conceptions of spatial identity. In the novel's schema, gentrified 'heritage
London' – 'Parliament, the West End, Bloomsbury, Notting Hill, [and] Hampstead' –
and the 'Millionaire's Toytown' of Chelsea Harbour exist beside 'bosky Surrey' (Ballard,
2007, pp. 101, 63, 105). Contrary to its bucolic overtones, 'bosky Surrey' connotes a
'roadside microclimate of petrol and diesel fumes', part of a 'terrain of dual carriageways
and industrial estates' (ibid., pp. 16, 97) shaped by consumerism and automobility.
The novel pointedly does not transpose a conventional city-country dichotomy with
a dualism of 'heritage London' and 'bosky Surrey' – the latter is not some form of
pastoral antidote to the former. With this, the identity of each term is not dependent
on the other. While central London is a subject increasingly devoid of interest to them,
Ballard's works do not posit suburbia as simply an authentic alternative.

The virtual city comes into play at this point. 'Brooklands seems to be off all the
maps' precisely because conventional cartographies such as the Hampstead perspective
fail to discern the changing social magnitude of the invisible suburbs (ibid., pp. 34,
155). Unlike the timeless idea of 'great cities', Pearson emphasizes a virtual state of
becoming: a 'suburban town had conjured itself from the nexus of access roads and
dual carriageways', just as a 'nearby town [. . .] materialized out of the empty air' (ibid.,
pp. 6, 7). This state of emergence corresponds with his departure from the historic
citizenry associated with his 'Chelsea flat' for the state of becoming 'a temporary
resident of Brooklands' (ibid., pp. 38, 52). Pearson's journey thus encompasses the
transition from the city to the *virtual* city. If the 'suburban outlands' of Surrey are fast
becoming the 'real centre of the nation' (ibid., p. 4), they inaugurate a modified concept
of the real that accommodates new patterns of virtual emergence. While trying to
find his bearings '[v]aguely south-west of Heathrow', Pearson concisely periodizes
the emergence of the virtual city: 'in one of the motorway towns that had grown
unchecked since the 1960s' (ibid., p. 7). In this context, the language describing David
Markham's journey in *Millennium People* is particularly suggestive. Leaving behind
South Kensington's 'warehouses of time', Markham is drawn to the 'magnetic fields'
of Heathrow Airport, a new 'territory' (Ballard, 2003, p. 128) which reconceptualizes
suburbia as the virtual city.[7]

In conclusion, Ballard's works do not simply make an *aesthetic* virtue out of praising
the unloved, as some critics have suggested (Sinclair, 1999, p. 77; Gray, 2009). Nor are

---

[7] Compare with the following analogy: 'as if the entire business park were a mirage, a virtual city
conjured into the pine-scented air like a *son-et-lumière* vision of a new Versailles' (Ballard, 2000,
p. 8).

they readily Ballardian in the sense of representing aspects of dystopian modernity. As this chapter has shown, Ballard's thematic distanciation from cities correlates with fundamental transformations in Britain's social and physical geographies. Typified by the 'unchecked' growth of the motorway towns over the past 50 years, the scale of these changes is such that they prompt a rethinking of the conventional terms – indeed, the ideological stock images – of British space. To this end, Ballard concludes the article 'Airports' by contending that:

> The light industrial and motel architecture that unvaryingly surrounds every major airport in the world [. . .] constitute the reality of our lives, rather than some mythical domain of village greens, cathedral closes, and manorial vistas. (Ballard, 1997)

Away from the 'mythical domain' of an Austen-esque iconography and the disparaging class myopia of the 'Hampstead perspective', the light industrial and motel architecture connote the socio-economic changes encapsulated by the thematic spaces of Ballard's later works. Far from the archetypal cities of industrialization or modernism, Ballard examines gated communities (*Running Wild*), tourist resorts (*Cocaine Nights*), science parks (*Super-Cannes*) and shopping centres (*Kingdom Come*) amid the context of city centres being transformed into spaces primarily dedicated to consumption (*Millennium People*). While there is seldom evidence of village greens, let alone manorial vistas, in these works, this absent bucolic iconography is for Ballard a sign of the times. Such a realignment of critical distance is necessary if we are to appreciate how the suburbs have finally come 'into their own'. In his own inimitable terms, Ballard's works can be said to chart the move from the 'dinosaurs' of city-centres to 'the terrain of business parks, marinas and executive housing that constitutes New Britain' (Ballard, 1999).

Part II

The Past in Its Place

5

The Shifting Ground of Commemoration in Suburbia

Hannah Lewi and Caroline Jordan

Alphington Park in inner eastern Melbourne is the setting for a bucolic scene that you might find in many suburban and regional neighbourhoods in Australia: residents walk their dogs in the morning dew, children play on the playground waiting for their older siblings to stream out of the nearby primary school on weekday afternoons and on the weekends the lawn bowls club and sporting ovals come alive with convivial matches. The grassy ovals and gardens are well kept but not overly manicured, and retain impressive eucalyptus trees (some predating European settlement). The park is bordered by late nineteenth-century houses on two sides, the muddy banks of the Yarra River to the south, and a large paper and cardboard recycling factory to the west.

Like many local parks, Alphington Park contains memorials and commemorative gestures spanning World War I to the present day. A statue to honour local soldiers stands in a gravel path in the northern gardens, one of a constellation of traditional memorials throughout suburban Melbourne and country Victoria built to commemorate some 114,000 soldiers who enlisted to fight in World War I and 19,000 who never returned from distant European battlegrounds. Next to this statue is a small memorial fountain and playground commemorating World War II. Entering the nearby Alphington Bowls Club building through its memorial gates, you will find other commemorative honour boards and faded pictures pledging allegiance to Queen and country. Such 'useful' recreation buildings and structures are another very common element in the commemorative landscape of Australian suburbia. Recently, this section of the park has been updated with the addition of a controversial new outdoor area commemorating local and national identities through a contemporary language of garden structures and plantings. This small suburban park therefore exemplifies a range of past and present practices of commemoration in public spaces across Australia.

'Lest We Forget' is the motto inscribed in the granite or marble surface of many Australian war memorials. But what are we collectively remembering today and how do local people now interact with these memorials of the past? Contemporary reactions undoubtedly fall across a broad spectrum, ranging from overt dislike of their outdated conservatism to an ongoing personal and emotional attachment.

Through no small amount of disinterest and amnesia, public opinion has typically settled somewhere in the middle. Local war memorials serve as inherited or found objects that ascribe a 'non-negotiable' status to public spaces that might otherwise be engulfed in the doggedly utilitarian terrain of suburbia. However, as this chapter will discuss, through Alphington Park and beyond, the making and keeping of memorials and commemorative markers in suburbia has often been controversial and contested, only finding settled ground over the course of time. A pertinent comparison is Bruno Latour's analysis of the making of scientific knowledge, which he characterizes through the two-faced Janus figure who looks both backward to the past and forward to the present. In the past, science and technology that is now seen as cold, unproblematic and 'ready-made' was once hot and still 'in the making' (1978, p. 4).

This chapter will examine this making at the local level of Melbourne's suburbs. We explore the impetus to build local community memorials after World War I and the counter-arguments for utilitarian or 'living' commemorations that won out after World War II, and conclude with a discussion of some contemporary and contested commemorative gestures that display a sense of lively anxiety about their language and shared purpose.

Diggers and obelisks: Suburban war memorials post-World War I

From the aristocratic parents of the true town life and the country estate came the bastard ideal of suburbanization.

Davison, 1978, p. 166

The suburb of Alphington was established along the Yarra River and a railway line connecting the centre of Melbourne to the eastern region of Heidelberg – known pejoratively in early years as the tediously slow line from 'nowhere to nowhere'.[1] The suburb was largely built in the extraordinary land boom years of the 1880s that gave rise to the moniker of 'Marvelous Melbourne', when large areas of land were bought by private developers, subdivided and sold for private housing. The construction of 'gentleman's residences' nearby to Alphington Park catered for the relatively affluent who could buy into the suburban dream with a sufficient family income to support a level of leisure and comfort (Davison, 1978, p. 170). Despite rapid boom and bust cycles of development in the late nineteenth century, Alphington grew steadily in the early twentieth century as housing in neighbouring inner suburbs became overcrowded (Mirams, 2011). Nine kilometers from the Central Business District (CBD), this was a 'middle landscape', with one footing in the country and another in the city (Ferber et al., 1994; Lewi and Jordan, 2010). It was seen as a fitting domain for women and families, set in close contrast to the workaday realm represented by the paper mill established in 1919 next to the park reserve.

Although successfully pragmatic, the suburban ideal has long been characterized by critics and chroniclers as a stark display of the consequences of rampant individualism,

---

[1] This quote describes the uncompleted train line, cited in *Darebin Historical Encyclopedia*.

and an emasculated zone of domesticity. Famously, the Australian architect and critic Robin Boyd, writing in the 1960s, represented suburbia as the fertile source of all that was mundane and mediocre (Boyd, 1961). Others posing a strong counter-voice cast this reality in alternative and more positive ways (Stretton, 1971). However with foundations built on individual speculation and pragmatism, public development could be conspicuously absent. Initiatives in civic beautification and recreation lagged well behind private housing, and it was largely left to individuals and citizen-led groups to foster development over and above the essentials (Davison, 1978, p. 283). With a very high rate of home ownership (already 45% in the early 1880s) there were certainly tangible incentives for working towards a direct contribution to and improvement of local neighbourhoods. The investment of communal energies into strengthening a public domain outside the boundaries of the home and garden can therefore be regarded as the flipside of rampant individualism. Commemorative initiatives, however small, show attempts to find some collective voice and shared ground upon which to build some sense of memory and place.

Returning to Alphington Park as a case in point, the reserve land was originally donated to the community by local residents who saw the proximity to the river as a popular drawcard. Indeed it would soon become a favoured destination for recreation and swimming once it was connected to the railway, and in 1921 it was chosen as the location for the building of a memorial to World War I. Parks and gardens were often seen as a sensible choice for the siting of memorials in suburban and country contexts – in part because there were few other public places deemed suitable and accessible for the creation of lasting expressions of commemoration. And in terms of symbolism, as John Stephens has suggested, parks were also seen as appropriate settings for the expression of 'regeneration and renewal' (Stephens, 2007, p. 246). The social status and cohesiveness of suburbs greatly impacted on their ability to solicit support for memorial projects.[2] In Alphington, the World War I monument was erected as a result of the efforts of residents to raise funding by public subscription, the selling of lapel badges, fancy dress parades and a large carnival staged in Alphington Reserve in 1921.

The resulting monument, a marble statue of an Australian 'Digger' soldier (Figure 5.1), is symbolic of the egalitarian structure of the Australian Military Forces (ibid., p. 247). As is customary with such World War I soldier statues, he wears the distinctively Australian uniform with slouch hat, is clean-shaven and stands looking forward with his rifle at ease by his side. The small ornamental garden of hedged rosemary in which he stands is symbolic of remembrance. The inscription on the grey granite pedestal tells the visitor that the statue was erected by the residents of Alphington in 1921, and honours the 25 Alphington men who lost their lives and the 75 men who served. This practice of commemorating both those who fought and those who did not return is common to about half the World War I memorials around Australia but is rare in other countries. As Ken Inglis observes: 'Only in Australia could most men home from the war read their own names on its memorials' (Inglis, 2008,

---

[2] This is something that would change in more recent decades when access to public works funding has become far more distributed through state and local government agencies, with a mandate of equity and accessibility across socio-economic grounds.

Figure 5.1 Alphington World War I 'digger' memorial statue, situated in Alphington Park, erected 1921

Photograph: Authors

p. 174). Naming individual soldiers on local monuments served important functions. It stood in for absent graves and created a tangible site for mourning, and recruited those who served into a statement of national identity and cohesive service (Scates, 2009, p. 127). It also inscribed a tangible three-way connection across time and space between soldiers' relatives, distant events and the local place of commemoration.

Active remembrance, enacted through memorial processions and ceremonies, further situated distant theatres of war in local places of peace. In Alphington, a procession and carnival day was held in 1921 when the statue was completed and consecrated. On a smaller scale, this localized commemoration is still re-enacted annually around Anzac and Remembrance Day ceremonies. Memorial parks and gardens thus provide a 'dramaturgical setting in which mourning and commemorative practices may be supported and played out' (Stephens, 2007, p. 258). Through the reporting and documenting of these local events in suburban and country towns, memorials are tied together as satellite locations in a broader network of commemorative spaces across Melbourne, the state of Victoria and the nation.

Despite commonly voiced assumptions that these kinds of World War I memorials are ubiquitous across every suburban park, street or plaza, in fact outdoor memorial statues were less commonly erected in Melbourne's suburbs, in comparison to less populated states and country towns where the concentration of war service and loss was acutely apparent. Soldier memorials like Alphington's are more common in Queensland and New South Wales.[3] A soldier bugler, as found in the Melbourne suburbs of Mitcham and Box Hill, is another sculptural variation. A range of other typologies of World War I memorials are also found in Melbourne. In Kew, across the south side of the Yarra River from Alphington, a grey granite memorial rotunda and obelisk sits at a major road and tram intersection (Figure 5.2).

Aside from individual names, inscribed in the circular cornice are the locations of the theatres of battles that Kew residents served in during World War I, thus extending the networks of commemoration outward from the homes of Kew to Salonica, the North Sea, Egypt, Belgium, Gallipoli, France, Palestine and Mesopotamia. The obelisk was the most popular form adopted for local memorials due to its relative cheapness and uniformity, but also its historical endurance as both a marker in space and as a non-sectarian symbol (Inglis, 2008, p.153; Vidler, 2011, p. 224). The stone obelisk situated in a prominent garden reserve in Williamstown, a port suburb, is flanked by flagpoles and Lombardy poplar trees, and composes a focus for ceremonies and processions on Anzac and Remembrance Days (Victorian Heritage Database).

Other World War I memorial structures built in suburban parklands across Melbourne include an elegant memorial rotunda in Edinburgh Gardens in inner Fitzroy, and an octagonal memorial rotunda and bandstand on the foreshore reserve of bayside Port Melbourne. This was erected by the members of the Port Melbourne women's welcome home committee, and is testament to the strength of engagement of local women in the conception and realization of suburban memorials (War Memorials Australia Database). Caulfield, a suburb with a large Jewish population, hosts three memorial structures erected in the local park. The eight columned classical pavilion on a stone platform commemorates

---

[3] A solder statue in the central suburb of Parkville, Melbourne provides one exception. See also War Memorials entry by Bart Ziino, in *The Encyclopedia of Melbourne* online: www.emelbourne.net.au/ biogs/EM01581b.htm

Figure 5.2 Opening of the Kew World War I memorial rotunda, 1925
Image courtesy of Hawthorn Library

army and navy service in World War I and later World War II, and provides the location for ceremonies in the park – with the memorial stone set in rose gardens creating a more intimate setting for the naming of individuals. There are a number of other interesting memorials specifically dedicated to Jewish history and individuals that are significant to the large Jewish population who settled in Melbourne suburbia during the twentieth century, but it is outside the scope of this chapter to describe them in detail.

Local memorials were thus multivalent in their type and expression, in part because each one possessed multi-vocal material biographies. Scates writes: 'War memorials were built at the busy intersection of private and collective memory' (2009, pp. 4–5). Their diversity illustrates the individualism at play in their instigation, and even a healthy rivalry between local community groups and residents to create a structure of solemnity and appropriateness that was nevertheless somehow 'unique'. Suburban memorials typically served a transformative function as agents of civic self-improvement through the beautification of existing gardens and parks, and the building of semi-useful structures like bandstands, bell-towers and fountains. Direct and localized community input allowed for some negotiation, if within a fairly small range, of broader national narratives. However, as Scates emphasizes, the overriding cohesive purpose that unites them arises as a direct consequence from the Australian policy not to repatriate the dead, thus making each local monument a 'surrogate grave, an empty tomb for "the boys" who would never march home, a "site of memory", a shrine of remembrance' (ibid., p. 1). The collection of localized and varied memorials across Melbourne's suburbs can therefore perhaps best be characterized as the dispersed gravestones of one large war cemetery.

Unsurprisingly, the flood of community enthusiasm for erecting their own self-styled monuments also prompted some dissonant voices. While Australians' 'open-heartedness' and eager commemorative work was praised, concerns were also expressed that too many were simply 'inartistic'.[4] Decisions around the type and utility of monumental structures escalated as a matter of great public concern in the 1920s. Larger municipal memorials were sometimes the subject of design competitions, and gave work to architects, artists and artisans, albeit within a restricted palette of expression.[5] However monuments created by professional sculptors remained few in comparison to the numerous obelisks, soldier monuments and fountains commissioned by amateur committees and made to a template by local stonemasons.

In the years immediately following World War I, debates over memorial design extended well beyond aesthetics, and would be greatly amplified after World War II. Fundamental doubts were expressed not just over small memorials but extended to the plans for the construction of the biggest memorial in Melbourne, the Shrine of Remembrance, which was almost terminally stalled by controversy. The campaign to build a grand and pompous memorial in the Domain Gardens in central Melbourne was not popular, and a people's plebiscite of 1924 returned a resounding 'No' to the competition-winning Greek-revival design by the returned soldier team of Hudson and Wardrop. Of those who preferred a non-utilitarian monument but did not like the Shrine design, a carillon tower was the favoured option, to relieve the flat monotonous sea of Melbourne suburbia. Not only was there dissent about the cost and design but also the setting – with many feeling that the city locale was wrong, with a bush setting being more appropriate to the image of the Digger soldier (Scates, 2009, p. 34). This reflected long-standing anti-urban sentiments, and perhaps further explained the preponderance of park-settings for suburban memorials, rather than urban precincts or major streets. But it was really the perceived waste of public resources that held most sway, with loud calls for the building of more civic works and services useful to both returned soldiers and the local population, including the repairing and building of new memorial halls, hospitals and recreation facilities. It was this voice that would become strongest after World War II.

Playgrounds and fountains: Suburban war memorials post-World War II

This fountain and playground are a tribute from the citizens of Fairfield and Alphington to the memory of those who served in the world war 1939–1945: 'lest we forget'.

[4] In 1919 a deputation of architects appealed to the federal Minister for Local Government on the need for state legislation and an advisory council with the charter of exercising more aesthetic design control over the building of local war memorials.

[5] Decisions on appropriate aesthetics for memorials were also sometimes scrutinized by professional bodies like the Australian Institute of Architects, in an attempt to 'professionalize' their design.

Next to the World War I statue in Alphington Park is a streamlined, granite memorial drinking fountain erected by local citizens after World War II (Figure 5.3). More modest and anonymous than its neighbour, there is no room for the inscription of the names of those who served – just a plaque recording the dedication of the fountain and adjacent playground. These kinds of more 'useful' memorial structures

Figure 5.3 Memorial Fountain and playground in background at Alphington Park
Photograph: Authors

and recreation facilities become more common in suburbs across Melbourne after World War II. Following the Repatriation Commission Recommendations, the favouring of monuments of a 'useful nature', or 'living memorials', had gained much ground in America after World War I. This was paralleled to some extent in Australia, with the Australian Labor Party promoting memorial construction projects like major roads, hospitals and parklands. There was far less enthusiasm in the United Kingdom and Europe for commemorative-led major construction projects where the building of essential services was seen as the responsibility of good government rather than private philanthropy.

Soldiers' Memorial Halls in particular were preferred by the RSL in inner suburbs where typically there was a denser population with greater numbers of returned soldiers to cater for. The inner suburbs of Richmond, Collingwood, St Kilda, Brunswick and South Melbourne all built halls or clubrooms, sometimes to complement memorial statues. These useful soldiers' memorials, it was hoped, would allay the sometimes pessimistic or even 'sinister' connotations of traditional war memorials which would be replaced by a more 'tangible, practical and indestructible form', that was of active benefit to the everyday lives of the community, now and into the future (Taylor, 1919, p. 46). Nor was utility seen as empty of symbolic capital: useful monuments were intended to both embody the motivations of soldier sacrifice and actively remind 'those that come after us of the many sacrifices by means of which we are enabled to remain in possession of our homes and fair land' (The Listening Post, 1924; Stephens, 2007, p. 247). However, after World War II there was certainly a more marked turning away from overly explicit political or nationalistic sentiments, in favour of more forceful commemorative gestures towards renewal framed within secularist understandings and a desire for cohesive community-building (Brown, 1995, p. 155).

A national opinion poll conducted in 1944 clearly revealed this swing in public opinion towards utility and the broadening of dissent across Australian towns and suburbs over the need for any more monuments – or at least any more traditional ones. Advocates for new kinds of living commemorations questioned the assumption that traditional monuments provided a potent or relevant focus for the 'work' of memory to be carried forward in society. Andrew Shanken has characterized the parallel depth of emotion invested in these debates surrounding memorialization in the United States: 'Choosing a form of memorial was tantamount to choosing a form of society' (2002, p. 130). Debates raged across all media from the scholarly to the popular, with features on the topic appearing in magazines like *Good Housekeeping* in the United States. As Inglis has suggested, in Australia those against utility thought that 'a community was not truly engaged in an act of commemoration when it gave the name of memorial to some public resource which should have been provided anyway' (2008, p. 132). Some saw utilitarian structures and services as less durable and in danger of being outmoded more quickly than stand-alone monuments. Others countered with the argument that with their loss of relevance to future generations traditional monuments would be more likely to fall into disrepair. Indeed it is true that a number of memorials have been engulfed by development or traffic and are no longer able to serve any mnemonic civic purpose.

Debates were further shaped by aesthetic and philosophical trends in architecture and planning that underpinned modern functionalism. Professional opinion after World War II, as reflected in architecture journals in Australia and internationally, was increasingly dismissive of traditional monuments that were deemed to contribute to the 'home-grown', unattractive and parochial clutter of local environs; the last thing that was needed in suburbs and town centres was another wave of cemetery sculptures.[6] Furthermore, what were regarded as unwanted 'white elephants' by some were also cast as an actual impediment to better civic planning. In contrast, the useful commemorative structure might indeed perform as a kind of Trojan Horse for bolstering civic renewal and beautification schemes.

Useful or living memorials therefore presented a way forward out of this commemorative dilemma, as 'a means of folding the sacrifices of war into the pattern of democratic community life, gently kneading the past into the present, in the process altering the relation between public space and memory' (Shanken, 2002, p. 130). The distinction between the useful and the purely monumental and ornamental was obviously open to interpretation, so it would be overly simplistic to position the traditional and the useful in clear-cut ideological or material opposition. In reality the two commingled; rather than supplanting traditional memorials, useful memorials 'complicated' memorialization (ibid.). Commemorative gardens, fountains, bell towers and lookouts were seen as places for pleasure but also as serving a social and civic function. Small-scale structures like drinking fountains and playgrounds in local garden settings offered this kind of compromise. In a few instances earlier monuments took on more useful functions following World War II. This was the case at the Kangaroo Ground memorial in Melbourne where a significant stone tower built in 1926 was modified 20 years later to become a fire-spotting tower.

Places and services associated with the health, education and welfare of children and families – including memorial kindergartens, libraries, women's rest amenities, infant health centres and playgrounds – were common targets for commemorative schemes that gestured towards future renewal, and went on being constructed long after the 1940s.[7] In Ivanhoe, for example, the neighbouring suburb to Alphington, a war memorial kindergarten was built in 1960. The well-known war historian C. E. W. Bean – a key instigator of the Australian War Memorial in Canberra – became an influential figure in the Memorial Parks and Playgrounds Movement started in New South Wales and a keen supporter of the view that local memorials should be of purposeful benefit. Bean's involvement in parks and playgrounds extended the pursuit of utility through outdoor recreation, which also resonated with his ideals of 'bringing the country as close as possible to the town' (Bean, 1969). Signifying the consolidation of a general shift in conservative attitudes after World War II, the Returned and Services League (RSL) also became actively involved in many local initiatives to create memorial parks and playgrounds. Significant memorial

---

[6] See Shanken (2002) for a description of Philip Johnston's critique of World War I statues on plinths in a 1945 issue of *Architectural Forum*, which parallels architectural criticism in the Australian professional journals of the same period.

[7] For instance, in the suburb of Eltham, the local community progress society felt that a war memorial should take the form of a kindergarten and children's library.

recreation buildings were also common in country towns and city suburbs, with a great number of war memorial Olympic swimming pools and bowling clubs built across Melbourne and the state of Victoria from the 1930s to the 1960s. They feature commemorative structures like decorative iron gates, seats, plaques and honour boards, as in the Alphington Bowls Club located next to the playground in the park.

To relax in a memorial park or playground, to drive down a memorial highway or to play bowls at the local memorial club was thereby assumed to indirectly honour previous sacrifices made to protect democratic freedoms that included communal leisure and recreation. The mainstream acceptance of recreation facilities doubling as memorials reflected more relaxed social attitudes after World War II, but perhaps also harboured the more conservative hope that against a backdrop of commemorative solemnity, public propriety and behaviour in leisure time might be constructively moderated. Patriotism and national identity was thus transformed to embrace a modern suburban-centred life, although sceptics could recognize this appropriation of leisure and recreation as at best hopeful or indeed dubious.

Cairns and crates: The commemorative suburban landscape

Uncertainty, people at work, decisions, competition, controversies are what one gets when making a flashback from certain, cold, unproblematic black boxes to their recent past.

Latour, 1978, p. 4

Suburban war memorials fold the ordinary man, his family and his suburban locale into a generic national symbolism. In the parks and boulevards of the Melbourne CBD, this national pantheon extends further to memorials to poets, generals, pioneers, workers and city founders. Relatively few equivalents to these exist in Melbourne's suburbs. An exception that commemorates a national figure is the 1914 replica of a statue of Captain Cook by British sculptor John Tweed, installed on the foreshore of the old beachside suburb of St Kilda in honour of the 'discoverer' of Eastern Australia. Other suburbs celebrate 'great men' who belong to that particular locality. Yarraville in the city's west erected a memorial to James Cuming, a local philanthropist and councillor. Cuming's portrait bust on a plinth (1915–16) is by Margaret Baskerville, a prominent female sculptor, who also produced an unusual husband-and-wife pair of memorial sculptures in beachside Brighton. Baskerville commemorated Sir Thomas Bent, a Brighton politician and land speculator who rose to become Premier of Victoria, and his wife in a full-length bronze statue mounted on a plinth (1911–13), with a small utilitarian drinking fountain nearby (Figure 5.4).

The fountain was commissioned by the couple's daughter and was produced at the same time as the paternal public statue. This affirms Chilla Bulbeck's observation that, compared to monuments to 'great men', 'monuments to women, workers or Aborigines are often less impressive . . . and more often utilitarian, taking the form of gardens,

Figure 5.4 Memorial to Sir Thomas Bent K.C.M.G (1838–1909) and drinking fountain to
his wife Mrs Bent, Brighton, Victoria. Artist: Margaret Baskerville. Date: 1913
Photograph: Authors

drinking fountains or seats, if they are not simple informative plaques on cairns'
(Bulbeck, 1988, p. 3).

Further, memorials to war and great men are usually visible, often located on a
main street or prominently situated in the better-frequented areas of public parks,
while 'smaller and utilitarian memorials are more hidden in parks, on private
property, or by lonely roadsides' (ibid., p. 21). Suburban pioneer memorials, for
example, are typically modest cairns whose out-of-the-way locations are explained
by their marking the exact spot of occupation. Hence a roadside cairn erected in
1964 along the foreshore in the beachside suburb of Beaumaris commemorates the
Moysey family, 'the first white settlers in the Beaumaris district', and was built as
close as possible to the site of the Moysey's original wattle-and-daub homestead
of 1844 (*The Age Newspaper*, 1964). Changing public consciousness in the 1960s
complicated this simple celebratory nationalist pioneer narrative by acknowledging
that the original white settlers had displaced the Aboriginal inhabitants. This led

to the uneasy compromise expressed in the inscription of a very similar pioneer memorial built only a few years later:

> This cairn was erected by the citizens of Mordialloc to commemorate the first permanent white settler in the district Alexander Macdonald whose homestead was built near this spot in 1845. And also to commemorate the Boonurrong Aboriginal Tribe whose camping grounds were along the banks of Mordialloc Creek. 24 May 1970.

Specific monuments to Aborigines are more recent but still rare. The William Barak memorial erected in 1985 by the Croydon Historical Society at Hughes Park in Croydon North commemorates the famous Aboriginal leader and artist of the Wurundjeri tribe who was born in the area, then known as Brushy Creek. The park is also home to various aging facilities including a sports oval, hall and pavilion, scout hall and homing pigeon club. Although technically a 'great man' monument, the Barak memorial is merely a cairn with a plaque featuring a profile portrait, located within a small native memorial garden. A recent master plan for the redevelopment of the park notes that 'the memorial is not prominent and there is no information available to alert the visitor to its presence in the park' (Maroondah Tourism and Heritage, 2009).

While there has been a notable resurgence of traditional lifelike bronze statues of politicians and sportspeople in the present day (exemplified by the 'Tattersalls Parade of Champions' at the Melbourne Cricket Ground by Louis Lauman, 2003–6), many progressive post-war local government councils actively looked for new opportunities for both civic utility and imaginative expression. Agency shifted towards the use of professional artists and designers and vibrant new forms, sometimes enlisting community involvement, were explored that questioned the language, purpose and subjects of commemoration. The community murals that became popular in the 1980s, for example, were often sponsored by councils in collaboration with the Trade Union movement and typically set out to include groups marginalized in traditional commemoration. The Women's Mural Project, 'Bomboniere to Barbed Wire', 1986 (Figure 5.5) survives as a large, cheerful, faded wall painting mural at the end of a main thoroughfare in inner-suburban Clifton Hill, adjacent to a placard explaining its intention:

> This mural was designed and painted by Eve Glenn and Megan Evans after 2 months talking with and photographing women in the Northcote/Preston area. The images are of local women. Our intention is to represent and celebrate the lives, work, recreation and cultures of all women in the entire community.

This process of lengthy community consultation and the basing of the artwork on donated photographs is typical of such murals of the 1980s, as is the desire to represent the community as multicultural and tolerant of sexual and racial diversity. This openly feminist mural with its prominent representation of lesbians, European migrants, Africans and Aborigines celebrates local and identifiable women, but also inserts women as a group in a new way into the nation-building story. Murals of lesser

Figure 5.5 'Bomboniere to Barbed Wire': The Women's Mural Project 1986, Collingwood, Victoria Artists: Eve Glenn and Megan Evans. Date. 1986
Photograph: Authors

quality and ambition continue to be common features in suburban shopping strips, usually commemorating some aspect of the locality and its history in the service of gentrification and commercialization. 'Street art', a term used to describe often elaborate spray-painted murals, stencils and paste-ups, was once seen as outlaw graffiti but today increasingly serves a similar function in contemporary Melbourne (Lunn, 2007).

Public memorials are now expected to be commissioned to commemorate major natural, industrial and other disasters in which lives were lost. A 2004 memorial park located under the West Gate Bridge, that links the western suburbs with the CBD, commemorates the 35 construction workers who died when the bridge collapsed in 1970 (www.westgatebridge.org, 2012). While the location of this park effectively turns the bridge itself into a giant memorial structure, the fountain memorial to the Bali terrorist bombings of 2002 blends almost invisibly into the paved landscape of a busy square in the inner-suburban university precinct of Carlton. The names of the 22 Victorians who were killed are inscribed in stainless steel around the edge of two pools divided by a granite slab. Like traditional war memorials, this memorial commemorates those who lost their lives elsewhere, in this case resulting in a generic monument that bears no direct relation to place and whose smoothly anonymous surfaces have proved attractive to skateboarders (Chadwick, 2011).

Arguably more successful are those contemporary memorials that are deeply rooted in local place and memory, such as the memorial to Port Melbourne's historic piers that

Figure 5.6 Sandridge Sea Wall, Port Melbourne, Victoria. Artist: Andrew Brophy (designer) and Dianna Wells (typography)
Photograph: Andrew Brophy, reproduced with permission

recycles the remnants of a defunct and no longer tangible industry. A low sand drift wall made from old wharf piles is inscribed chronologically with the names of the men who built the piers, their timber and their dates of construction. The text is strung out along the horizontal line of the shore, so that rather than reading a plaque as one would on a traditional memorial, we must combine the act of walking along the beach with the act of reading. By working with this landscape, the form of this memorial invites an experiential approach that animates memorialization. The ritual of walking along the beach, although intensely private, is also in some sense quintessentially 'Australian', so that this memorial also draws its larger meaning from a recognized element of national identity (Figure 5.6).

Artist Julie Shiels' 'Aunty Alma's seats' (2005) in St Kilda's O'Donnell Gardens is another contemporary memorial that is defiantly local and specific in its frame of reference. At the same time, Shiels' work inserts itself into a national debate as a deliberately provocative political intervention that exposes the lack of consensus about what and whom to memorialize in contemporary Australian suburbia. The sculpture was inspired by the familiar presence in the park of two Aboriginal elders, Aunty Alma and 'Boom Boom' Forbes, who would drag in milk crates to sit upon and hold court. After their deaths, Shiels sought council sponsorship to commemorate these well-known local identities with a humble and informal memorial: three bronze milk crates, one for each of the deceased elders and one 'for the living' (Figure 5.7).

Figure 5.7 'Aunty Alma's Seats', O'Donnell Gardens, St Kilda, Victoria. Artist: Julie Shiels and Bill Perrin Foundry. Date: 2005

Photograph by artist, reproduced with permission

Shiels said she consciously set out to make an anti-monument, 'an ironic comment on the sorts of monuments that are generally erected to honour dead white men, like the imposing statue of Captain Cook gazing out to sea from the St Kilda foreshore' (Hagan, 2005). The work was unveiled on the National Day of Healing, reinforcing its status as a gesture of reconciliation. Not all were impressed, however. Right-wing columnist Andrew Bolt declared it patronizing, destructive and racist, asking, 'do Aborigines really want to be celebrated as park dwellers?' But the response from the local Aboriginal community was overwhelmingly positive, suggesting that to them, at least, the commemoration of their lived experience outweighed pious symbolic representation (Bolt, 2005).

Shiels and Bolt occupy positions on opposite sides of a political spectrum, but both recognize the power and threat of vernacular challenges to the national language of memorialization, challenges that we have seen have historically been played out on a small scale in suburban parks, including Alphington Park. A new ornate garden has recently been built on the northern perimeter of the park, adjacent to the two world war memorials, lawn bowls club and playground. This latest addition to the existing ensemble replaces a typical municipal park space of perimeter rocks, trees and lawns. The design has been controversial with local residents, to the extent that works were suspended by the council in late 2011, while their concerns could be addressed. The new linear garden, modest in scale but grand in ambition, is designed around a series of six thematic representations of Australian cultural and natural landscapes including: a desert-like dry rock garden with indigenous (although not local) plantings; a cottage garden with rectangular metal climbing frames forming a symmetrical axis and pathway; a representation of the vernacular, Aussie suburban backyard space complete with shed façade, corrugated iron dog kennel and water-tanks, 'Hills Hoist' clothes line, and a retro-style table setting that would look at home in the bowls club just behind; and a series of totem poles and skate ramp-seats painted red, yellow and black, with Aboriginal motifs created by the local Alphington Primary School children. A new seat made by the school children and local artist sits under an existing great eucalyptus.

This conjunction of professionalism instigated by local government bodies, and community engagement involvement, often involving children, reflects an increasingly typical way in which everyday public places are now adorned in Australia. In the case of Alphington, however, residents felt they were insufficiently consulted on the design, and that the result was 'inappropriate' to the suburban setting. One said: 'This was always such a serene area with its green grass and shady, established trees. Now it's a sudden jolt to the senses and inappropriate for the space, with its gentle, dignified memorial statue' (Schetzer, 2011). Some locals think the new garden is ugly for apparently deeper reasons than simply not being asked. It seems that the attempt at overt symbolism of both indigenous and suburban identities, reminiscent of the design sensibility of a number of gardens and civic places in Australia in the last two decades, is seen as out of place here. One vocal neighbour is quoted as saying the themed design is better suited to a garden show than a community park: 'It's not what a park like that should be all about. Our neighbourhood would have been happier with some good quality trees.' In response other locals have voiced their support for the new design, indicating a battle of traditionalism versus modernism at play: 'There are many people, as it turns out, who love the modern aspects and art on display', said one resident. And another suggested that Alphington, as home to a number of artists, was an ideal suburb to host such a statement: 'The structures lend themselves to that sense of avant-garde associated with modern art – and what better suburb to do that in than Alphington. What is there to complain about?' (ibid.). However in March 2012, as a result of a resident ballot, the more abstract and colourful elements of the new design were removed and later relocated to a less prominent setting.

That a seemingly staid and harmonious scene such as Alphington Park can harbour such community friction suggests a parallel with Andrew Shanken's observations about a 'crisis' of memorialization in the United States. He sees recent acrimony over memorial design as evidence of a more long-standing problem that Americans have with commemoration: 'a typological quandary that points to a deep discomfort with memorials and memorial practices as they have developed since World War II' (2002, p. 130). In the suburban context, where broader national concerns are referenced – if through a contracted and sometimes distorted lens – there exists not only a quandary as to what kind of memorials should be created but also what events, people and places should be publically commemorated and with whose cultural narratives. As we have seen in this chapter, the commemorative fabric of Melbourne suburbia has always been more complex, diverse and contested than may now appear. The stumpy obelisks and soldiers on plinths that make up the familiar furniture of the earlier twentieth-century memorial landscape may have already represented tradition and stultification by the 1960s, but they were born into controversy. Every monument represents some sort of compromise forged at the local level between those who rejected 'useless' and 'morbid' symbolic statues for those who favoured utilitarian or 'living' memorials. Similar challenges have been mounted more recently to other traditional monuments that knit the local and suburban into founding national narratives. Ordinary events, migrants, women and Aborigines have all also found a small foothold within contemporary commemorative landscapes. Our study of Alphington Park demonstrates that these traces of contested commemoration can co-exist, if often uneasily rubbing together in contemporary suburbia. This park site also reveals that, far from being considered a dead weight from the past, threats to traditional memorials can be expected to be vigorously defended, and new memorials just as vigorously debated by those local communities that they purport to represent.

6

The Future Has Come and Gone: Managing Change in the Ageing Suburbs

Alan Mace

Introduction

Since the seminal work of Tuan (1977) on space and place, where he highlighted the work of people in engaging emotionally with place, there has been ongoing interest in how people actively develop and maintain a sense of belonging, and this body of work has sometimes had a specifically suburban focus (Savage et al., 2005; Duncan and Duncan, 2001). Tuan argued for the need to take into account the relationship between time and place seeing it as an 'intricate problem' (Tuan, 1977). He identified three aspects of time-place: first, place as pausing; second, time as a function of becoming attached to place; and third, place as time made visible where place serves as a memorial to times past (ibid., p. 179). This chapter focuses on the latter two aspects of time-place and argues that they can be usefully employed alongside the idea of phantasmagoria (Pile, 2005b) to help understand how the temporal feeds into the process of belonging in suburbia. Following a more general discussion of the differing ways that time impacts suburbia, attention is given to the role of time in the construction and maintenance of a sense of belonging for residents in the ageing suburbs of outer London. In particular, attention is given to personal memory and to the embedded memory of place (including the imprinting of history through the built form).

The suburbs have always been intimately related to space-time; in economic terms, once the time gap between the centre and the periphery was reduced by transport solutions, capital could exploit these new frontiers, in the case of outer London farmland used for grazing could realize far greater value as land for housing. The suburbs can be categorized as sets of isochrones, half an hour from the centre, 45 minutes and so forth. This space-time gap between the centre and the new urban edge was often present in studies of newly establishing suburbs (Durant, 1939; Gans, 1967) where women were 'a long-time away' from former communities as there was poor public transport links and limited or no access to a car. However, the significance of the space-time gap between the centre and the edge changes over time. The gendered impacts in the 1930s and 1950s were related to the economic dependence of women who were less likely to be working and less likely to have access to a car than in later decades. The experience of women is now understood to have more to do with the compression of space-time in everyday life (Jarvis et al., 2001). Whereas in the earlier period the focus was on the isolation of the stay-at-home suburban 'housewife', now the issue of connectivity is quite different as women seek to manage homes and family – driving children to school, accessing work, servicing the household, etc. These changes are not driven by, or unique to, the suburbs; as Clapson (2003) argues, the suburbs are a barometer of broader changes in class and gender relations in the society in which they are located.

The suburbs are too often viewed as static, as stuck in time – as the unquestioning inheritors of the bourgeois values running through almost uninterrupted from the early pioneers of the eighteenth century (Stone, 1977), to the Victorian mass suburbanization of the upper-middle classes (Dyos, 1966) and finally, through the sprawling interwar manifestation (Orwell, 2001) to the present day. Yet if we foreground the lives of people as lived, rather than accepting assumptions about the inherited and inherent social attitudes and form of the suburbs, we see considerable change over time; it is precisely this sense of suburbia as a place of change that leads McManus and Ethington (2007) to call for more longitudinal studies of suburbia in order to understand better the ways in which these places, and their residents, adapt through time. They note that while community formation in newly established suburbs – at a point in time – has been the subject of a number of studies, it is less common to trace how residents manage change over time.

Belonging, time and phantasmagoria

Having argued that becoming attached to a place is a function of time, Tuan (1977) asks an obvious yet difficult question: how long does it takes to know a place? We can quickly obtain abstract knowledge from guide books or government documents but what about getting 'under the skin' of a place? He argues that we need to become aware of the rhythms of place, daily and seasonal, so that the particularities of place become familiar (ibid., p. 183). An additional question is posed by Savage et al. (2005): what it is to belong in place in a globalizing world? While Tuan considers the way that different societies imbue place with meaning in situ, Savage et al. (ibid.) ask how the meaning of place is impacted by transnational flows of people and culture. They contrast the entertainment industry to housing with the former offering people the chance to express a set of cultural preferences that are highly internationalized and not linked to a particular place – allowing people easily to become cultural omnivores. In comparison, housing choice represents a relatively static and fixed item of consumption; they conclude that residential location remains particularly important in terms of providing a sense of self that remains place-based. Therefore, argue Savage et al. (ibid.), the relative inflexibility of housing choice make it important in producing a sense of cultural identity. Housing (in suburban areas in this instance) becomes important precisely because it is relatively static as compared to many other choices. This, they argue, provides a strong case for the local to be defined apart from global forces, so justifying a 'local studies' focus and supporting Massey's (1993) argument for not losing sight of the importance of a place. In this context, Savage et al. conclude that to be local is not – following Massey – necessarily a reactionary matter; it is not that one has simply staked a claim on place by living there longer than someone else. Rather, belonging is the result of a more active engagement with place leading them to propose the concept of elective belonging; being local results from active work in relation to place.

The idea that residents are engaged in meaning-making is reflected in the writing of Blunt and Dowling (1977) on the sense of home which, they argue, is something actively constructed by individuals: something to be negotiated, made and remade. As part of this active engagement with a place, suburban residents carry time through into a place. Residents carry their own past around with them: memories of previous homes, and of family members who have lived in and departed the present home. For some, these memories will have an international aspect; they will encompass space – 'homelands' left, distant family and cultures. For others, who have lived for a long time in a place, the stretching of time-place similarly leads to the familiar becoming distant. This reflects the other aspect of Tuan's time-place focus that is the subject of this chapter: place is also time made visible; place serves as a memorial to times past. We can hold on to memories through personal objects interior to the home but the public realm can also hold memories. In some cases, notes Tuan, society may confer a particular status on this by developing conservation areas and listing buildings (rarer in the suburbs than the inner city but not unknown). Therefore, residents do not only carry personal memory through into a place, there are also societal memories of a place. There are also inherited impacts of particular places that are bespoke. The quality of the present-day built environment varies considerably from place to place. In outer London, the health-related qualities of different sub-soils and topography mean that higher quality, more desirable property was built away from clay soils, usually on higher land. Not infrequently, new estates of semi-detached houses were developed on the open land of former country estates. These would often include a manor house and landscaped gardens. In some cases, the latter survive as municipal parks hinting at past exclusivity and privilege such as Kelsey Park in Beckenham or Grovelands Park, Southgate. Longstanding transport connections still impact: some suburbs connect their residents straight to City careers, other to less lucrative parts of the centre; while still others draw more on road connections – proximity to the motorway being good, for example, for the self-employed tradesman with van (see Sinclair, 2003, for a psycho-geography of the M25).

There are also generic memories of suburbia: from their inception the cognoscenti have long pilloried the mass suburbs as places of uniformity and conformity – as lacking social imagination and being vested with petty self-interest (Gordon and Gordon, 1933). Through dominant discourses, including popular culture (Medhurst, 1997), elite judgements are passed between generations, for instance, suburbia as apologetically middle England (Gilbert and Preston, 2003). Elite critiques of suburban middle England are transmitted through the built form including the low status attributed to the semidetached house by commentators – often architects (Swenarton, 2002). This has practical significance; Savage et al. (2005, p. 103) argue that, to belong, people must actively develop an emotional link which is likely to require compromise with more instrumental reasons for choice of residential location. Bridge (2006) shows how this tension between the instrumental and emotional aspects of place can lead to considerable psychological dissonance on the part of some suburban residents. In the case of Bristol, he tracks residents who move from gentrified areas of the city to the suburbs in order to access higher quality schooling for their children. Although driven to suburbia by instrumental reasons, Bridge reports that a number of his interviewees felt uncomfortable in the suburbs, for these were places that did not reflect their values. Arguably part of this failure to transmit the right values rested in the historical baggage of the suburbs – the cultural meaning of the semi-detached interwar house and so forth. As Nicolaides (2006, p. 97) argues, despite 'all of the scholarship that has both deepened and complicated our understanding of post-war suburbia', particularly in the United States, it is the stereotype of 1950s mass-suburb that still informs the public imagination.

The role of personal and social history in informing belonging in the suburbs resonates with the work of Pile on phantasmagoria (Pile, 2004; 2005; 2005b), and in particular with dreams and ghosts, which Pile identified as two aspects of his understanding of phantasmagoria. Following Tuan, dreams and ghosts suggest a possible way of working with aspects of the temporal in suburbia. In referring to a form of late eighteenth-century magic lantern, which projects images while hiding the means of their production, the concept of phantasmagoria indicates the need to go beyond appearances and at the same time suggests the dream or ghostlike quality of the image (Pile, 2005, p. 19). Therefore, phantasmagoria allows us to start with appearance – as with investigations of the everyday – and it also affords the opportunity to go beyond to what lies behind the surface appearance of things. Phantasmagoria, like Tuan's time-place focus, draws our attention to the affective, to the emotional work of suburban belonging.

Pile (2005b) divides phantasmagoria into four aspects or experiences: dreams, magic, vampires and ghosts. Unable to rehearse all of these aspects here, in this chapter I will focus on dreams and ghosts, both of which appear to offer the most promising application, alongside Tuan's work on time-place, for interrogating belonging in the suburbs. Turning first to dreams, Pile outlines Freud's use of dreams which, he notes, emphasizes the work of interpreting our dreams: they do not simply reveal their 'truths' to us; rather the real meanings and motivations are often obscured and so must be excavated. Like analysing the everyday, there is a need to work to attach meaning beyond the immediately apparent. This engagement with meaning-making resonates with the sense of the active work of belonging (Savage et al., 2005). Dreams, notes Pile, are everywhere in the city not least in the imagery provided by the marketing industry (Pile, 2005, p. 27). Suburbia has its own dreams – or at least dreams can have a suburban emphasis and can attach themselves to suburban space: consider for example early posters for the Underground. Seeking to sell these new places the posters often combined images of a bucolic past and an idealized petit-bourgeois family. The suburbs were built on dreams: the dream of the ideal home in the park (Fishman, 1987), the dream family with dream children and access to the husband's dream job in the city. Dyos (1966) in his study of a Victorian suburb finds the suburbs to be almost dreamlike – finding it hard to arrive at a physical definition of suburbia he concludes that the suburbs are more a state of mind – perhaps more of a dreamlike state than a physical reality.

Another aspect of phantasmagoria for Pile is that of ghosts. Drawing on the work of Avery Gordon (2008) he describes ghosts as '[introducing] a haunting affect that permits an emotional recognition of that loss, trauma and injustice' (Pile, 2005, p. 131). While we might, in a more grounded way, simply use the vocabulary of memories, speaking of ghosts draws our attention to the personal and impersonal nature of ghosts – they may be ghosts of public memory, of past events. Moreover, the notion of ghosts suggests the unpredictable and involuntary nature of their appearance: 'Ghosts appear and disappear. In so doing, ghosts destabilize the flow of time of a place' (ibid.). However, in his accounts of anti-capitalism riots in London in 2000, Pile (2004) notes how both protesters and the state 'appropriated' the ghosts of the war dead, and in particular how these were evoked through the Cenotaph monument in Whitehall, and how these weighed on the present. As with dreams, ghosts are something that we can be conscious of and work with; they can be actively engaged with as part of the work of belonging.

But phantasmagoria in suburbia can be disturbing, hinting at inevitable dislocation and disappointment. The ghosts of former country estates act as reminders of the early bourgeois drivers of suburbanization – following the cultural lead of the gentry, merchants escaping the city separated family from business – but also they can remind us of the loss of this wealth and the urbanization of what was formerly rural. Through phantasmagoria we might glimpse the fleeting nature of our own dreams; the ideal family form, the dream of a safe and ordered society, the dream of combining country and city (of *rus in urbe*), and of the ideal home. If the original dreams of suburbia still resonate when combined with the ghosts of past glories, we might expect suburbia to be experienced in terms of loss or of expectations disappointed; the unrealized dreams of the 'ideal home' might undermine a sense of belonging in the suburbs. Here the work of Blunt (2003) on nostalgia may have some purchase, in particular on the idea of nostalgia as helping people accommodate separation. She argues that nostalgia too is a process that we manage, that we work with. Nostalgia, she argues, may be about a certain longing for somewhere or sometime other than the present-place but despite this, perhaps because of this, it has a comforting aspect to it. For Blunt, when nostalgia ceases to have some comforting element it ceases to be and becomes grief or loss. In this respect, nostalgia can help people to make sense of present places, it brings comfort to the present-place; it is a way to resolution by allowing in to the present missing or lost times and places, so aiding belonging in the here and now. Are dreams and ghosts similarly worked with to support belonging? In the following Part I draw on empirical work in outer London including interviews with residents to offer examples of where time has entered into belonging. I seek to show how phantasmagoria – and in particular dreams and ghosts – can help in exploring the significance of time in the work of belonging.

Belonging and the phantasmagoria of outer London

The suburbs of outer London have always played with a mix of spatial-temporal imagery – they were originally marketed as the new arcadian past – a place of both tradition and modernity. We see this in a certain architectural schizophrenia (Green, 2009; Saint, 1999); Pick and Holden's stations of the extended Underground network, other public buildings and some private homes drew on European modernism. At Southgate and Arnos Grove on the newly extended Piccadilly Line new stations were symbols of the future – a future powered by electricity. Southgate prefigures 1950s science fiction, appearing as though a spaceship had landed on the largely Victorian settlement; Arnos Grove's design drew directly on the modernist architecture of Stockholm's new public library. Clearly these stations were a connection to somewhere very different – they were invitations to another place, to the city but also to another time, they ushered in the future. They reflected the modernity of suburbia itself, the new city as suburbia – low density, dispersed, owner occupied, anticipating mass car ownership and so on. However, the majority of private-sector-built homes were developed for more conservative market tastes and reflected an Arcadian ideal with their gabling, timber cladding and cottage porches. These suburbs have always looked back as well as forward.

This dualism of the built form was to some extent reflected in the social representation and reality of these suburbs. Following Stone (1977) who traces the link between the suburbs and the – initially – bourgeois family, the interwar suburbs sold a certain ideal of family life. Yet while the 'housewife' was to be found at home nurturing the children she was also 'mistress' of a range of new technology which supported a home without staff and which eventually came to be associated with creating time to seek paid work beyond the home. Moreover, the semi-detached of the interwar years was much smaller than its Victorian predecessor, reflecting a changing family form: no extended family and fewer children. The interwar semi was, then, both symbolic of a 'traditional' family form and the harbinger of change. These suburbs are now over 80 years old; they have aged, or maybe matured. As part of an evolving London, now a mega-city region (Scott, 2001; Hall and Pain, 2006), these suburbs have in some instances appeared incredibly stable and in other instances have accommodated substantial change over their lifespan – what have been the impacts of this for belonging?

In the rest of this part, I examine residents' experience of belonging in outer London using Tuan's 'time as attachment' and 'place as embedded time' alongside the usage of ghosts and dreams by Pile (2005; 2005b). As Figure 6.1 indicates dreams are associated with the internal, created imaginings and ghosts with external memorializations; however, they are not entirely discrete. Suburban ghosts such as the social meaning of the semi-detached house or the landscaped park will be mediated through personal dreams, through personal imagining of the suburban. Dreams can indicate a future point but as people's lives pan out in a particular place so past dreams will come to be evaluated (time as an aspect of belonging): has a place lived up to our dreams, has it confounded or confirmed the ghosts of suburbia?

First, in the context of ageing, the ghosts of family are considered; do these ghosts support or disrupt a sense of belonging? If the passing of time helps people to associate with place, does the passing of too much time lead them to disassociate? Second, attention is turned to place as memorial – in particular to the local high street as a place of memory. Finally, and as a counter case, the experience of British-Asian communities

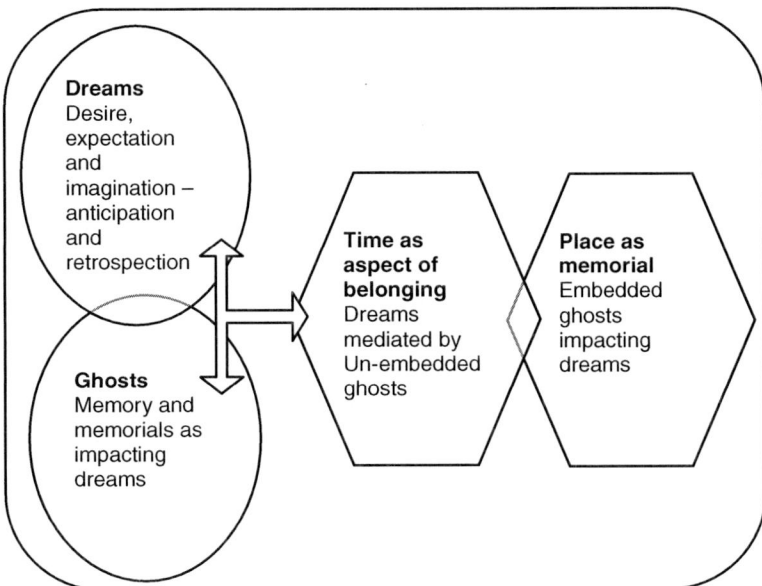

Figure 6.1 Time-place aspects of belonging in outer London as interpreted through ghosts and dreams

in outer London is considered in order to ask how place as memorial might look from a different cultural perspective; what alternative dreams of suburbia inform suburban belonging? The empirical material employed below is drawn from interviews in three parts of outer London, Beckenham (London Borough of Bromley), Queensbury (London Borough of Harrow) and Collier Row (London Borough of Havering). These were selected as containing the three most typical groups of residents (as categorized by Mosaic-Experian data). Interviews were carried out with 60 households in the three parts of outer London; volunteers were drawn from an earlier questionnaire which had been sent to 1,305 addresses representing all households in the three selected study areas. The number completed was 332, a 25 per cent return rate. The original focus of the study was on people's sense of belonging; the questionnaire required both factual and evaluative answers; for example, before moving in did you have family in the area? Is your neighbourhood a good mix of city and country (rated on a five-point Likert scale)? The questionnaire included some sense of the passage of time; for example, respondents were asked to reflect on their impression of the area before and after moving in (when they had not always lived there). While the questionnaire phase was valuable in testing early theorizing and developing interview questions it was the interview data that drew the researcher's attention to the potential of ghosts and phantasmagoria as elements in constructing a sense of belonging.

The interviews were semi-structured and were carried out in people's home at a time of their choosing. The interviews were coded (categorized) using Nvivo – a qualitative data analysis programme; the initial coding reflected categories from the literature; for example, references to 'owner occupation' were sub-coded to show references to affordability, aspiration, hardship, investment. However, codes were added to reflect unanticipated themes; for example, repeated reference to the local high street had not been anticipated and so a series of codes were added to capture these references. Through the process of coding, as the importance of the loss of local shops, the outward movement of family and the importance of the inherited fabric of the area (such as landscaped parks) all emerged the potential of ghosts and phantasmagoria as an analytical tool emerged and eventually these too were added as separate coding categories. The interviewees were self-selected volunteers and did not exactly match the demographic of their area. Overall, interviewees over-represented older age groups and those who had lived longer in the area. In Collier Row the 65–74 age group was the most over-represented, in Queensbury it was the 45–64 group and in Beckenham the 25–44 group. The proportion of respondents to the questionnaire and interviewees who had lived in their present home for over ten years was higher than the English average and in Collier Row and Queensbury was in excess of half of all participants. This may have led to greater emphasis on the passing of time and change than would a more representative range of residents; and indeed, Tuan (1977) observes the different relationship between time and place for the young. Notwithstanding this, the empirical work provides an insight into the importance of time for those interviewed which might be tested in other areas and with different cohorts of suburban residents.

The twentieth-century suburbs have been closely connected with the petit-bourgeois family but more mundanely with social reproduction; yet what happens as families grow up and move on? In one case an account both describes the inevitable losses through death but also how proximity to the family has been lost to economic forces too:

> My parents have died. I have got a brother in Bedford and one in Australia. In my formative years, when I was 15, my whole family used to meet up in the summer holidays at a caravan in the Lea Valley Park. All of the aunts, uncles, cousins used to meet up there for the weekend, stay overnight. You would meet; you had contact with your aunts, uncles, cousins. But that sort of thing doesn't happen very often now. I have got cousins in Spain, they have moved to Switzerland for work. Aunts and uncles live in different parts of the country again, because of work. So that closeness that you had when you're younger with your immediate family is totally decimated. (CR07, male, 45–54, white British)

With its medical/military implications of pestilence/warfare, the use of the term 'decimated' communicates the sense of scale of loss and also its finality. For CR07, the area contains both the ghosts of close family gatherings, and a network of extended family and also the present-day certainty that these have gone forever. In some cases the interviewees almost seemed to describe themselves as ghosts from a past place inhabiting a present-day landscape so changed that they only belong in a remembered place. Here both ethnicity and age play a part in creating this sense of being part of the spectral: 'Well I'm not really part of it because they are all Indians here now, I am the exception, I am the leftover from an older generation really. But it doesn't bother me' (Q05, female, over 75, white British). While Q05 may feel as though she has assumed something of the spectral she also inhabits a place filled by ghosts. As with a number of longstanding residents when asked what they would be leaving behind, if they were to leave the area the response was emphatically, their memories: I would leave behind my life, wouldn't I? I met my husband that I married, I had two children. My parents died, my husband died. I would be leaving my life behind, wouldn't I? (Q05, female, over 75, white British). In this instance, the ghosts of family have kept the person in the area and seem to add some solace or comfort to being there – familiar ghosts have accompanied her through the changes that have been taking place in the area. In other cases nostalgia and the spectral come together as in the instance of CR08 (male, over 75, white British). Here his remembered wife fills the area with meaning – yet the area itself is no longer as she would remember it, she would be a stranger in the present day. His wife remains as a reassuring presence sharing his sense of how the area once was. Also implicit is a sense of being lost without her, it is she who knows her way around the Romford of his memories – her spectral presence that makes the area familiar despite the physical changes:

> My wife's been dead 14 years; she wouldn't know Romford now and she knew it like the back of her hand. She certainly wouldn't recognize it now. The new shops, the malls, the buildings going up. The only thing recognizable is St Edmunds Church, it's been there centuries. That's the only thing that hasn't changed. (CR08, male, over 75, white British)

While for some these ghosts of those now gone were a strong reason for wanting to remain in close contact with the site of these memories, for others there was a preparedness to leave the place behind – the memories would travel with them; they are not place-specific:

> There have been a lot of happy memories because obviously we lived in this house with my mother. [. . .] There were three generations of us in this house. My son grew up here so, for us, it would be about family. I could leave Beckenham without a lot of regrets because that phase of my life is past. My mother and my aunt have both died and my son has grown up and moved on. (B12, female, 45–54, white British)

Therefore, it would overstate the case to say that ghosts tie people to the area but they do seem to help people to belong, and to manage change, while they are there. Overall the ghostly memories of family and friends seemed to provide a comfort and a means to belonging that was reflective of the mechanics of Blunt's (2003) nostalgia.

Moving from personal ghosts we next look at a place as a memorial as expressed through the local high street. This tells a more ambiguous story, one where suburban change seems to be more unsettling, at least for some. Local shops are significant in terms of their symbolic value, and the responses of interviewees resonate with the argument of Griffiths et al. (2008):

> In Britain, the term 'high street' carries cultural connotations of reassuringly small town or suburban neighbourhoods characterised by social stability and enduring local identity. According to the popular image, the high street functions as the communal hub. (p. 1155)

Local high streets are intertwined with a sense of neighbourhood and by extension with a sense of local community. They do cartographic work by delineating neighbourhoods through their catchment areas; they define places:

> So there are smaller geographic areas that people would identify with rather than saying we are all from Beckenham. We think we are part of Beckenham Village because we walk down the road to the shops but people who live half a mile further away would get in the car and drive, they would probably go to Bromley. That's why people in these roads would say Beckenham is local; we would eat there, whereas people in Elmer's End would probably eat around Elmer's End. (B05, male, 55–64, white other)

Given the role of local shops (or in Romford the market) in defining places it follows that threats to these are viewed as having a broader impact than the mere inconvenience of having to travel to an alternative elsewhere. In some sense the local shops act as a barometer for the fortunes of the area. For example:

> I would be much more inclined than I used to be to leave the London region behind, but that is hardly likely at my age, to a place with a more local shopping. The local shops are abysmal here. The high street used to be very good thirty years ago. (B06, male, over 75, white British)

The loss of local shops reflects the inability of people within the area to resist outside forces of change, and so the inability to maintain their definitions of the area. Here, the big supermarkets are perhaps regarded more as a symbol of global forces impacting on the area than as simply an alternative type of retail offer – they represent the loss of the local. The change in local retail could also be a powerful symbol of the new communities that have established themselves in outer London over several decades. Queensbury, along with other parts of north-west London, has become home to a significant Asian population – with their roots primarily in the Indian sub-continent. Naturally enough, as this population has established itself, various services have followed including places of worship and shops. White interviewees were generally measured in observing the loss of local shops that were regarded to have been more valued than the current offering. However, one person expressed this sentiment more strongly and employed the symbolism through reference to the loss of the 'English butchers': 'Every shop has gone, we have not even got an English butchers no more. Every shop, Queensbury is the same, [and] Kingsbury. Every shop that is opening up is an Asian shop' (Q01b, male,

55–64, white British). The shops are there but they are not there, his memorials have gone. The dream of neighbourhood, place-based community even of self-sufficiency and perhaps of desired detachment all seemed threatened by the changes to or losses of local shops. The fate of local shops seems most strongly to represent the impotence of place in the face of structural forces working across space. In her writing on difference, fear and habitus, Sandercock (2005) argues that changes in local shops can impact at a range of spatial scales. Writing on the Australian experience she argues that as the local is changed so the sense even of national identity may be challenged. From an Australian perspective she argues that the change in the local area from an 'Aussie' to a Halal butchers, from a Protestant church to a Buddhist temple, from an 'Aussie' pub to a gay bar threatens an invented (but nevertheless pertinent) sense of nation as, she suggests, the 'imaginary' of the nation is, 'embodied in the real local spaces of one's street, neighbourhood and city, where it is either reinforced or undermined' (p. 223).

This is, of course, a matter of perspective; while the decoupling of the suburban experience from an imaginary of (white) national identity certainly seemed to resonate with some residents in outer London, it is only one side of the story. For the British Asians in Queensbury, the development of an ethnic infrastructure in the area provided a strong and secure sense of belonging. For some of the British-Asian population the distinctiveness of the area, its quality of place, was more often linked to the support found in the security of like others and the social infrastructure that followed on from this:

> As far as I'm concerned, I think it's the best place in the world for Indians. We have everything Indian that you could possibly need in this area. The shopping for Indian stuff is on your doorstep, Indian food; the best Indian restaurants in the UK are in the north-west of London without a doubt. Good community, we have good social functions, different functions, good it's all good, really fantastic. (Q15, male, 45–54, British Asian)

British Asians were drawing on dreams of the local shop, of community, neighbourhood and self-sufficiency but for them this was a dream being increasingly realized rather than an invocation of memorials being eroded by time; it was a dream of the future not of the past. As Trienekens (2002) investigates, in relation to the valorizing of 'high' culture, ethnic immigration has the potential to disrupt; the historic cultural judgement and meanings of particular urban forms and expectations and dreams linked to these forms may simply not carry over (though these interactions certainly merit further investigation).

Conclusion

The purpose of this chapter has been to look at how Pile's 'dreams' and 'ghosts' might make a contribution to understanding some of the multiple ways that time seeps into our understanding of place (Tuan, 1977) and into the work of belonging, in particular in relation to temporal aspects of maturing suburbs. Pile contests those who argue that we must break free of the dream in which we live, from our false consciousness of capitalism. While Harvey (2000) would have us wake from a nightmare to find utopia, for Pile (2005b) there is another possibility, one which Freud and Walter Benjamin articulate. In this possibility our dreams may still deceive us, the desires that they represent may be hidden from us; but rather than waking from them and discarding them, we need to work with them, to excavate what it is in the dream that we want to hold on to and nurture – in so doing we might wake up to our true hopes and aspirations. Similarly with the monuments of place, these, like our dreams, can present false – or at least multiple – realities; the former landscaped estates, high streets and even the 'semi' itself provide a ghostly reminder of times past that can disturb and unsettle us, but their meaning can also be disturbed and unsettled as new residents move in, for whom memorials of place may have quite different meanings.

The suburbs of outer London are well on their way to their centenary. As they age, so it seems increasingly important to factor in the 'intricate' interweaving of time and place as we seek to understand the ongoing work of belonging in the suburbs. This chapter has sought to focus on the extent to which belonging in the present is dependent on both the ghosts of the past and on dreams of times both gone and still to come. These elements of phantasmagoria, like time itself, can both settle and disturb the act of belonging; they bring both comfort and the potential of suburban futures as well as dissonance; in so doing they illustrate the complexity of the ongoing work of belonging in the ageing suburbs.

7

Where the Heart Is: Cinema and Civic Life in Singapore

Gaik Cheng Khoo

Introduction

This chapter deals with the recent attempts by filmmakers and communities to represent the housing estates that predominate outside of Singapore's Central Business District. For a long time, the representation of the HDB (Housing Development Board) flats was limited to the homogeneous housing blocks of Eric Khoo's *12 Storeys* (1997). A film about alienated HDB dwellers, *12 Storeys* reinforced Rem Koolhaas' view of postmodern Singapore as a 'Potemkin metropolis' – an inauthentic place that features 'the coexistence of the strictly orthogonal super-blocks of average modernity that comprise the vast majority of its built substance' (Koolhaas, 2000, p. 22). Koolhaas' description gives an impression of HDB high rises as homogenizing and somewhat sterile, one perhaps incapable of producing creative, interesting selves. A decade into the new millennium has seen more films that deal with place, history and memory in Singapore, some focusing on particular estates and fast-disappearing landmarks.[1] In contrast to Khoo's representations, the films I focus on seem to actively work against the pragmatic developmentalist and present-futurist orientation of the state which allegedly has little room for sentiment and nostalgic feeling. Singapore is a city of constant face-lifts: HDB flats have to be upgraded every few years and old buildings are destroyed to make way for newer ones, making permanent landmarks impossible. How then does one make sense of oneself in an ever-changing landscape? I demonstrate how filmmakers make the supposedly sterile HDB more interesting by representing the environment as places of sensuous and affective memory that generate, authenticate and anchor a personal yet collectively shared Singapore identity.

---

[1] Examples include Tan Pin Pin's documentaries *Moving House, Singapore Gaga* and *Invisible City*; *Diminishing Memories 1* and *2* (Eng Yee Peng, 2006 and 2008) about the kampong, Lim Chu Kang; the early films by Jack Neo which focus on the problems faced by Singaporean heartlanders and take place in and around housing estates (*Money No Enough* 1998; *That One Not Enough* 1999, etc.); and *Singapore Dreaming* (Colin Goh and Yen Yen Woo, 2006) and *Invisible Children* (Brian Gothong Tan, 2009).

My selected texts include both amateur and professional films: the 90-second short films from 'Where The Heart Is', which is part of an ongoing community arts project called *Civic Life: Singapore* (http://civiclife.sg/); and works by two well-known Singaporean filmmakers, documentary filmmaker Tan Pin Pin and Royston Tan. Led by the British Council and the National Museum of Singapore, *Civic Life: Singapore* explores identity, memory, architecture and civic space, functioning to embed place in personal memories and to 'humanise space'. The short films offer a glimpse of diverse Singapore neighbourhoods from ordinary people and amateur filmmakers, yielding a richer canvas for me to be able to draw some generalizations about cinema, place and civic life in Singapore. I then turn to the works of Tan Pin Pin and Royston Tan to discuss the cinematic techniques 'professional' filmmakers have deployed to evoke memory and place, techniques which emphasize a capturing of the senses (via food, sound, touch). Both offer two contrasting aesthetics of (re)presenting the Singaporean self and its relationship to time and space: Pin Pin's stark documentary realism in *The Impossibility of Knowing* connotes a present self unmoored from the past while Royston's aesthetics of nostalgia rely on the haptic possibilities of film to connect the present with the (reconstructed) past. Collectively, these films which focus on capturing community and human stories suggest that all Singaporean estates and communities face similar issues: a realization that geography is temporary and that the only way to transform space into place is through the artful form of storytelling, recounting memories, archiving and recreating a past that is no longer visibly present. However, I conclude that the affective civic life created on film is not entirely independent of the state's development goals. This is because the state has become attuned to the effects of emotional geography and strategically deploys the discourse of affect in its urban planning schemes.

Singapore's sub/urban development

Eighty-two per cent of Singaporeans live in government-built flats (most of which are owner-occupied) (Teoalida, 2010). Set up in 1960 to solve the nation's housing crisis when many were living in unhygienic slums and crowded squatter settlements, the Housing Development Board built 21,000 flats in less than three years, exceeding in efficiency its colonial predecessor, the Singapore Improvement Trust (which was responsible for building the Art Deco-style Tiong Bahru flats). By 1965, the HDB had built 54,000 flats and within 10 years of its formation, had the housing problem under control (Housing Development Board, 2012a). From 1960 until 31 March 2010, the HDB was estimated to have built a total of one million apartments, alongside creating new towns or housing estates with integrated infrastructure while continuously 'rejuvenating and regenerating' older HDB blocks (Teoalida, 2010). A result of this constant renovation is the demolition of older structures built in the 1970s and 1980s and replacement with newer buildings and styles. Even old HDBs are not immune to demolition – the first two 10-storey HDB blocks at Tanjong Pagar, Duxton Plain, was redeveloped into the 48-storey Pinnacle@Duxton, the tallest HDB blocks.

The HDB heartland is understood as everyday space, inhabited by ordinary Singaporeans and distinguished from the CBD which caters to tourists with its 'grandiose shopping mall[s]' (Toh, 2011). Planned to be self-sufficient, these townships (the earliest being completed in 1960) contain commercial and retail shops, food courts, recreation centres, cinemas, wet markets, nearby primary schools, community and welfare facilities, and open spaces – all serviced by public transportation such as buses and the MRT (light rail transit). For these reasons, the Singapore housing estate resembles planned suburbs elsewhere such as the Zoetermeer or Alphen aan de Rijn in the Netherlands or a number of recent German conglomerates around the Frankfurt and Taunus area. Nevertheless Singapore's HDB dwellers, known as 'heartlanders', are conceived in uniquely discursive ways.

Heartlanders are to be distinguished from cosmopolitans. An ideologically loaded distinction first introduced in 1999 and used by the state for political expediency, it was 'a new way of referring to shifts in the traditional bourgeois and proletarian class formation' (K. P. Tan, 2008, p. 66). Heartlanders typically live in mature public housing estates and their values are conservative, communitarian, 'Asian', ethnic and sometimes religious in character (ibid., p. 67). The HDB heartland is also associated with linguistic diversity, and heartlanders speak Mandarin, Chinese dialects, Malay and Tamil, with Singlish serving as a common language across ethnic groups. They supposedly form the mainstay of support for the People's Action Party, which has been in government since independence, and are seen as 'the "keepers" or "protectors" of national values, culture, identity and a sense of belonging' (ibid.), particularly at a time when Singaporeans are feeling the brunt of the global economic downturn. Heartlanders and heartlander concerns are featured in films like Jack Neo's *Money No Enough* (1998). Here the HDB is home and the kopi-tiam—the ethnic Chinese coffeeshop found in the housing estate—the 'Good Third Place', which Ray Oldenburg (1989) argues is where workers can go to relax and seek community, away from both home and work and essential to community and public life. The ideal 'cosmopolitan', on the other hand, lives in private housing, is English-educated, sophisticated and has enough cultural capital and competitive edge to enable global mobility (K.P. Tan, 2008, p. 67).

Excerpts from *Where The Heart Is*: Favourite little haunts

In the online film competition *Where the Heart Is,* participants are invited to 'show us the places that matter to you' (www.civiclife.sg/competition.html). While the selected locations include some cosmopolitan spaces such as private housing, shopping districts and tourist sites, most of the short films are tributes to the heartland neighbourhood that filmmakers recall from their childhood. Unlike Royston Tan, or those from a generation before who would have experienced the relocation from kampongs to high-rise living, the majority of the filmmakers under 35 years of age spent their childhoods growing up in the 1980s and 1990s, when Singapore was already 'developed'. Some of the films focus specifically on the memory of physical structures such as a bridge, the long communal HDB Corridor, the stone table which becomes a gathering place for teenagers to hang out, the 'mama stall' (a small convenience/corner shop traditionally run by Tamil Muslims that is located on the ground floor where the void deck is), and the void deck itself.[2] Others found subjects like a field, bus stop, playgrounds, schools that either had been demolished or relocated; two were about supermarkets (like NTUC which can be found in every major township); two were about going to IKEA.

While many reflected the rather sheltered and homogeneous middle-class Singaporean upbringing of the young, a few managed to be more creative or affective. For example, the winner *Corridor*, delivers the memory of a HDB flat with a single dolly shot along an old HDB corridor, using sound effects and English titles to tell the story of what people did along the corridor. The film begins with orchestral music and the camera on a dolly at one end of the corridor. The text tells us 'A passageway. Even though it is narrow, it was more than just a passageway.' As the camera passes a wall that frames the corridor, the text reads 'A goalpost' and we hear crowds cheering (while the music continues). The camera moving backwards reveals the staircase on the left: 'It was a football field.' The text goes on to describe how the corridor was also their battlefield where wars were fought. This is accompanied with the sounds of gunfire and explosions. As the camera passes some potted plants, the text tells us 'there were forts and jungle to help our platoon', and so on. The film uses a child's imagination to turn domestic objects into a child's playground and to make connections to the filmmaker's past. For example, passing a bicycle, the text mentions the film *E.T.* and BMX bicycles, which were all the rage in the 1980s. To its credit the film ends without sentimentality. The camera comes to a stop when the text reads: 'These days, corridors are empty.' The screen turns to black, the sound of childish laughter in the background stops and the text appears: 'Gone are the joy and laughter.'

Many films in the *Civic Life* project are nostalgic for a different time, especially the slower time of childhood. As Svetlana Boym reminds us, nostalgia is 'a rebellion against the modern idea of time, the time of history and progress' (2001, p. xv). And nowhere is 'the time of history and progress' more ardently adhered to than in Singapore where progress is signified by '[first and foremost, economic] improvement in the future, not reflection on the past' (Boym, 2001, p. 10). Progress in the form of urban redevelopment to make way for a spatial expansion of the downtown core have therefore sparked nostalgia for old coffeeshops like Hock Hiap Leong (demolished after 55 years at Armenian Street in 2001). Thus, nostalgia, 'as a historical emotion', as Boym notes, 'is a longing for that shrinking "space of experience" that no longer fits the new horizon of expectations' – for '[n]ostalgic manifestations are side effects of the teleology of progress' (ibid.). In Singapore, such longing manifests as a kind of obsessive-compulsive need to capture on film what one helplessly cannot control in reality (Royston Tan interview with Ng Yi-Sheng in 2010). For Tan the loss of his childhood place in Lorong Chuan leads to a shortened sense of self in history: 'I feel like part of my life is gone.' After all, 'no one can become what he cannot find in his memories' (Amery, in Young, 1993, p. 1). As if to anchor self to memory and place, Tan named his film production company Chuan Pictures in early 2009. He concludes that '[Singaporeans have] their own favourite little haunt, their own little

---

[2] The void deck together with the stone table and 'mama stall' are unique architectural features to Singaporean HDB flats: located on the ground floor, the void deck is an open communal space used to hold weddings, funerals and other social gatherings for residents living above since most units cannot accommodate large numbers of people.

space. And because we have so little space, it matters so much more to them' (Royston Tan interview with Ng Yi-Sheng in 2010).

Nevertheless filmmakers also understand too well that there is no going back, and that the expression of nostalgic sentiment may well be 'a symptom of our age, a historical emotion' and one that is 'not necessarily opposed to modernity' (Boym, 2001, p. xvi). Royston Tan explains: 'It's a conflicting thing I think, because you need to remove some old things to progress. But then again, some of the old things means [sic] a lot to a lot of people. And Singaporeans, I think, these two years, are getting very nostalgic. . . . .' (2010 interview with Ng).

These films invest the physical estate with differential histories and memories associated with affect, play, bonding and, sometimes, solitude and psychological recovery. For example, thinking about the place he grew up in, his grandmother's HDB flat, helps the filmmaker/narrator Tang Kang Sheng recall what he was like as a child in the short film, *Remember*:

> And I remember things like missing my parents the entire day. And just at the end of the day, I'll rush out to look at the car park, to see if their car had arrived back already. Or if it was just as simple as going down and being excited to, you know, go and buy potato chips with my uncle at the nearest convenience store. Or also you know hating to go to the market, really hating it, because it was wet and dirty . . . but then you just wanted the company of my grandmother. And it's things like that that sometimes remind me how I was, and it doesn't make things better. But it makes me want to become better. And that's all I can hope for.

The narrator/filmmaker's memory of the HDB is supported by a mix of old happy family photographs taken at his grandmother's flat and film footage of the current flat (which had gone 'en bloc' and therefore seems empty).[3] Interestingly the lapse into childhood memory reveals ambivalence: the boy's loneliness from missing his parents, his anxiety, his feelings of revulsion towards the dirty wet market (perhaps evoked as much by touch as by smell) all do not provide a sense of relief for the young man who might have done something he regrets in the present. Instead he can only strive to 'want to become better'. Despite the ambivalence, he is able to draw from this memory of the self embedded in the place of the building; the memory operates as a kind of resource for the renewal of faith to go forward into the future.

Different aesthetics of representation: Tan Pin Pin and Royston Tan

I would now like to turn to a comparative analysis of two Singaporean filmmakers' works which in their own varying ways represent the housing estate: Tan Pin Pin

---

[3] 'En bloc' in Singapore is the Selective En bloc Redevelopment Scheme (SERS), an urban redevelopment strategy employed by the HDB in maintaining and upgrading public housing flats in older estates in the city-state. Displaced residents are offered a new 99-year lease in a supposedly nearby flat or compensated.

and Royston Tan. Both these filmmakers have very different personalities and filmmaking styles, with Pin Pin mostly making documentaries and experimental work that is much more minimalist and subtle. Being a more technically oriented and cerebral filmmaker, Tan Pin Pin's most popular film *Singapore Gaga* (2006) asks viewers to consider the role of sound in cinematic representations of the city: the soundscape of eccentric buskers at MRT stations; world-famous Singaporean pianist Margaret Leng Tan playing John Cage's *4'33"* on a miniature piano at a void deck; the sounds of English-language chants at a madrasah (Islamic school) sports day; and the female announcer whose familiar voice is used on all the MRT trains to locate passengers to specific stations, who would otherwise not be recognized by her appearance in real life. This film dramatizes Gwen Lee's point that Singapore has its own 'auditory thumbprint [such as the familiar Singaporean accent and the city's symphony of urban noises] which cannot be erased by en-bloc sales, economically driven planning decisions and market forces' (Lee, 2010). Present-day sounds maintain a familiar sonoroscape even as the city has undergone physical transformation.

Conversely, flamboyance and nostalgia are signature traits for Royston Tan, whose recollection of sensuous details evoke our haptic senses. He relies heavily on sound and texture, the latter being the kind that makes the viewer want to reach out to touch 'the skin of the film'. Laura Marks in her book *The Skin of the Film* suggests that 'memory is encoded in objects through contact' and also that 'cinema itself appeals to contact – to embodied knowledge, and to the sense of touch in particular – in order to recreate memories' (2000, p. 129). Marks makes a distinction between haptic and optical vision. For her, most cinema privileges the visual over other senses of perception such as sound and touch and her objective is to explore cinema's capacity to render memory through the haptic. Touch provides information about objects in the environment and our relationship to them and our participation in that environment (Rodaway, 2002, p. 44). Touch involves more than the action of the fingers feeling the texture of surfaces. Instead, it involves the whole body reaching out to the things constituting the environment and things which come into contact with the body (Boring, 1942, in Rodaway, 2002, p. 44).

The documentary eye of Tan Pin Pin: *The Impossibility of Knowing*

In *The Impossibility of Knowing* (2010), Tan Pin Pin visits banal places where tragedy has occurred, some of which take place in housing estates. For example, these sites include a HDB in Toa Payoh Central from which two lesbian lovers jumped in a death pact, a burnt and empty flooded mosque on Marine Parade Road, the site where a tunnel collapsed, an expressway where a rare deer was knocked down, a flooded canal where a schoolgirl was washed away. Her artist statement reads:

> Despite Singapore's hyper-urban and sterile appearance, this terrain is still wrought over with human emotions. A place may just be a place to some but be fraught

with meaning for others. It is the subjectivity of emotional nodes connected to geography that fascinate me.

The title *The Impossibility of Knowing* refers to the limits of images, the limits of what we see and can know, from what we see. It also refers to the act of construction of meaning by the director. The process is tenuous and highly mediated.

The camera uses still shots to portray these sites with a narrator reading in English excerpts taken from the newspapers (in a neutral voice). There are no people in these still shots although there is traffic. What little movement there is in the documentary is associated with traffic and nature: water gathered in puddles inside the mosque, in the canal, the gentle ripples on the surface of the pool, the wind on the leaves of a tree, a lone scarf blowing over a tree branch. Pin Pin expressly wanted still shots without people so that the audience can contemplate in silence (SINdie, 2010). The auteur's rational voice guides her realist representation of space in the film: indeed, it is impossible to know that these places are places where tragedy has struck because the visual evidence has disappeared with the constant change in the landscape and the drive towards sterility. Her camera captures and restricts our senses of perception to the optic alone. In the aftermath of these efficient clean-ups by the road sweepers, who or what remains as witnesses? The trees along the expressway? Nature? What gives meaning to these banal 'non places' (Augé, 1995)? Only the voice-over provides hints of narratives, newspaper accounts, neighbourhood gossip. But the voice-over is just as dry as the visual representation:

Night. Stereotypical long still shot of an HDB.

Text: Downstairs of HDB 179 Toa Payoh Central

Another shot from the HDB flat upstairs looking down.

Male V/O: Yong was found on the footpath and her lover Wee on the second floor parapet. Both women had red thread around their ring fingers. They were dressed in red t-shirts and blue jeans. Police found the pair of scissors and 3 cigarette butts on the 25th floor directly above the two bodies. Yong left a note for her mother saying that she was leaving and to take care.

The leanness of the representation requires that the viewers only rely on the visuals and narration. What available sound there is in the documentary is purely incidental (birds, watery sounds and effects of wind, the hum of passing traffic) rather than social, identifiable sounds that would narrativize the landscape. In conclusion, this documentary suggests that we can never know the kinds of personal relationships, social networks and emotions that are attached to these places through visuals alone. Ultimately it is up to the viewers to produce their own version or memory of these places. But what if you were a stranger to Singapore and are not familiar with these spaces, like a foreign viewer at the Singapore Biennale 2011 where this film was screened? These sites of past trauma would then just remain as impersonal spaces.

Royston Tan's haptic perception: Nostalgia and cinema of the senses

Here I contrast Pin Pin's austere documentary realism with Royston's fictional film in order to demonstrate that the limits of filmic representation that she mentions only exist if we do not move beyond optical vision. Royston's works are evidently infused with sensory perception: rich visuals, touch and sounds. Both *Ah Kong* [Grandpa] (2010) and *Hock Hiap Leong* (2001) employ the phonograph sound of a Mandarin song by famous Chinese songstress, Ge Lan, to evoke 1950s' nostalgia. Antiquated technology becomes part of the cache of nostalgia that is communicated, ironically, through new digital technology.

A short film about dementia, *Ah Kong* is set in the heartland. Royston marks the filmic space with layers of time using music and sepia-toned images. Unlike the cosmopolitan city which signifies the country's present and future, the heartland is 'a representation of the past' (Tan and Yeoh, 2006, p. 164). The film begins with talking heads of diverse people (Chinese, Indian, Malay) in heartland spaces that can be construed as 'old places' – the old-fashioned barber shop, the wet market and in front of an old beautiful shophouse with a tiled-wall frontage.[4] They are all describing to the grandson in Mandarin and Singlish their memories of his grandfather as a young man. This series of sequences is followed by a scene where the grandson interacts with the senile grandfather inside a HDB flat. This part is shot in close-ups but the nostalgia is still palpable in the sepia-tinted colour of the facial skin of the two men and the use of light and shadow: these devices highlight the pigmentation on the old man's face, his toothiness, his wrinkled fingers on the boy's smooth cheek, the youthful grandson's pimples and scar across his eyebrow, the glisten in their eyes as the boy seeks connection from his grandfather who mistakes him for his father. Unlike the sterile empty physical spaces in *The Impossibility of Knowing*, it is the texture of the skin in these facial close-ups, represented through the sepia photograph-like nature of the film (the 'skin' of the film), that stimulates our haptic pleasure and evokes an aura of nostalgia. The senile grandfather, caught in a time warp, only remembers the past and forgets the present. When he thinks he hears his chickens calling (he no longer raises chickens), he goes out to the corridor and asks his favourite 'son' to help him feed them. The boy indulges his grandfather and pretends to feed the chickens 'in the yard' (actually the HDB corridor) with him.

In 'The Making of *Ah Kong*', psychologist Sng Yan Ling explains that a good caregiver like the boy in the film should attempt to share the memory and step into the world of the person with dementia.[5] Here I would like to use dementia as a metaphor to think about the films in *Where The Heart Is*. What would it be like to grow old and senile in an ever-changing landscape like Singapore? How would I find my way home when home is no longer where it used to be? In recalling the relationship between the filmmakers

---

[4] A shophouse is a form of vernacular architecture common to urban Southeast Asia. Usually a low-rise building comprising of two or three stories, it has a shop on the ground floor for mercantile activity and a residence above the shop.

[5] The short film 'The Making of *Ah Kong*' can be found here: www.youtube.com/watch?v=iV9Z7jw5GIQ&feature=watch_response.

and the past lives of specific spaces are these nostalgic films forgetting the present in the process of representation? Could they be said to be suffering from the same symptoms of dementia (disorientation, confusion, memory loss, apathy and withdrawal, personality change), except that these symptoms are triggered not by an illness in the brain but changes in their physical environment? Are these 'moments of dementia' socially useful tools to theorize a country suffering from what Singaporean poet Alfian Sa'at calls, 'a history of amnesia' (2001)? Similarly if the dementia patient needs a caregiver to share the memory and step into his or her world, if only temporarily, how do we as viewers (or the state officials and urban planners) learn to be that caregiver? Royston offers this challenge in his earlier short film, *Hock Hiap Leong*.

Hock Hiap Leong (2001) was made to commemorate an eponymous kopitiam or coffeeshop that shut down after 55 years on Armenian Street to make way for urban renewal.[6] Although Armenian Street is not considered heartland because of its proximity to the city centre, its story mirrors that of many older kopitiam found in older housing estates (or where housing estates have sprouted up). It shows that what is being memorialized is not the space itself as much as the social actions and spatial practices that give it its distinct qualities: the two food operators who turn out art forms 'borne of a lifetime of sweat and toil', the coffeeshop owner calling out the orders in Hokkien, the constant flow of customers throughout the day, the sounds of rhythmic chopping on the wooden chopping board, the clanging of the steel spatula in the iron wok and the smell of freshly brewed coffee all converge to 'dissipate one's loneliness and evok[e] ephemeral bliss', the narrator observes. Not only does this filmed memory evoke sight, sound and smell, it also invites the viewers to make meaning out of what it pictures and delivers in the Mandarin voice-over (with English subtitles). The camera lovingly pans over the neatly arranged cigarette packs, the rows of opened cans of sweetened condensed milk, the cups lined up on the shelf, the brown-stained coffee filters hanging on the wall and the charcoal-toasted bread, as if to register and memorize each sight and sound. The narrator says 'every little item seems to have its own story to tell. In these stories are found my childhood memories.' Here the eye for the everyday detail that designates a kopitiam a kopitiam á là Georges Perec (in *Species of Spaces and Other Pieces*, 1998) does not merely offer a list of objects which on their own have no meaning except for their use value. This filmed memory evokes sight, sound and smell, and invites the viewers, especially Singaporeans (and Malaysians) sharing a common cultural experience and memory of the kopitiam, to piece together the 'elements of the paradigm' to form a syntagm and ultimately meaning (Thwaites et al., 1994). In other words, the camera picks out the ensemble ingredients (or paradigm set) of a typical kopitiam breakfast and makes the viewers imagine the finished product: of eggs (to be boiled), bread to be toasted and buttered over with margarine and kaya (egg jam) served with local coffee and sweetened condensed milk in the cups on display. Without the cultural, communally shared understanding about how these ingredients come together, and with whom we have meals, on what occasions, etc. these objects do not resonate with any memory.

---

[6] The short film *Hock Hiap Leong* can be viewed here: www.movieola.ca/video_streaming.php?id=04018001.

Returning to my metaphor of dementia, the viewer as caregiver (with this shared memory) is invited in to share Royston's momentary dementia, the lapse into childhood memories, and to 'fill in the blanks' as it were. The voice-over claims that if the stories about each detail in the kopitiam were transposed into a movie, the camera would only capture their form not their essence and asks, 'How does one begin to uncover the true soul and humanity' of the coffeeshop? Royston does this through rendering everyday life in the kopitiam appropriately as a campy 1960s' musical – a genre that offers a 'profoundly aesthetic vision of utopian human liberation' (Feuer, 1993, p. 84). Royston's queer kopitiam fantasy is equally utopian for being a 'third place' (Oldenburg, 1989) that includes a transvestite, played by the only visibly ethnic Malay actor in the film. As Boym reminds us, 'nostalgia is a sentiment of loss and displacement, but it is also a romance with one's own fantasy' (2001, p. xiii). In fact, Royston did not frequent Hock Hiap Leong as a child (as is suggested by the male narrator in the film) but was born only a few years before it was demolished. Here in the space of dementia, fact and fiction become enmeshed and different times coalesce: the past is rendered as a nostalgic longing for the old, the idyllic slower tempo of a simpler Singaporean kampong life. Thus the costuming (which ranges from 1960s to the disco fashion of the 1970s) and the music (from the 1950s) do not authenticate the 1960s but stems from a vague idea of the past that pre-dates the filmmaker's birth.

Conclusion

While it might seem that filmmakers' recourse to haptic devices help viewers treat the HDB heartland as emotional geography filled with personal memories that construct an 'authentic' or unique sense of Singaporean identity and a collective self 'where the heart is', one wonders whether the endeavour of constructing civic life on such popular/ populist terms is entirely independent (of the state). For ultimately the nostalgic discourse of home in the heartland does not operate solely among the arts community and individuals. In their promotional material for the plan to remake the heartland starting from 2007, the HDB relies on the same rhetoric: 'Remaking our Heartland: realise, rejuvenate, regenerate' and 'Home . . . where the heart is' (Housing Development Board, 2012b). Is this nostalgic sentiment, a sentiment that has usually no place in the pragmatic mindset and policies of the PAP, a sign of a good caregiver playing along with the dementia patient? Rhetoric aside, these plans received overwhelming support from residents surveyed at the Remaking our Heartland exhibition in April 2011. One of the proposed plans to remake Hougang includes a Heritage Corridor and an acknowledgement of Hougang's rich Teochew and Hainanese cultural heritage dating back to early Singapore. In then MP George Yeo's speech (8 January 2011) on the remaking of Hougang, he spoke of connecting the future to the past: 'We are not only concerned with physical development but also with community development. Our heritage is something to treasure. Community development means involving those who live here or have connections here with our plans for the future.'[7] These policies

---

[7] It is uncertain what will happen to these plans for the area of Aljunied after Yeo lost in the 2011 elections.

demonstrate the determination of the government to re-position itself as the master builder of homeland and homes and its awareness that space is crucial in forming identities, particularly national identity and good citizen-subjects.

However, these policies are neither new nor do they reflect some sudden change of heart: citing Ghassan Hage, Velayutham traces the attempt on the part of the Singapore state to manufacture the 'affective building blocks of home' (Hage, 1997) as early as the 1997 *Singapore 21* report (Velayutham, 2007, p. 102). The report was the result of the government's growing consciousness that 'a high standard of living could never, on its own, be enough to create any kind of affective attachment to the nation among the population' (ibid., p. 97). Thus *Singapore 21*'s rationale was to create 'a citizenry with both emotional and economic stakes in Singapore' (ibid.). A committee was set up to develop 'the heartware' to make Singapore more homely and to deter cosmopolitan Singaporeans from migrating overseas (ibid.). Velayutham quotes a passage from Prime Minister Goh Chok Tong's speech from 14 October 1999: 'Singapore risks becoming like one of those well-run, comfortable international hotels which successful business executives check in and out. What makes a home different from a hotel is where the heart is' (ibid., p. 82). To achieve its goal, the state set out on an agenda to use affect in combination with economics to develop a stronger sense of civic nationalism.

Royston Tan's popular aesthetics of affect and nostalgia were to suit this agenda perfectly. Indeed several of his short nostalgic films were commissioned by various state institutions (*The Old Man and the River* by the Singapore National Museum and *Ah Kong* by the Health Promotion Board). The *Singapore 21* document outlined five ideals to represent Singapore's vision for the future, two of which included wanting to see citizens take a more active role to make a difference in community and civic affairs, and fostering passionate feelings about Singapore (ibid., p. 100). These ideals were followed up in the recommendations of the 2003 report *Remaking Singapore*, some of which are reflected in the current policies of urban planning around the heartland. They include enhancing a heritage programme identifying significant 'memory' sites around the island, developing a series of social and cultural history museums and transferring state management of communal land surrounding HDB apartments under strata-title to the owner-residents themselves to manage in order to foster a greater sense of proprietorship and pride in communal spaces, and to promote increased civic involvement (ibid., p. 101).

When contextualized within this greater state discourse that produces affective and effective neoliberal citizens, the Singapore Civic Life project sounds less and less like a community project that stems organically from the people themselves (after all, it is sponsored partly by the National Museum). For example, the apparently positive message about food sharing as binding the quarrelling family members in the HDB flat from the 90-second short film *Home*, in retrospect seems to compromise the individual's ambivalent feelings about family and space and the need to escape the squabbling parents/household. This neat affective ending secures a 'fundamentally instrumentalist logic at the heart of these home-building efforts' (ibid., p. 109) such as the call for strong families outlined in *Singapore 21*, which would help alleviate the lack of social welfare in a nation with an ageing population and declining fertility rates. Escape is not possible if the citizen-subject is fully interpellated through the state ideology and discursive tools of national place-making and home-building. To put it another way, the state wants children to learn how to be good caregivers to their parents with dementia in order to absolve itself from the responsibility of looking after its ageing population. This is not to negate the genuineness of feeling and communal participation of Singaporean filmmakers, writers and others involved in the *Civic Life* project. Rather it is to acknowledge that these civic actions are only rendered possible when they are not perceived as threatening to the state. Needless to say, space and place are implicitly always already political in and outside of Singapore.

Part III

Aesthetics of Affect

8

'The ssshh of sprays on all the little lawns': Imagining the Post-war American Suburbs

Jo Gill

This chapter examines the often-overlooked contribution made by poetry to the establishment and maintenance of what we might call the suburban imaginary. Focusing in particular on the lyric poetry of the post-war American suburbs and drawing on work by a number of writers, I argue that poetry has played a critical – by which I mean vital *and* interrogative – role in the construction of suburban experience and the dissemination of its meanings.

By way of illustration and case study, I take a number of poems about suburban gardens and lawn care spanning the 1950s and 1960s including Howard Nemerov's 'Suburban Prophecy', Hollis Summers's 'The Lawnmower', Mona Van Duyn's 'Notes from a Suburban Heart', William Stafford's 'Elegy' and Richard Wilbur's 'To An American Poet Just Dead'. Each evokes the peculiar topography of the contemporary suburbs and, more importantly, its historical, social and discursive parameters. A close reading of such poems reveals traces of an emergent anxiety about the environment; an anxious testing of the relationship between centre and margins; an exaggerated – and, as Catherine Jurca has noted of contemporary suburban fiction, self-pitying – vision of the burdens of modern manhood; an awareness of the pressures of post-war, Cold War surveillance culture and an acute sensitivity to the significance of suburban space on the construction and mediation of subjectivity. As such, poems about suburban lawn care provide a particularly useful lens through which to view the material and ideological pressures of this place and time.

Suburban lawns

The lawned lot has long stood as a synecdoche for the seductions of suburban living. It represents access – in safe, domesticated form – to the natural landscape and, by association, to the promise of personal and social fulfilment. It offers jaded ex-urban migrants the opportunity to reconnect with the soil and thereby – if only in their own fantasies – to identify with the pioneering traits of American citizenship. The lawn reifies that conflation of civilization and wilderness, *urbis* and *rus* that has long been at the heart of the suburban project as evidenced by the emergence of borderland developments from around 1820, picturesque enclaves from around 1850 (Hayden, 2003, pp. 4–5; Stilgoe, 1998, p. 152), romanticized 'arcadian villages' later in the century (Martinson, 2000, pp. 20–2) and the single-family detached homes, surrounded by lawned lots, of the mid-twentieth century. As Leo Marx, writing in 1964 in his influential study *The Machine in the Garden: Technology and the Pastoral Ideal in America*, notes: 'the pastoral ideal has been used to define the meaning of America ever since the age of discovery, and it has not yet lost its hold upon the native imagination' (p. 3).

Late nineteenth-century suburban villas and cottages provided space for productive kitchen gardens at the furthest reaches of the plot, with decorative lawns, terraces and flowerbeds close to the home itself. As land became scarcer and thus more expensive, and as the economy shifted from one based primarily on production to one sustained by consumption, suburban gardens shrank in size until in the new developments of the post-war years, they might comprise an open lawn at the front and a minimal enclosed yard at the rear. In middle-class suburbs, houses continued to be spaced apart by as far as was economically feasible with a plot surrounding all four sides of the home, and strategic planting was used in order to soften the overall look. Modern designs such as Mies van der Rohe's Farnsworth House (1945–51) in Piano, Illinois were conceived so as to give the impression of hovering or floating over its surroundings:

> Eight slender columns of white-painted steel support a transparent glass box, two horizontal planes   crisp, parallel bands of steel hovering above the ground – represent the floor and the roof. Though barely making physical contact with its site, the house seems securely anchored in the green sea that surrounds it. (Friedman, 2006, p. 126)

New innovations in house building – and in particular in the manufacturing of load-bearing steels and robust sheets of plate glass – stimulated a vogue for open-plan designs which made much of the potential for merging outside and inside spaces. A January 1945 article in the *Ladies Home Journal*'s regular feature, 'Homes for Modern Living', depicts a modern, single-story, three-bedroom family home with an innovative 'inward-sloping' roof (chosen because it is easier and cheaper to construct and maintain than conventional structures), open-plan living areas designed to promote 'the pleasure of family living' and 'glass walls' which would make the house economical to heat and light and promised to 'make possible and practical such charming features as the indoor-outdoor garden' (Pratt, 1945, p. 116).

In many newly built, post-war suburban communities, hedges at the front and between properties were banned so as to give the impression of more space. Stilgoe notes precedents for this practice in turn-of-the-century borderland developments where 'Fences, hedge, and other defenses, including high foundation planting, struck nearly everyone as un-American [. . .] Federalist' (1998, p. 197). Bill Levitt prohibited fences in his developments – with mixed success. As James Gallagher notes, 'few houses today are fenceless. In this paradox is the end of Bill Levitt's dream of a one-garden community. The dream died because, living in the city himself, he forgot that good fences make good neighbors' (1958, pp. 80–1). Thomas Hine discusses the status of what he calls 'symbolic fences – a few lengths of split rail or a bit of picket fence in the front yard – that established boundaries without disturbing the pastoral community.' More substantial boundaries, he argues, 'were generally disapproved of even more strongly than unmowed lawns. Because you only erected such a barrier out of utter loathing for your neighbors, these became known as "spite fences", and they were almost universally illegal' (ibid., pp. 33–4).

The grassed lawn had, by the post-war years, become 'an essential aspect of the suburban dream' (Jackson, 1987, p. 57). A lawn of one's own allowed suburbanites to believe themselves to be back in touch with their native soil and reconnected with their (mythical) past after years of exile in the concrete city. Less cynically, it gave settlers and their children welcome and safe spaces to play. But the upkeep of the lawn was not without its frustrations. Women were under pressure to maintain the domestic interior. For men, lawn care posed what they perceived to be an equal challenge. A. C. Spectorsky notes in his influential 1955 book, *The Exurbanites* that 'every commuter suffers additional physical strains to varying degrees in the daily need to keep up his home and grounds' (p. 2). Pressure was such that in the post-war boom years, as Ted Steinberg reports, some householders privileged investment in the perfect lawn over furnishings for the inside of the home (2007, p. 61).

Contemporary commentators were nervous about men's ability to deliver to the socially mandated standard, fearing that years of city work and indeed, the influence of overbearing suburban Mom-figures, had softened and deskilled them. Lawn care – as the single most visible sign of a man's obligation to his home and family – became a highly charged activity and one wherein failure to discharge one's responsibilities might be held against one as in Richard Yates's 1961 novel, *Revolutionary Road*, wherein Frank's abdication of his duty to mow the lawn becomes an open invitation to his wife, April, to assume that role and thereby to expose his inadequacy. The garden, as the visible sign of the aesthetic, moral and social values of the suburban family was scrutinized carefully by neighbours and visitors. Although in some newly built developments, formal covenants established minimum requirements for lawn care, in others, neighbourly scrutiny was enough to accomplish the same aim. In Levittown, the dual pressures of 'social control' (Gans, 1967, pp. 176–8) and clauses in the tenants' agreements (Kelly, 1993, p. 71) ensured that no man neglected – or indeed took too much care of – his lawn. The consequence was what David Riesman, writing in 1957, called 'a kind of compulsory outdoor housekeeping' (p. 139). Gardening, from this point of view, was to be seen 'less as a cultural amenity than as a minimum contribution to civic decency' (ibid.). Harry Henderson writing in 1953 in *Harper's* confirms the point: 'Failure to cut one's grass and "keep the place up" causes "talk" or hints in the form of offers to mow it. Constant attention to external appearance "counts for a lot" and wins high praise from neighbors' (p. 81).

Suburban gardens feature in an astonishing number of poems by a range of poets across and beyond the immediate post-war era. These are sometimes used for comic or observational effect as, for example, in Phyllis McGinley's 1952 poem, 'Fifteenth Anniversary', which parodies her husband's proprietorial – even feudal – relationship with his garden. His parade around the suburban plot on his evening return home from the office is likened to a military manoeuvre. As set in McGinley's collection, *A Short Walk from the Station*, where the poem is accompanied by a pen-and-ink drawing, the householder is depicted in the armour-plated costume of a medieval knight. The visual and poetic idiom draws on the rhetoric of contemporary marketing campaigns for new ranges of lawn-care products, devised to sustain the suburban man in his battle against the weeds; Steinberg notes of the introduction after the war of the herbicide 2,4-D that it 'gave new hope to lawn warriors everywhere' (2007, p. 45).

Light-hearted mockery aside, many suburban garden poems across the mid-century 'boom' years offer a collective account of male frustration and discontent, directed ostensibly at the trials of garden maintenance but synechdochally representing a deeper and broader set of anxieties and complaints. The male speakers identify themselves as members of an oppressed group, charged with shouldering an unbearable load. Like Sisyphus, their work seems never-ending; the more they water, the more they need to mow in a never-ending cycle of care. In defining themselves as the pitiable souls charged with such a responsibility, these poets signal their own simultaneous disempowerment and rage, their suburban subordination and, paradoxically, their capacity to rise above, critique and remain aloof from this domain. In other words, by lamenting their lot (in both senses of the term), they signal their distinctiveness and reassert their agency. At the same time, each individual, by protesting his incommensurability with such a regime unwittingly signals his indistinguishability from his equally frustrated peers. Even in moments of supposed leisure, then, there is no escaping the homogeneity and hegemony of the widely noted role of *The Organization Man* or *the Man in the Gray Flannel Suit*, to quote the titles of William H. Whyte and Sloan Wilson's well-known books.

The frustrations of the position are manifested often, as in the image of the suburban gardener as warrior cited a moment ago, in metaphors of conflict and aggression. In Hollis Summers' apparently tongue-in-cheek 'The Lawnmower' (published in *Poetry* in March 1954), the speaker constructs a caricature of suburban constraint – represented by the 'clipped boulevard' of line four, and by the oppressive demands of a mechanized modernity (epitomized by the 'Juggernaut of the yard' in line two and by the dominant lawnmower which, at the end of the first stanza, forces the subject into 'the role of the machine'). Similar figures appear in Philip Levine's 1963 poem, 'Lights I Have Seen Before'. Levine's poem opens at dawn in the suburbs with a male speaker passively registering his subservience to the machine of the house (manifested in extended images of 'the buzz of current / in the TV / and the refrigerator' heard 'groaning against the coming / day'), and closes at twilight with a glimpse of the speaker's next-door neighbour, waving as he plods obediently behind his 'power mower' (3–4). The dehumanizing properties of suburbia – soon to be indicted by studies such as John Keats's *The Crack in the Picture Window*, Gordon, Gordon and Gunther's *The Split-Level Trap*, and by Lewis Mumford's *The City in History*, as a spiritual and cultural waste land – are epitomized in line five by the 'the mower, unhampered by soul' which, as the final lines of the octet reveal, dominates even as it disaggrandizes the 'miniature pastoral scene'. The palimpsest in both poems, which is traduced even as it is invoked, is Elizabethan poet Andrew Marvell's 'Mower' poems. There is no place, it seems, in the post-war suburbs for the hero / labourer of pastoral (or more specifically georgic) tradition; the human figure (the mower 'Damon' in Marvell's poems) is explicitly dehumanized, emasculated, while the ideal of the suburban peace and plenty is demeaned by the gratuitous allusion – in the case of Summers's poem – to the 'miniature pastoral scene' of the conclusion to the first stanza.

In Summers's poem, the lawnmower and, by extension, the forces of suburban convention are no match for the plants themselves which, in stanza two, spring back into life 'As soon as our backs are turned'. The perennial battle between householder and crabgrass, between suburban development and a resurgent and irrepressible American landscape, persists. In the final and defiant quatrain, the poem shifts register, positing the battle between power mower and turf, householder and the organic environment as just one element of a larger – and seemingly timeless – conflict between art and nature, civilization and barbarism (manifested by a veiled reference in the penultimate line to Keats's 'Ode on a Grecian Urn', a poem which itself alludes to Marvell's 'The Garden'). The natural world, it seems, will never surrender to 'The superior beauty of truth'. Defeated by the task in hand, Summers's speaker's only option in the poem's final lines is to assert the qualities of the intellect (superior, in his own perception, to the suburban environment) over the mindless 'muscular weed' (319).

Four years later, Howard Nemerov's sonnet, 'Suburban Prophecy', from his 1958 collection *Mirrors and Windows*, similarly suggests that neither man nor machine (representing the seemingly inexorable rise of the suburbs) will defeat the forces of nature. The poem opens with the weekend ritual of grass cutting:

> On Saturday, the power-mowers' whine
> Begins the morning. Over this neighborhood
> Rises the keening, petulant voice, begin
> Green oily teeth to chatter and munch the cud.

Weekends, as Gary Cross points out, were an 'essentially suburban phenomenon' (that is, they emerged as a consequence of the separation of home from place of work) and although an ostensible time of rest and recuperation were also, as many of these lawn poems show, a period of conflict and frustration (Silverstone, 1997, p. 17; Cross, 1997, pp. 108–31). In 'Suburban Prophecy', as is characteristic of this sub-genre, the lawnmower is anthropomorphized. Again, the suburbanites' stresses and complaints (the 'whine', the 'keening petulant voice') are displaced onto the machine. The process mirrors that in contemporary poetry by women writers such as Anne Sexton and Sylvia Plath wherein, for example in Plath's 'Lesbos', the frustrations of female domesticity are transposed onto appliances such as fridges, food mixers and washing machines.

The suburban lawn, though, is a male domain. Like in McGinley's 'Fifteenth Anniversary', the suburban men imagine – and aggrandize – themselves as brave soldiers tackling a dangerous foe. It is as though only in their fantasies can they ever hope to triumph. Aligning himself with his weapon (the lawn mower), the speaker of Nemerov's 'Suburban Prophecy' seeks to boost his own and his machine's morale by painting a vivid portrait of the enemy, described in the poem's second, ten-line section, as a 'Monster', as an army in camouflage ('battalions green and curled'). In the speaker's imagination, if nowhere else, the 'neighborhood' (signifier of civilization and modernity) risks being subsumed by the primordial past – populated by 'dinosaurs in swamps' – such that in the poem's closing lines by the next morning: 'All armored beasts' (that is, all lawnmowers) will have been 'eaten by their lawns'. The 'Suburban Prophecy' – or, more properly, the vengeful fantasy – is of the demise of the suburbs and of masculine liberation from the monstrous tyranny of lawn care (Nemerov, 1958, p. 60).

As already indicated, and as Ted Steinberg's fascinating account *American Green: The Obsessive Quest for the Perfect Lawn* confirms, lawn care became big business in the post-war years with a plethora of new products, processes and services appearing and adding to the pressure on suburbanites to achieve and maintain the impossible. One crucial weapon in the suburbanite's arsenal was the lawn sprinkler. First patented in 1871 (Steinberg, 2007, p. 12), by the middle of the twentieth century, the sprinkler had become essential to the upkeep of the 'perfect' lawn – not least because the ideal of perfection (the manicured, verdant lot) to which suburbanites were impelled to strive was modelled on English examples, and thus sustained by an entirely different climate to that which pertained even in Eastern states of the United States.

Julian Mitchell's poem, 'Sprinkler in the Suburbs', first published in the *Sewanee Review* of 1961 (269–70), uses the lawn sprinkler as the catalyst for a broader meditation on suburban anomie. Interestingly in this poem, unlike in the others, the machine is characterized as feminine and thereby, in the poem's rhetoric, as weak, superficial and yet persistent in its demands. As the opening stanza puts it:

> After its day-long dizziness and swirl
> The sprinkler slows, subsiding on the grass,
> Flipping one final, skittish curl,
> Collapsing necklace of warped glass.

In this way, the speaker portrays himself – the man subordinated to the machine – as the victim of a suburban matriarchy, or of what Mary F. Corey describes, appropriately enough, as the 'snake in the grass – women' (p. 173). The opening stanza thus establishes the tone of resentment which persists throughout. The image of the feminized (and much-despised) lawn sprinkler – sign of a claustrophobic and emasculating suburban domesticity – is countered in stanza two by the returning male, the 'last commuter [who] turns to watch his train'. The exaggerated polarity between home and work, women and men, the wife's neediness and the husband's independence is further emphasized by the metaphor in stanza two of the train's 'couplings strained as marriages'. The homogeneity and deathliness of the scene are evoked by the lament in stanza five, 'The sameness of it all appals', where 'palls' invokes a funereal cloth.

Mitchell's speaker's frustration and self-pity are evoked in three parts of reported speech. In the first (stanzas three and four) he laments his wife's passivity and the tedium of his suburban life: '"There should be something more than home, / Supper and slippers and a grate."' In the second (stanzas six to eight), he complains about his son's timidity (according to contemporary observers such as Phillip Wylie, author of the notorious *The Generation of Vipers*, the fault of the overbearing 'mom'). And in the third and final stanza, he turns again to his own disappointments and frustrations, complaining about being tied, like other organization men of his generation, to his job, family, mortgage repayments and, to cap it all, his tyrannical garden:

> 'Too late I count the rising cost of pay,
> Yoked, no way back, (and all I might have been!)
> A sprinkler scattering all day,
> The grass intolerably green!'

The final line offers an awful reminder of the superficiality and garishness of the suburbs and invokes the contemporary pressure – stimulated by post-war innovations in fertilizers and agrichemicals – to bring a perpetual and ultimately synthetic colour to the lawn. The vivid, technicolor green seems as out of place here as the speaker feels (or fantasises) himself to be. Where Howard Nemerov's later poem 'The Beautiful Lawn Sprinkler', discussed in a moment, closes with a lawn sprinkler scattering its blessings, in Mitchell's poem – here epitomizing the suburban speaker's sense of his own redundancy – it simply, and apparently endlessly, wastes its potential. The excess – of water, of effort, of green – cumulatively prove unbearable. According to William Whyte, untended suburban lawns are to be taken as a sign of 'malaise' (1963, p. 330). In 'Sprinkler in the Suburbs', the well-watered lawn masks an equally devastating discontent.

Nemerov's 'The Beautiful Lawn Sprinkler' (from his 1973 collection *Gnomes and Occasions*) offers a different view. Indeed, it ends on a poignant note of hope for the suburbs of the future. The poem is one single sentence, maintained across seven lines which mimic the constant motion of the lawn sprinkler as it rises, arcs and sinks again. Here, as in numerous other examples, the material accoutrements of suburban life, such as the humble lawn sprinkler, are given sentience; in the opening line we are told that 'What gives it power makes it change its mind'. The effect is to portray the suburbanite himself as subservient to the machine – as little more than a cog in a mechanized world. There is something beneficent, though, in the subordination of self to environment, in the dedication of the individual to the greater good. The animation of the lawn sprinkler allows the speaker to see in it, or project onto it, some of the emotional demands of his own life. In the movement of the arc of water, the speaker sees a healing 'exchange' of 'humility and pride' in which both 'reverse, forgive, arise, and die again' (Nemerov, 1977, p. 439). 'The Beautiful Lawn Sprinkler' offers a form of blessing; its ritualized movement, spanning 'both ends of the day', provides reassurance of the promise of a better future. The allusion in the final line ('The rainbow in its scattering grains of spray') invokes God's promise and the renewal of his faith in humanity (ibid.).

Women poets of the post-war suburbs infrequently consider garden and outdoor maintenance; exceptions include McGinley's light-verse 'Fifteenth Anniversary', noted earlier, and Mona Van Duyn's 'Notes from a Suburban Heart' from her 1964 collection, *A Time of Bees*. The title of Van Duyn's poem – with its allusion to the heart of the suburbs – confirms the perfect lawn's place in the popular imagination as embodiment or 'visual symbol' (Berger, 1968, p. 98) of the suburban dream. It also establishes the explicit theme of the poem: an exploration through the sustained metaphor of lawn care of the affairs of the speaker's 'heart'. Ted Steinberg traces the introduction and proliferation of lawn-care products such as nitrogen-rich fertilizers, combined fertilizers and weed-killers, and even ready-mixed applications of seed, mulch, feed and weed-killer, across the 1950s and 1960s. Suburbanites were encouraged to apply products on frequent – and in some regions – excessive cycles. Van Duyn's speaker is trapped within such a regime; the opening lines of the poem evidence a weariness with its demands: 'It's time to put fertilizer on the grass again'. As in Mitchell's poem, the effect is excessive – and dangerously so. Previously when she had bought the fertilizer, the speaker recalls:

> the stuff was smelly and black,
> And said 'made from Philadelphia sewage' on the sack.
> It's true that the grass shot up in violent green[.]

In Van Duyn's poem, care of the lawn allows the speaker to sublimate her feelings for her absent partner, hence the poem's epigraph: '*Freud says that ideas are libidinal cathexes, that is to say, acts of love. NORMAN O. BROWN.*' The suburban regimen, documented across the poem's three eight-line stanzas (e.g. in stanza two where a voyeuristic neighbour castigates the speaker for over-indulging, and 'mak[ing] bums out of the birdies') proves, in the end, ineffective against the incontrovertible truth of love. The idiom of the penultimate line and one-line coda return to the qualified definition of the epigraph in their assertion – first in the metaphorical framework of the body of the poem, and then the simple words of the final line – of the message that lies at the poem's 'heart': 'I love you, in my dim-witted way' (2003, pp. 33–4).

Suburban elegies

In Van Duyn's love poem, as in Hollis Summers's 'miniature pastoral scene', we see the suburban environment offering a novel and unexpected context within which established poetic forms might evolve and change. The same might be said of suburban elegies which, like Mitchell's 'Sprinkler in the Suburbs' and Nemerov's 'The Beautiful Lawn Sprinkler' use the accoutrements of suburban garden maintenance to situate loss and rituals of mourning in modern times and places. In particular, the lawn sprinkler takes the place of the weeping fountains of elegiac convention; the neighbourhood men following in the wake of their machine substitute for the funereal procession, and the sound of the power mower stands in for the haunting lamentation of pipes. On one level, the emergence of a distinctively suburban form of elegy is to be expected. The elegy offers a ready-made set of conventions with which to signal the alleged deathliness of this community and environment; it provides a framework within which one might lament the passing of time and the inevitability of change, and it permits the speaker to bring intimate and abstract, social and natural worlds into productive proximity.

William Stafford's 1962 poem 'Elegy' (from *Traveling Through the Dark* (p. 13)) commemorates the speaker's father, a suburbanized America, and a changed self. The poem uses seven seven-line stanzas, followed by a single final line and deploys irregular, often assonantal rhyme, on lines which tend to expand in length as the poem proceeds, as though in an attempt to encompass the immensity of the life being commemorated. In tracing his debt to his father, the poem opens with an allusion to the specific duty that he has inherited from him (cutting the grass), and by metonymic extension, to his newly assumed role as man of the house. The first stanza depicts the closing in or down of a now-exhausted suburban environment; this is the site of conformity, safety and constraint (hence the 'net' as a sign of security or of entrapment), and of suffocation (the rather clumsy metaphor of the refrigerator door):

> The responsible sound of the lawnmower
> puts a net under the afternoon;
> closing the refrigerator door.

The first stanza then moves on from the depiction of the inhibited, grieving suburban poet via the father to a narrative of the past which is full of evocative, sensual, even synaesthetic details, condensing taste, sight, smell and touch in one image (the 'melonflower breath' that the speaker recalls from a long-ago August night of walking in a cornfield). The representation prompts us to question the values ascribed by contemporary readers to different measures of success or wellbeing. In Stafford's 'Elegy', the 'lawnmower' and 'refrigerator' – icons of suburban comfort – are as nothing compared to the rich flowering of the speaker's memories of the past even if that past was, by material standards, relatively impoverished.

The past is remembered in terms of its silences (represented by a stealthy creeping through 'cornfield farms' in stanza two, and by the long-passed train in stanza three). These memories in turn contextualize the evident difficulties of communication between father and son. As stanza four exclaims: 'If only once in all those years / the right goodby could have been said!' The son can 'hear' the father receding into the distance, and can 'hear' the closing of doors (lines three and seven of stanza four) but he cannot find a voice with which to make contact. In subsequent stanzas, though, even the aural contact is denied: 'I can hear no sound'. We recall the image of the closed refrigerator door in the opening stanza; the poem constructs and sustains a vision of suburbia as a stultifying, numbing place. The father's apparent death by drowning in the final stanza ('When you left our house that night and went falling / into that ocean, a message came: silence') in part explains the muted quality of the elegy.[1] More than this, though, the emphatically suburban setting (established from the beginning and reinforced by references to 'our house' and 'our door' in the final stanza) precisely because it is thought to be empty of signification, becomes unexpectedly receptive, attentive and always ready to be inscribed by others; the rustling leaves of the unkempt lawn seems now full of meaning as they 'come spinning / back into sound with just leaves rustling'. As the poem's final line urges: 'Come battering. I listen, am the same, waiting.'

One of the most notable examples of the suburban elegy is Richard Wilbur's well-known poem, 'To an American Poet Just Dead' which was first published in *Poetry*

---

[1] Other poems, too, for example, James Wright's 'Miners' depict death by drowning as a particularly suburban fate (1963, p. 24).

magazine in December 1948 and reprinted in his 1950 collection *Ceremony and Other Poems*. 'To an American Poet Just Dead' offers a suggestive, and at first deceptive, portrait of suburbia. The poem opens with an apparently inconsequential reference to an obituary in the 'Boston Sunday Herald'. The effect is to establish, from the outset, the difference between Boston (America's *ur* city) and the nameless, generic suburban locale from which the 'I' of the poem speaks. There is a primary uncertainty in Wilbur's poem – one which the poem itself leaves unresolved – about whether the 'American Poet Just Dead' of the title is himself a Boston poet or one who, like the speaker, made his home in what stanza three dismisses as the 'comfy suburbs'.[2] Either way, his life appears to have come to little; it is recalled in a sequence of approximations or near-misses (the 'no point' type in which his obituary is set, the allusion to his propensity to praise 'imaginary wines', and his death, casually related, 'or so I am told, of the real thing').

Wilbur's poem thus far has exploited and replicated a contemporary tendency to see a cultural schism between city and suburb, and to portray the latter as a moribund, inferior and synthetic milieu – hence the allusion in stanza three to the 'comfy suburbs' with their characteristic 'yawns / of Sunday fathers loitering late in bed' and the 'sshhh of sprays on all the little lawns'. The tactic is to an extent effective; critic John A. Myers, writing in 1963 in the *English Journal* reads the poem as an indictment of a 'deadened' suburban society which has failed to appreciate the poet in its midst (378) and observes of the speaker that: 'He lives in a Boston suburb (feeling, no doubt, a little trapped) but is obviously not a part of it spiritually' (377–8). Yet this is an interpretation from which I wish to demur. 'To An American Poet Just Dead', I suggest, proposes something rather more unsettling, and more defiant. It sets up a contradictory set of interpretative possibilities or, at the very least, establishes a tension between the surface and depth of suburban experience. For Wilbur's speaker, the suburbs are potentially full of meaning; against the odds they prove to be poetically fruitful, provocative, compelling spaces.

In stanza three, the speaker / subject immerses us in this suggestive suburban world, exaggerating by the use of emphatic alliteration, sibilance, onomatopoeia ('the ssshh of sprays') and regular rhymes ('yawns' and 'lawns'), his ability to bring this supposedly unpromising poetic landscape into vivid life. From one perspective (for example, that adopted by Myers), the poem regrets the suburban community's inability to comprehend their poet's death and, by extension, the suburbanites' ignorance of wider cultural values. And certainly the poem questions the ability of a modern consumer society (evoked in images of lawn sprinklers, refrigerators and the latest automobiles) to recognize its loss. As stanza four asks:

> Will the sprays weep wide for you their chaplet tears?
> For you will the deep-freeze units melt and mourn?
> For you will Studebakers shred their gears
> And sound from each garage a muted horn?

[2] James Longenbach names the dead poet as Phelps Putnam.

The abrupt 'They won't' that opens the next stanza answers the rhetorical question. Yet the poem also sets up the possibility that the suburban community *will* recognize and value its dead – its own bard – when the moment comes. The emphatic 'you' of the stanza quoted above invokes a silent 'me'. This is to say: the suburbs may not value 'you' (the dead poet of the title), but they may well register and approve and, when the time comes, mourn the qualities which the implied 'I' has demonstrated throughout the poem.

In effect, 'To an American Poet Just Dead' asks whether it is possible to have a suburban elegy and, against the odds, proves that it is. Although rooted emphatically 'out' in that most unpropitious of places, 'the comfy suburbs', the poem commemorates the poet's passing, affirms the place of the suburbs as a viable locus for poetic representation and posits – and indeed proves – the potential of a suburban poetics. Its own scepticism (and its readers' doubts) about suburban society's ability to rouse itself, to notice and to care, is defeated in and by its own poetic process. Wilbur's poem forges a new kind of elegy appropriate to the post-war suburbs. These silent spaces (hence the 'sshhh of sprays' in stanza three, the 'muted horn' of stanza four and the 'sleep of death' in stanza five) may not toll the resounding bell expected of the elegy, but they do produce a new kind of threnody – one which is quiet, subtle and deceptive. For this suburbanite (the speaker) has recognized the poet's death, and has commemorated it. The dead poet can 'save [his] breath' in the final line of the poem in part because the surviving poet has taken up his song.

The suburban pastorals and elegies discussed in this chapter exploit a set of expectations, figures and tropes associated with post-war suburbia. Each poem, knowingly and productively, engages readerly expectations in order to challenge popular perceptions of what, and how, the suburbs mean. Lawn care figures throughout as the catalyst for male dissatisfaction, as a sign of the pressures of a surveillant society, and as an index of the coercive power of the marketplace. Yet this also proves to be unexpectedly fertile poetic territory. Here a new – if sometimes conflicted – vision of suburban subjectivity might be constructed and tested; here, signs of community might be found. Here one might devise a new poetics – new forms of pastoral, elegy and more broadly of lyric poetry – appropriate to this particular place and time.

9

'Nothing seemed familiar, yet everything was very, very familiar': Rethinking Bill Owens's *Suburbia*

Bridget Gilman

In 1972 Bill Owens, a young newspaper staff photographer, published a photobook titled *Suburbia*, the result of a year of documentation of his Northern California community. Filled with images of middle-class families and the trappings of their domestic milieu, *Suburbia* became a commercial success, selling more than 50,000 copies and receiving three internationally distributed editions (Zanfi, 2007). Yet, in 1982, after two additional documentary publications, a Guggenheim fellowship, and work for such prominent publications as *Life* and *Newsweek*, Owens stopped photographing, sold most of his equipment, and became a brewer (ibid.).[1] *Suburbia* had become iconic, but Owens found life as a photojournalist physically trying and conceptually confining, and his subsequent documentary efforts proved financially unsustainable (Owens, 2011).

Owens's photobook was reissued as a revised edition in 1999, capitalizing on a resurgence of nostalgia for its earlier moment of suburban habitation. In the interceding years *Suburbia* has been harnessed as evidence for period celebrations and condemnations, alternately read as a paean to mainstream domesticity and an ironic indictment of white middle-class values (Hayden, 1984; Mora, 2007). Such contrary interpretations reveal the seemingly banal territory of Owens's book as an ambiguous, highly charged social document. Yet, though the work remains a cultural touchstone, comprehensive critical analysis of its form, tone and import remains sparse.

Though the patina of nearly four decades undoubtedly affects present-day views of *Suburbia*, that distance also serves to clarify the book's social and art historical context. Situated between the rise of the 'new documentary' giants Diane Arbus, Garry Winogrand and Lee Friedlander and conceptual and postmodernist developments, Owens's images rest – perhaps uncomfortably – on the boundary of multiple image-making strategies. Owens captures at once the typical and the idiosyncratic, the eccentric and the profound, that flourish within the banal. Made during a period of political and social upheaval and growing awareness of humanity's encroachment

---

[1] Owens has continued to photograph, but not as a primary occupation.

on the natural world, Owens's work is an engrossing document that gives voice to its subjects while also complicating their identities and aspirations. The book remains a central artefact of pivotal shifts in the American landscape, registering the effects of a new domestic spatiality in distinctly personal terms. It is thus an essential case study of both the reformulation of documentary photography and the national discourse surrounding middle-class lifestyles.

The making of *Suburbia*

Suburbia charts the territory of Owens's proverbial backyard, yet being close to home did not result in a series synonymous with the character of his youth. Raised in what is now 'Silicon Valley', Owens was the son of a one-time Oklahoma coal miner and later subsistence farmer – part of a family that grew produce and livestock to put food on the table (James, 2000). After flunking out of college, Owens discovered photography while serving in the Peace Corps in Jamaica and India in the mid 1960s.[2] Yet returning home to San Francisco State University (SFSU) for formal training, he found the formalist rigour of art school distasteful, preferring to practice what his mentor John Collier termed 'visual anthropology' (Zanfi, 2007). Hired by the local *Livermore Independent* in 1968, Owens's newspaper job paid $110 per week. With a wife and baby on the way, the Owens family moved into a rented house in Livermore for $120 per month (Owens, 2007). As Owens (2000, n.p.) himself recently recalled, 'Everyone was moving to the suburbs, you could buy a house for $2,000, with only $99 down. A two car garage, a swimming pool, and a Kenmore washer and dryer . . . all of the things that come with the good life.'

Yet, if Owens's background seems to suggest a smooth ascent from working-class upbringing to middle-class suburbia, the reality differed from this apparent trajectory of class mobility. Owens first made his name with a series of pictures devoted to the social upheavals and counterculture that inundated the San Francisco Bay Area in the late 1960s. During his brief stint as a graduate student at SFSU, Owens photographed the student protests there and across the bay at UC Berkeley in 1968 (Zanfi, 2007). His big break came in 1969, when he was contracted by the Associated Press to cover the Altamont Speedway Free Festival. The event, promoted as 'Woodstock West', ultimately turned chaotic and violent, resulting in four deaths. Perched on one of the sound towers, Owens captured the only glimpses of the Hells Angels security guards' fatal beating of an audience member during The Rolling Stones' performance that were published in the national press (Owens, 2007). Thus his initial encounter with the domestic, consumption-oriented lifestyle of suburbia came as 'something of a shock' (Owens, 1978). Visual proof of the Owens's incongruity lies tucked in the back of *Suburbia*: amidst a yearbook-like montage of portraits of couples and families, Bill and his wife Janet appear, marked as outsiders by their hippie-ish dress and white Volkswagen Beetle.

---

[2] Owens's dyslexia made formal education a struggle (Owens, 2008).

But if Owens and his family felt somewhat estranged from their new surroundings, *Suburbia* was by no means a document made from the outside looking in. Owens writes in his pithy introduction:

> This book is about my friends and the world I live in . . . To me nothing seemed familiar, yet everything was very, very familiar. At first I suffered from culture shock . . . Then slowly I began to put my thoughts and feelings together and to document Americans in Suburbia. (1972, n. p.)

As is clear from the tensions that his description articulates, suburbia was both a home and a foreign land for Owens, an oscillation of the strange and the familiar that reveals much about his picture-making strategies and the images that resulted.

Suburbia's photographs exhibit an awareness of the local community gained from Owens's position at the *Livermore Independent* but also retain some of the distance native to photojournalism. Taking pictures on 52 consecutive Saturdays, holidays, and, towards the end of the project, additional Mondays, Owens adopted a strategy that lay somewhere between the scripted mode of the Farm Security Administration and the conceptually based projects of photographers like Bernd and Hilla Becher and Ed Ruscha. Both approaches utilize predetermined subject matter to define their photographic search, though the resulting images are quite different in aesthetic and intent. The earlier model, a product of its Depression-era aims of social and economic uplift, valued the authenticity and emotional candour of intimate photographs. Later photographers often shunned such 'sentimental' goals, instead laying bare the ideology of image construction, or, as contemporary photographer Jeff Wall observes, parodying traditional reportage with a purposefully amateur aesthetic (Wall, 1995). Recounting his own process, Owens (2000, n. p.) remarks: 'The photographs for "Suburbia" weren't done by accident. I put together a shooting script of events that I wanted to photograph.' Indeed, many critics characterize *Suburbia* as part of the FSA legacy, in line with the 'straight style' of the 1930s (Sholis, 2005).

Although Owens can claim direct lineage to the earlier documentary model – Collier, his influential professor, worked for the FSA – elements of chance and familiarity alter the rigidity of that approach (Collier, 1967). The photographer sets himself apart from both photojournalists and the FSA method in emphasizing,

> I was not an outsider coming in from a big magazine, shooting hundreds of rolls of film and departing, never to see those people again – I had a relationship with the people who were my subjects, and I retained complete control over the project. (Owens, 1978, p. 17)

Furthermore, while Owens's structure enumerated certain desired events and locales, other elements opened the work to chance encounters. Though many of his *Suburbia* subjects were friends, acquaintances or neighbours, Owens also resorted to more impersonal forms of recruitment, placing classified ads in the paper that read, 'I am working on a photographic project about suburbia. I would like to photograph your home, your children, pets, or whatever' (ibid.). As *New York Times* critic Roberta Smith (1999) suggests, he could be characterized as a 'folk Conceptualist', documenting vernacular details within an established framework and appending various kinds of text. If, in light of the cool distance of such Conceptual projects as Dan Graham's *Homes For America*, 'folk Conceptualism' sounds slightly oxymoronic, Owens's work repeatedly courts such confusion. Blurring the boundaries of an idea-based practice and the intimacy of a sustained documentary project, *Suburbia*'s style is difficult to define. Such stylistic elusiveness is compounded by the fraught task of dealing with ubiquitous subjects. The book itself is deceptively ordinary looking – at first glance it could simply be an assortment of family scrapbook photos captioned with humorous quotations. Yet, *Suburbia*'s visual and linguistic construction is far from haphazard: perusing its images and text one finds not a singular or simplistic narrative of suburban living, but subtle indications of social and environmental commentary and insights into the shifting discourse on post-war American domesticity.

Structuring suburban lifestyles

Owens sought to achieve a combination of naturalism and studied clarity; *Suburbia* had to look familiar, not just presenting recognizable aspects of middle-class living but also revealing that milieu in greater detail. Using large-format cameras, wide-angle lenses and off-camera flash, he aimed for evenly lit, clear, detailed images (Owens, 1978). Explicating there aesthetic preferences, Owens states:

> In the documentary tradition, you must be able to 'read' and comprehend the photograph. And so I require sharp photographs with rich middle greys; this kind of printing communicates information without over-dramatizing the subject. It's the sharpness of my photographs that marks my style – and *style* is what the photographic business is all about. (1978, p. 34)

These comments recall the Depression-era work of Walker Evans, whose 'documentary style' produced a rich dialectic between art and document (Eisinger, 1995).[3] Like Evans, Owens defines his method as one that is direct but by no means stylistically void. If *Suburbia*'s portraits mimic the frontal poses and simple, direct aesthetic of vernacular image-making practices, their crisp detail, precise lighting and strategic compositions are calibrated to yield more information about their subjects than the average casual snapshot. Owens's self-imposed mandate was not simply to record, but to make audiences 'aware of their environment and their lifestyle' (Owens, 1979, p. 9).

This awareness is achieved not only through the purposeful staging of individual photographs, but also the structure of the book as a whole. An advocate of self-publishing, Owens paid great attention to the formats of his books, oftentimes

---

[3] *Documentary Photography* (1978) was intended for aspiring professionals, but the commercial practicality of Owens's approach does not negate the important tension articulated between document and style.

I put it off until I can't stand it anymore. The rottenest job in the whole house is cleaning the bathroom.

Figure 9.1 Bill Owens, from *Suburbia*, 1972
Courtesy Bill Owens

culling from thousands of images in order to produce his desired content and layout.[4] *Suburbia* consists of 126 photographs mostly printed one or two per page, with the exception of four album-like layouts.[5] There are no page numbers or titled parts. To locate an image, one must flip through the book, encouraging awareness of sequencing and, if one is particularly involved, development of associative links based on image juxtaposition.

For instance, one might recall a woman mopping her bathroom is unexpectedly placed next to an aerial view of the city (Figures 9.1 and 9.2). Oftentimes the images on facing pages are thematically linked, though this is not always the case, as is clear with the mopping woman/aerial view pair. Here the link may be formal: the expanse of houses crowding the middle ground in the bird's eye photograph loosely resembles the

[4] See Owens (1979, pp. 120–1) for an account of his book design process. Unfortunately Owens does not address how he chooses to sequence images.
[5] There are also frontispiece and cover images, though these are repeated from the book's body.

Figure 9.2 Bill Owens, from *Suburbia*, 1972
Courtesy Bill Owens

all-over floral patterning of the bathroom wallpaper. The woman's lament is amplified both by the wide angle shot – note the distorted elongation of her mop handle – and the repetition of the sprawl in the adjacent image, suggesting the vast quantity of domestic labour suburbia requires. There is likewise a subtle play between the natural and artificial, the horse pasture in the aerial view giving way to manicured greenery and cleared ground, while the bathroom offers up a plethora of artificial flora. A viewer seeking metaphoric associations might extrapolate that the similitude between row house and wallpaper is a visual pun, with subdivision development becoming the architectural equivalent of a 'wallflower' – an unremarkable surface, offering no further depths to be plumbed. But such symbolic correspondences remain at the level of interpretive possibilities rather than overt or didactic correlations. *Suburbia* hovers somewhere between discernible structure and random order, providing intriguing suggestions of formal and thematic juxtaposition, but retaining enough openness that the viewer is both free to generate her own connections and challenged to comprehend the whole of its disparate parts.

The book does contain several sequences with subject associations: couples and families posing in living rooms, the all-important suburban lawn care, couples and children in their bedrooms, women and families in kitchens, social gatherings, housework, children at play, yearbook-type photos, and holiday events. Often the connection is the activity pictured, but almost as frequently it is the site that unites the images. In sum, *Suburbia* is a document of social roles and the spaces in which those roles are enacted. Fundamentally intertwined, these broad investigations are fleshed out by a multiplicity of sub-categories, providing a highly multifaceted view of life in the suburbs. For instance, the issues pertinent to social roles include not only the expected studies of family and gender dynamics, but also elements of class and racial politics, and sexuality and violence in the everyday. Likewise, the book's spatial locales are not merely defined by the de rigueur lawn, kitchen or living room gathering, but also macro and micro views, offering a sense both of the significant detail found in still life studies of pantry cabinets and of the large-scale comprehension provided by an aerial view of a prototypical cul-de-sac.

Essential to *Suburbia*'s tone and interpretation is Owens's integration of text. The photographer's own written word is scarce. Apart from the very short introduction (quoted above), he provides little guidance for precisely how to 'read' the book: the images have no formal titles or dates nor are there part titles to divide the book. There are, however, captions for many images. Owens (1972, n. p.) tersely explains, 'The comments on each photograph are what the people feel about themselves.' Yet, unmarked with quotations, it is hard to know how these comments were selected. Though most images have accompanying text, some do not. The latter type fall mostly into the landscape or still life category, but there are several exceptions. Furthermore, while most captions seem obviously to come from the central figure pictured, in others the speaker is harder to pinpoint. In images of couples, families or social gatherings, who is the commentator? The frequent use of 'we' in these cases implies a collective voice, though whether the remarks are truly consensual is impossible to determine.

One further textual anomaly deserves particular attention. These are the captions where an authoritative narrator suddenly appears. For instance, beneath an aerial shot that reveals the suburban street grid, a disembodied voice tells the history of Dublin, California, noting that 14 years prior:

The population was less than 1,000 (most of them cows). Today Dublin is the crossroads of Interstate Highways 580 and 680 with a population of over 25,000 people. We now have fifteen gas stations, six supermarkets, two department stores and a K-Mart. And we're still growing. (Owens, 1972, n. p.)

Though one might expect the meta-view presented in text and image to appear at the start or conclusion of the book, they are in fact placed about two-thirds in. Likewise, the passage upends expectations by switching from historical recollection to a voice of the collective present. 'And we're still growing', may simply imply that Owens, as the photographer and presumably the writer here, identifies himself as a part of the community he is documenting. But perhaps the phrase can be interpreted more broadly, a reflection of the national phenomenon of rapid suburban expansion, intended to make viewers consider their own part in the redefinition of the American domestic landscape. Both the content of the commentary and placement of the image subtly engender audience immersion: by the time these factual titbits appear, one has already met many of *Suburbia*'s residents and entered many of its homes, thus making the 'we' a revelation not only of Owens's intimacy with his subject, but also plausibly a measure of 'our' identification with this representative sampling of middle-class America.

Another case of an unidentifiable narrator presents an intriguing moment of more overt social commentary (Figure 9.3). Next to an image of an apathetic-looking young girl in her nightgown, her Barbie dolls arranged on the shag carpet, the caption reads:

This is Valerie's world in miniature. She makes it what she wants it to be . . . without war, racial hate, or misunderstanding. Ken and Barbie (dolls) are man and woman rather than Mom and Dad. They enjoy living and having a camper truck is the good life. Today Valerie has the chicken pox and can't go out to play. (Owens, 1972, n. p.)

Quite possibly this is one of Valerie's parents speaking, but the formality and content bypass familial intimacy to focus on larger questions of social discourse. The issues raised by her play are described as deeply embedded in currents of gender, racial and national politics. In later interviews, Owens has revealed that the captions were not recorded simultaneously to the photographs, but rather were gathered on return visits, prompted by the fact that the photographer had not originally obtained releases from his subjects. Owens (2000, n. p.) explains, 'When I went back to get the releases, people would sometimes comment on the photograph, and I would write those comments on the back of the picture. This is photography after all, it's not rocket science!' Yet if he is fairly nonchalant about his own practice, Owens (2000, n. p.) is fully cognizant of the striking juxtapositions that sometimes resulted from these return visits:

Sometimes when you photograph a person, they have something completely opposite to say . . . you find contradictions. 'Damned Dishes' is an example of this kind of contradiction. This is a photograph of a woman in her kitchen holding a baby, with the sink full of dirty dishes. The woman said to me, 'how can I worry about the damned dishes when there are children dying in Vietnam?' You don't expect people to have those concerns, but they do!

This is Valerie's world in miniature. She makes it what she wants it to be . . . without war, racial hate or misunderstanding. Ken and Barbie (dolls) are man and woman rather than Mom and Dad. They enjoy living and having a camper truck is the good life. Today Valerie has the chicken pox and can't go out and play.

Figure 9.3 Bill Owens, from *Suburbia*, 1972
Courtesy Bill Owens

These competing visual and verbal messages enrich our understanding of the subjects, generating a more complex image of suburbia and recognizing in its inhabitants both acute self-awareness and the sociopolitical implications of their domestic circumstances.

Perhaps the most frequently cited photograph in *Suburbia* is of a couple standing in their kitchen, mom feeding her child, dad standing behind them with drink in hand (Figure 9.4). One could equate the nuclear family with the manufactured gloss of the abundant fake fruit on the table – they are nearly a living advertisement – though several details puncture the appealing surface of their existence. Through the glass doors at the rear of the room electric pylons loom, filling the outdoor vista and disrupting the sense of a non-urban idyll. The ambiguity of the image is further complicated by the text: 'We're really happy. Our kids are healthy, we eat good food and we have a really nice home' (Owens, 1972, n. p.). Though their words seem genuine, their vision of simple contentedness reads as an insufficient measure of the complexities of raising

We're really happy. Our kids
are healthy, we eat good food
and we have a really nice
home.

Figure 9.4 Bill Owens, from *Suburbia*, 1972
Courtesy Bill Owens

a family in the late twentieth century; is the family truly happy or simply ignorant of
the ominous industry that lurks outside their door? Yet one element is missing from
this discourse on the ramifications of consumer-bound family lifestyles – it ignores
an eccentricity plainly on view. The subjects were chosen not because they perfectly
embodied the nuclear family, but because they had 23 cats, several of which appear in
the shadowy corners of the kitchen.[6]

Owens frequently performs such visual sleights of hand, often with cunningly
comic effects. The older couple who express their fondness for collecting rocks at first
glance appears to occupy themselves with one of the most clichéd pastimes imaginable,
until one notices the plethora of topless pin-up pictures in their geological archive
(Figure 9.5). Perhaps were the husband pictured alone one might dismiss this detail
as a decorating impulse typically marking a 'male domain', but the wife's presence and
the odd montage of gemstone cross-sections and nude women on the upper right wall
suggest other possible scenarios. Does the couple run a trade in pornographic imagery?

---

[6] Jeffrey Kastner (2000) appears to be the only writer to notice this detail.

We've been collecting rocks
since 1958. It's enjoyable to
get out into the open and hunt
for rocks, and it's really fun
to cut open a rock and find
a gem inside.

Figure 9.5 Bill Owens, from *Suburbia*, 1972
Courtesy Bill Owens

Or is the woman in the photo to their left the wife in her more youthful days? Certainly there is a strange resonance between the gesture of the pin-up girl's gloved hand and the wife's display of a large rock.

Other details of décor and abode evoke similarly charged gendered and sexual implications, such as the woman who claims to 'believe in women's liberation' (Figure 9.6). Though she asserts, 'Staying at home with and taking care of the kids doesn't help', she is nonetheless pictured sitting on the couch in her robe, contentedly absorbed in bottle-feeding her infant while her toddler sprawls out next to her (Owens, 1972, n. p.). Moreover, what is to be made of the large painting of a woman's face that hangs over the fireplace? Is the figure's kitschily rendered glamour a model of women's liberation? Or does she simply represent one more image of commodified beauty akin to the images promulgated by Helen Gurley Brown's recently revamped *Cosmopolitan* magazine (Benjamin, n. d.)? The fireplace filled with discarded product packaging, the 'industrial size' box of laundry detergent, and the 'WHILE SUPPLIES LAST . . .' slogan printed across the television screen imply the consistent call of commodity consumption – a potentially stifling environment for a woman hoping to break free from society's mandated gender codes. Politics lurk in many corners of suburbia, subtly infiltrating the realm of the everyday. What is compelling about the images is their resistance to simplistic commentary: unlike the world of mass media that brandishes its consumerist messages so blatantly, once integrated into the home these messages become one of many voices. Perhaps suburbanites are overwhelmed by

I believe in women's liberation. I'm tired of the image of
the woman who has the most
⋯⋯⋯ toilet bowl, the clean-
est floor and the brattiest kids
as the supermother. I want to
be able to change with my
children and to change with
my life as I grow older. Staying at home and taking care
of the kids doesn't help.

Figure 9.6 Bill Owens, from *Suburbia*, 1972
Courtesy Bill Owens

the commanding lifestyle aspirations of their 'stuff', but such a judgement requires a
univocality that Owens's densely layered juxtapositions of image and text often refuse.

Contextualizing *Suburbia*: Critical views and demographic realities

Though the post-war era brought affordable, government subsidized homes to many
Americans, for critics the uniformity of the built environment and the advertising
culture that promoted the suburban lifestyle signalled a vicious attack on the values
of individualism and personal liberty.[7] Many of the resulting realities were indeed

---

[7]   Suburbia has been critiqued from its very inception; for an overview of period criticism in the United
      States, see Archer (2010).

grim: highways built to support legions of commuting suburbanites destroyed urban neighbourhoods of colour, mortgage insurance programmes often excluded women and minorities, and housing developments frequently exacted an enormous environmental toll (Hayden, 2003). Nonetheless, these drawbacks – both real social inequities and perceived cultural shortcomings – generally did little to inhibit this potent incarnation of the American dream.

Owens's book is not only representative of a national phenomenon, but also indicative of particular patterns of geographic development. Post-war economic growth in the San Francisco Bay Area was largely fuelled by rapidly expanding manufacturing and technology industries: the fertile orchards of the 'Valley of the Heart's Delight' were quickly ploughed over to make way for the engineering hub of what would become Silicon Valley, while southern Alameda County – *Suburbia*'s location – exploded with newly minted cities founded on the backs of corporations like General Motors and Ford (Wollenberg, 1985; Self, 2003). This growth incurred reciprocal damages in urban environments both near and far. Older East Coast and midwestern industrial cities became the 'Rustbelt' to the South and West's 'Sunbelt', the former shrinking in both population and economic productivity as the latter drew corporations and workers with ample space and pro-business policies (Shermer, 2011). In California suburban growth spurred the 'taxpayer's revolt', resulting in the 1978 passage of Proposition 13, an enormously influential statute that severely limits property taxes and thus reduces the fiscal burden of suburban homeowners. Though the movement was a response to real increases for individual taxpayers, it was also fuelled by a larger attack on the government programmes which helped support the economically disadvantaged who mainly resided in urban areas; southern Alameda County was a hub of support for Prop 13 (Self, 2003).

By the time Owens undertook *Suburbia,* deed restrictions and mortgage availability had somewhat loosened, slowly encouraging a greater diversity of residents. As the book reflects, whites still constituted a clear majority, but racial hegemony was noticeably lessened. Spatial shifts, however, were less positive. New growth looked less like the tightly gridded early model developments of Levittown and Lakewood and instead opened up on the rural fringes, thus drastically increasing domestic and commercial sprawl (Self, 2003). Attention to sprawl also spread through the art world, most notably with the 'New Topographics' work of such photographers as Robert Adams and Lewis Baltz. Like Owens, Adams and Baltz use large format cameras to produce images of human impact on the landscape, though Owens deals more explicitly with the people inhabiting these spaces. New Topographics photographs frequently probe the aesthetic possibilities and formal structures embedded in vernacular architecture – Adams's work in particular can be seen both as social critique and an exploration of the visual pleasures of such landscapes. The most direct parallels to these works lie in Owens's framing images: the book's last image, which is reprinted in smaller form as its frontispiece. Here, opposite a bulldozer clearing the land for development, new and old worlds meet, a small wooden cistern set amid tall grasses and wildflowers, with suburbia encroaching in the distance (Figures 9.7 and 9.8).

Figure 9.7 Bill Owens, from *Suburbia*, 1972
Courtesy Bill Owens

Figure 9.8 Bill Owens, from *Suburbia*, 1972
Courtesy Bill Owens

Certainly the smog-like haze that sheathes the mountainous horizon and the tractor operator's ominously unreadable face can be interpreted as subtle indictments of suburbia's environmental destruction.[8] Notably though, this land clearance documentation is separated from the book's most explicit plea against development. Many pages prior, two boys on bikes relay a youthful resistance to the cruel consequences of new building:

> They cut down our tree forts to put in some new houses. We don't want houses. We want our trees back. They paid us five dollars to keep people back while they cut up the trees, but we're not going to keep anybody out. (Owens, 1972, n. p.)

Had these three images been arranged successively, they would undoubtedly constitute a collective rebuke. Refusing such a clear narrative sequence does not divorce the landscape images from their direct connections to the suburban milieu, but likewise one cannot view these photographs of development-in-progress apart from *Suburbia*'s many expressions of domestic contentment. It is ultimately left to the viewer to decide whether the cistern image's seemingly harmonious balance of nature and culture is a portent of hope or despair.

Compounding the critical weight of these social and environmental debates, the rise of photographic postmodernism in the late 1970s and early 1980s brought with it reformulated mandates for documentary practices. As photographer and writer Alan Sekula (1984, p. 57) urged, 'frame the crime, the trial, and the system of justice and its official myths.' Sekula, along with Martha Rosler, Abigail Solomon-Godeau and other postmodern critics, desired a form of photography that acknowledged the medium's place in a larger discursive framework, and banished notions of 'objectivity', 'neutrality', 'photographic truth' or the self-sufficiency of the 'artist's vision'. For Sekula (1984, p. 71), Owens's work should be categorized along with that of his predecessor Diane Arbus as simplistic 'grotesquery'.

Perhaps responding to these demands, Owens (2008, p. 11) has recently claimed: 'I'm a socially concerned photographer *à la* Robert Capa. I wanted to change the world and make it better . . . I wanted people to be aware of the crass consumerism of the American culture.' Did *Suburbia* present a clear message of need for change? Or has Owens's own view shifted with time? Key to answering these questions is the revised 1999 edition of *Suburbia*, a collaboration between Owens and his longtime supporter and collector, Robert Harshorn Shimshak (Owens, 1999).[9] While much of the original content remains, a number of changes substantially alter the book's structure and tone. Most noticeably, additional colour photographs yield a more vibrant immediacy.[10] But perhaps more crucial are sequencing shifts, frequently rearranging the photographs to suggest clearer subject links. For instance, the

---

[8] The tractor operator's dark face does not seem to imply racial bias; rather the mid-day shadows and his sunglasses obscure his face.

[9] Owens confirms the re-issue was a joint effort. Owens (2012), Email sent to B. Gilman, 16 May.

[10] Owens has always made colour photographs; expense prohibited their inclusion in the original publication (Owens, 2011).

aerial view paired with the woman mopping is replaced by a close-up of a red toilet. Such changes not only make thematic comprehension easier – just as the addition of page numbers makes the book more 'functional' – but also forfeit many of the subtle nuances of the original juxtapositions. The captions, too, are occasionally edited, again altering context and interpretation. Two men jogging are originally accompanied by the remark that work 'as an engineer at Lawrence Radiation Laboratory causes a certain amount of tension and frustration', while the later edition eliminates the reference to the national defence research centre and thus elides a fundamental political component of Bay Area economic development (Owens, 1972, n.p.; 1999).

Above all, a few pivotal additions to the opening and closing pages decidedly shift the work's environmental perspective. In place of the framing cistern image, the title and introductory pages are paired with photographs that speak to a significantly more abstracted, didactic view. In the first, horizontally composed strata of freeway, open land, suburbia and smoggy hillsides plainly illustrate human impact on the natural world (Figure 9.9). The subsequent photograph of a sign for the 'Sunsetown' development plays on the evident disparity between the advertised utopian promise and its humble setting – a scrubby open lot, plain, identical white ranch houses, and a sunless sky. The close of the later edition also evinces increased attention to macro-suburban effects. Of the last four photographs, two are carried from the first edition, but here they are shifted from mid-text placement and re-contextualized by two new images. The aerial photograph paired with Owens's mini-history of Dublin is now accompanied by an elevated view of a single street (Figure 9.10). The electric pylons that disrupted the quirky feline-loving family's abode here dominate the entire neighbourhood, unmistakably displaying the discomfiting costs of suburban living. Finally, next to a highway vista from the original book, the revised edition closes with a sign announcing a new shopping centre development on a lush, grassy field. These additions shift *Suburbia* from a work that remained mostly ensconced within the confines of its suburban enclave to a study that attempts to reveal larger spatial networks and implications – a move from personal perspectives towards the territory of jeremiad also evidenced in the exclusion of Owens's journal-like original introduction.

Though these alterations generate a clearer macro-critique, the original work more effectively implicates the viewer. The core strength of Owens's book lies in his immersion with his subjects. This impact is evidenced by the remarks of a contemporaneous reviewer – one who was, like many, not favourably inclined towards the suburbs: 'That suburbia and the quality of life there ought to be condemned goes without saying . . . Owens goes further by requiring that we also recognize our part in it. Condemnation is no longer enough' (Hardiman, 1975, p. 260). For instance, William Garnett's arresting aerial images of Lakewood are frequently used to illustrate suburban histories and critiques. Such bird's eye views are essential to understanding the breadth of suburbia's footprint and recognizing the rigid architectural schema developers invented in the quest to produce mass quantities of assembly-line style affordable housing. But the power of aerial abstraction cuts both ways – such visual

Figure 9.9 Bill Owens, from *Suburbia*, 1972
Courtesy Bill Owens

extrapolation is less effective in communicating personal implication, and can transcend into an aesthetic appreciation of patterned landscapes.

Owens's most powerful photographs, by contrast, evoke a more intimate, idiosyncratic experience. Against the commonplace view of suburbia as a monolithic, tedious existence, Owens's pictures illuminate its subtly variegated contents. *Suburbia* takes pleasure in exploring the slightly awkward and the comically banal, but the

Figure 9.10 Bill Owens, from *Suburbia*, 1972
Courtesy Bill Owens

photobook is also a prime exhibit of the exemplary comforts of suburban living; it reminds viewers that while many claim to abhor suburban values, a great number has found contentment in such communities. Nonetheless, the recent revisions are an essential part of *Suburbia*'s historical journey, reflecting not only Owens's evolution, but also tilts in the critical discourse. As always, suburbia is as much about our perceptions as the realities of the place itself.

10

'A more interesting surgery on the suburbs': Richard Ford's Paean to the New Jersey Periphery

Tim Foster

In his introduction to the 2001 paperback edition of *Revolutionary Road*, Richard Ford notes that Richard Yates's novel presents the two main protagonists, Frank and April Wheeler, as characters who, while they dislike the suburbs, 'complain . . . about it too much', to the extent that they are 'finally done in by circumstances . . . [they] simply lack the moral vigor to control'. In Ford's view, *Revolutionary Road* is a fiction that requires us to consider 'just how bad can it literally *be* out there in the 'burbs . . . where almost nobody's character shows capacity to change, but only to suffer' (Ford, 2001, pp. xv, xvii, xx). In this chapter I argue that in his trilogy of novels *The Sportswriter* (1986), *Independence Day* (1995) and *The Lay of the Land* (2006), Ford presents his narrator, Frank Bascombe, not as a victim of his environment like the Wheelers, but as someone who, through experience, understands that space means nothing in and of itself, and that it can always be transformed if its inhabitants are willing to do so. To do this I will draw on the work of Henri Lefebvre and his ideas about the social production of space to suggest Frank as someone who enacts this process as a virtue. Lefebvre claims that, 'physical space has no "reality" without the energy that is deployed within it', and that the 'modalities of this deployment', or the 'spatial practice' of a society is derived from the mutually interdependent forces of 'representations of space' (the conceptualized space of 'planners, urbanists, technocratic subdividers and social engineers') and 'representational spaces' (the space that is 'directly *lived*' by its inhabitants, the space 'which the imagination seeks to change and appropriate') (Lefebvre, 1991, pp. 13, 38–9). While Brian Duffy has asserted that the three Bascombe novels 'characterize human becoming through time' (Duffy, 2008, p. 16) in their representation of Frank's developing moral and ethical code, in what follows I want to build on this idea by pointing out the ways in which Frank 'becomes' through a Lefebvrean engagement with space, and explore how his relationship with the developing suburban landscape in New Jersey allows the reader to consider the texts free from a perception of the suburbs as a static, pernicious environment.

In *The Sportswriter*, set over the Easter weekend in 1983, what quickly emerges at the outset of his narrative is the importance of language to Frank's capacity to engage with the world on his own terms. Ford has Frank assert that 'I have a voice that is really mine' (Ford, 1996, p. 17). Frank's engagement with his environment is notable for the way in which his language allows him to intervene in, and recapitulate, the received wisdom on the suburban landscape. Ford has spoken of his desire to foreground through Frank's idiom the qualities of language that are 'not specifically communicative' but that are, instead, 'expressive and sensuous' (Thompson and Ellis, 1996, p. 118). As Ford elaborates, 'if you can somehow persuade yourself by the artful use of language that such and such a thing is real, that you're happy in the suburbs . . . sometimes you can actually connect yourself to the bottom of experience' (ibid., p. 123).

Thus, Ford satirizes the clichéd view of suburban social relations as he fills in some of the details of Frank's life in Haddam. Frank tells us that one of the reasons he has forsaken his life as a writer of fiction is because he felt he was 'stuck in bad stereotypes' with 'all . . . [his] men . . . too serious, too brooding and humorless'; they were 'characters at loggerheads with imponderable dilemmas' (Ford, 1996, p. 52). So, we have Frank recounting the dissolution of an old Haddam friendship of his, a hangover from the 'old cocktail-dinner party days': following an evening at his friend Bert's house, during which the host got 'jittery as a quail' and 'ended up downing several vodkas' before 'threatening to throw . . . [Frank] through the wall' the two of them now see each other only infrequently 'on the train to Gotham'. Frank, though, is able to laugh this off for the triviality that it is in concluding his story with the pithy observation that this outcome may be the 'essence of modern friendship' (ibid., pp. 50–1).

This sense that Ford is actively countering the sorts of *mise en scène* found in so much writing about the suburbs is confirmed later on during an interior monologue in which Frank ponders the Easter Sunday dawn. Again, as with his tale of Bert's psychological implosion, Frank's language initially seems to draw on the same hysterical stock as that of some post-war sociological studies of the suburbs (see in particular Gordon et al., 1960, and Keats, 1957). On hearing a noise in the nearby cemetery, he remarks: 'Early is the suburban hour for grieving – midway of a two mile run; a stop-off on the way to work or the 7–11. I have never seen a figure there, yet each one sounds the same, a woman almost always, crying tears of loneliness and remorse' (Ford, 1996, pp. 209–10). Ford's use of the modifying phrase 'I have never seen a figure there, yet . . .' serves to alert us to Frank's scepticism about just how real the 'suburban hour for grieving' actually is, and Ford encloses in parenthesis a remark of Frank's which completely undercuts the notion of a particularly suburban register of grief. Frank confides – in a sort-of aside to the reader – that, '(Actually, I once stood and listened, and after a while someone – a man – began to laugh and talk Chinese)' (ibid., p. 210). There is no suggestion here that embittered Haddamites are slowly dying from despair-induced ulcers, as supposedly were the subjects of the Gordons' *The Split-Level Trap* (1960), and Frank continues his present meditations by laying 'back on the bed and listen[ing] to the sounds of Easter – the optimist's holiday, the holiday with the suburbs in mind, the day for all those with sunny dispositions and a staunch belief in the middle view' (ibid., p. 210). Thus, instead of a space that is associated with psychological and psychosomatic affliction, in *The Sportswriter* Ford scripts suburban New Jersey as a landscape entirely without any overwhelming immanent affect. Frank extols his home state as a place where 'Illusion will never be your adversary' saying that if you are prepared to 'Stop searching' for some ideal and 'Face the earth where you can' (ibid., p. 59) then there is the possibility of finding pleasure in your surroundings.

Similarly, Ford represents Walled Lake, a peripheral part of suburban Detroit to which Frank travels in order to interview an ex-pro footballer, Herb Wallagher, as the extreme edge, literally and figuratively, of suburban insularity and introspection. But Ford also suggests, in a manner redolent of Lefebvre's idea about the production of space as a dialectical process, that it is an environment that has been compromised by its inhabitants' negative outlooks, as much as it is a space that has sullied the minds of those that live there. As Frank reflects, 'A hundred years ago, this country would have been . . . A perfect place for a picnic' but now it is a place of 'gray crust[ed]' snow-melt, 'uneasy silence[s]' and mess where people have 'tossed their refuse' (ibid., p. 161). For Frank, then, 'location isn't actually everything' (ibid., p. 223). His imperative to 'face the earth where you can' celebrates the fact that social relations and location are inextricably linked but rejects the idea that identity is predominantly influenced by environment. His flight from Herb's isolated existence is a flight from a state of mind that Frank abhors, and a flight from a space which is both tainted by and reinforcing of that defensive mindset.

Furthermore, in a continuation of the idea that space is socially produced, Frank associates settling contentedly in a location with learning and maturation, not with the enactment of purchasing power. Describing his particular place in the Haddam community, Frank explains that he is part of the . . . group who're happy to be residents year-round, and who act as if we were onto something fundamental that's not a matter of money . . . but of a certain awareness: living in a place is one thing we all went to college to learn how to do properly, and now that we're adults and the time has arrived, we're holding on (ibid., p. 55).

What Frank imparts here is the knowledge that satisfactory emplacement in an environment requires work and engagement rather than whimsy and abstraction. To Frank's mind, apprehending Haddam as a 'straightforward . . . plumb-literal . . . simple [and] unambiguous' town 'makes it the pleasant place that it is' (ibid., p. 109) and means that suburban life unfolds in ways he can understand. If we are to see Frank in Lefebvrean terms as a prime agent in the social production of Haddam as a suburban spatiality, even allowing for the impact of late capitalism and institutional planning, *The Sportswriter* seems to posit the pragmatic foundations of Frank's part in this process. Kevin Brooks, in a perceptive essay on the philosophical tenets of Ford's fiction, avers that, broadly, Ford's work evinces a rejection of simple truths and universal rules. More specifically for Brooks, the Bascombe novels construct Frank as a figure who consciously employs the pragmatist's tactics – identified by Richard Rorty in *Philosophy and the Mirror of Nature* (1979) – of 'coping' and 'edification', terms which Rorty uses, according to Brooks, 'with the connotation of figuring things out or making one's way in the world' (2009, p. 848). This pragmatism is given fictional expression by Ford in the opening pages of *The Sportswriter* when Frank describes how 'Nowadays I'm willing to say yes to as much as I can: yes to my town, my neighborhood, my neighbor', to 'Let things be the best they can be' (Ford, 1996, p. 58).

In embracing contingency and shunning the abstractions of an idealized notion of the suburbs, Frank nonetheless enjoys what he terms the 'meaningful mystery' (ibid.,

p. 54) that Haddam and suburban New Jersey offer. Paradoxically, this enjoyment of the enigmatic derives from Frank's literal appreciation of the everyday spaces around him; but, Ford suggests, this is not an untenable outlook. Martin Corner points out, in an essay on spirituality in recent American fiction, that Frank's desire for mystery is grounded in the innate *mysteriousness* of the material world and does not seek to transcend the stuff of tangible reality. As Corner puts it, for Frank, 'mystery might be a feature of the given world, not the disclosure of some special, distinct, marked-off reality' (Corner, 2006, p. 148). With such a philosophical outlook, Frank Bascombe becomes the polar opposite of Frank Wheeler, a character who fails utterly to believe that the suburbs can be anything other than a token of some malign existential force.

We can begin to see, then, that *The Sportswriter* presents Frank as someone who acknowledges the way in which the suburbs are the product of a postmodern capitalist economy but who nonetheless is able to determine them, through his own wilful thought processes, as 'representational spaces' of possibility. Several of Ford's critics have struggled to accommodate this seemingly unironic take on Frank's New Jersey existence (e.g. Dupuy, 2000; Guinn, 2002; Hobson, 2005). But Ford has confirmed that this was precisely his intention: 'The suburbs have been written about ironically so often that I thought it might be a more interesting surgery on the suburbs to talk about them in unironic terms' (Smith, 1987, p. 54). So, Martyn Bone's reading of the novel conflates Frank's background as a writer who profited from the sale of his literary product (his short-story collection *Blue Autumn*) with an inseparable complicity in the economic production of place; for Bone, when Frank sells the option on his stories to Hollywood and moves to Haddam his 'speculations in the literary market . . . [become] equivalent to, exchangeable with . . . [his] speculations in the property market' (Bone, 2005, pp. 102–3) and it is this investment in the market that means Frank is unable to see the developments in the Haddam surrounds as anything other than a good thing.

And yet, such an insight can be qualified by the recognition that speculation, in its purest sense, is an imaginative act, an act that is bound up with language and the social. In Frank's view, the best way to ensure a sense of locatedness is through an imaginative engagement with the reality of place. As he remarks while sat on his girlfriend's porch in a subdivision near to Haddam, the 'snaky peninsula is the work of some enterprising developer who's carted it in with trucks and reclaimed it from a swamp. And it has not been a bad idea. You could just as easily be in Hyannis Port if you closed your eyes, which for a moment I do' (Ford, 1996, p. 262). Bone's reading follows that of Edward Dupuy in its reliance on the idea of Frank 'relenting' to the capitalist 'world-as-text' landscapes around him. Although, while Dupuy argues that this allows Frank to recover from the dreaminess that has been afflicting him, Bone posits that Frank is diverted from any critical engagement with such places, further prolonging his journey back to some sort of equilibrium (Bone, 2005, p. 103; Dupuy, 2000).

However, I want to argue that Frank neither relents to, nor fails to engage with, his suburban surroundings. In a postmodern landscape of multifarious architectural signifiers detached from historical context and animated by the creative/destructive energies of capital, Frank pointedly persists in making what is signified something that works for him. This particular scene, in which Frank imaginatively reconstructs

Barnegat Pines as a Cape Cod seaside town, marks the beginning of a continuing effort to acknowledge the constructedness of reality and turn it to his own ends. Matthew Guinn's argument, that Frank is a figure Ford knowingly sends up by consciously implicating him in the valourization of an inauthentic postmodern suburban landscape, is entirely dependent on viewing Ford as an ironic commentator on the suburbs. But, Ford scripts Frank as a figure who positively embraces the suburbs and rejects a view of this environment as a breeding ground for what Guinn calls a 'truly exiled sensibility' (Guinn, 2002, pp. 204–6). Frank's relativist coping strategy deploys an optimistic rhetoric that defines the terms of his engagement with the suburban landscape in a positive light. While it is overly simplistic to conflate Ford's and Frank's attitudes to the suburbs, at the level of narrative technique, what Ford's use of the first person does not allow for is the sort of authorial reproach that Yates reserves for Frank and April Wheeler by flitting between a free indirect style and a more omniscient third-person perspective. Thus, through the rejection of an ironic tone, Ford's style facilitates the defamiliarization of a clichéd view of suburbia.

At the end of the Easter weekend Frank contemplates what the suburbs mean to him. It is early evening, a time when 'we all want to sit down in a leather chair by an open window, have a drink near someone we love or like, read the sports and possibly doze for a while'. Frank opines that, 'It is for such dewy interludes that our suburbs were built' and that 'entered *cautiously*, they can serve us well *no matter what our stations in life, no matter we have the aforementioned liberty or don't . . .* It is a pastoral kind of longing, of course, but *we can all have it* [my emphasis]' (Ford, 1996, p. 318). Gregory Dart has written about the way in which the highly systematic nature of late capitalist spaces 'is always, however inadvertently, giving birth to its opposite – fantasy, reverie, daydream – as a form of resistance' (Dart, 2010, p. 79). While Dart is referring to city space in this statement, his point is equally applicable to suburban space: the excerpt from *The Sportswriter* quoted above amply demonstrates Frank's urge to resist through the utilization of the imagination, a practice that he believes all suburbanites can engage in.

But this idea of Frank as a daydreamer able to resist the hegemonic domination of abstracted suburban space relies upon an imaginative pursuit of suburban mystery that is grounded in the real. While waiting at Haddam train station, Frank reaffirms his commitment to his home:

> I will say it again, perhaps for the last time: there is mystery everywhere, even in a vulgar, urine-scented, suburban depot such as this. You have only to let yourself in for it. You can never know what's coming next. Always there is the chance it will be – miraculous to say – something you want. (Ford, 1996, p. 348)

As Frank goes on to say, 'you can learn not to be cynical – if you're interested enough' (ibid., p. 367). It is through Frank's willingness to muse on the suburban spaces that surround him that Ford challenges entrenched views about this environment. Frank refuses to acquiesce to what he terms the 'fragrant silly dream' of the suburbs, the sense that they are utopian spaces that offer a 'Life-forever' (ibid., p. 325). Frank understands this perception to be promulgated by the 'bad stereotypes' of advertising and literature and he flatly dissociates himself from it as an insult to the real tribulations of what he calls – in a very Lefebvrean idiom – 'lived life' (ibid., p. 84).

Early on in *Independence Day*, set five years after *The Sportswriter*, we learn that Frank has left the world of sportswriting behind and transformed himself into a realtor with a local firm called Lauren-Schwindell. Duffy posits that in the second and third parts of the Bascombe trilogy the practice of real estate functions 'as a metaphor for the hazardous negotiations and choices of adult life' (Duffy, 2008, p. 64) but this suggestion risks reducing Frank's relationships to the level of market transactions. Contrary to this, I read Frank's new immersion in real estate as indicative of his developing outlook on life and his belief that 'contingencies and incongruities' – so evident in the course of buying and selling houses – are not to be feared, but rather embraced. In an interview with Kay Bonetti, Ford ponders the terms of man's dialectical relationship with space: 'I think that you have to be imaginative in your relationship with place. You have to be sensitive to the fact that it makes a claim on you and then try to make up what that claim is' (Bonetti, 2001, p. 21).

As I explored in my analysis of *The Sportswriter*, such imaginative acts are not comparable to a deference to abstraction. They are, instead, the means by which exigency and uncertainty are dealt with. So it is that *Independence Day* begins with Frank acknowledging a 'wild world' (Ford, 2003, p. 5) of economic and social change in the Haddam area, but Frank is quite willing to countenance a suburban landscape that is being transformed. While Frank recounts that Haddam is becoming, in many of its residents' defensive reactions to changing circumstances, a town that exhibits the behaviours of an ailing listed company (ibid.), he himself prefers to take his chances with contingency. As he says when expanding on the functioning of market economies, 'The premise is that you're presented with what you might've thought you didn't want, but what's available', with the challenge being to 'start finding ways to feel good about it and yourself' (ibid., p. 41). Later, when talking to Mr Tanks, a truck driver he meets at a freeway rest area, Frank concludes that Mr Tanks's desire to move from California to Connecticut is one that is explicable in the sense of it 'having to do with the character of eventuality' and 'not rust-belt economics or the downturn in per-square-foot residential in the Hartford-Waterbury metroplex' (ibid., p. 204). Being a realtor allows Frank, paradoxically, to keep himself at a distance from the dictates of the economy, and profess the belief that there is more to a spatiality than its exchange value.

Some critics of the novel have taken it to be exclusively concerned with mapping the contours of this economically perilous 'wild world'. For this group of readers, Ford's exploration of the theme of independence reflects a sense that American society has become one of diminished expectations, with the novel's representation of the celebrations of the titular holiday revealing the ways in which getting on in America at the end of the twentieth century is only possible through the pursuit of selfish gratifications. For Nick Gillespie, *Independence Day* is a novel that advances a 'funereal vision' (Gillespie, 1996); for Catherine Jurca, it 'pivots on the sacrifices people are willing to make to protect themselves and their property' and the novel is read as proof of 'a further literature of suburban victimization, in which characters mourn the spiritual hollowness of their lives' (Jurca, 2001, p. 171). With this as her critical outlook, I suggest that Jurca misreads Frank's fealty to the epiphanies provided by the everyday and, rather than seeing such a disposition as the means by which Frank re-makes his environment, sees him instead as a narrator who indulges in 'endless naval-watching' thereby 'tak[ing] suburban self-consciousness and self-pity to a new level' (Jurca, 2009, pp. 176–7). By contrast, my reading is predicated on a belief that the various tactics and strategies Frank employs in order to better understand his suburban environment are not the symptoms of self-absorption. In *Independence Day*, his relationship with suburban space is ego-free to the extent that it enables him to come to a fresh understanding of what it means to be independent in a culture where independence is synonymous with a withdrawal from society. Indeed, the many interviews that Ford has given on the genesis of *Independence Day* clearly reveal that his intention was to do more than make the novel a reflection of a sociocultural moment that seemingly engenders interpersonal dysfunction and atomization. Instead, Ford asserts, the novel is an attempt to reconsider the nature of independence in order to see if it is not only compatible with community-mindedness but also integral to it. In an interview from 1996, the year following *Independence Day*'s publication, Ford asserts that in writing the novel he was 'interested in how and if the historical brand of independence upon which the country is founded had any peculiar relevance to how independence is achieved subjectively.' He concludes that 'Human independence is not so much founded on wanting to cut yourself off . . . but . . . to make other hints of rapport, other kinds of relations' (Thompson and Ellis, 1996, p. 107).

Frank sees his work as a realtor in terms that flatly oppose a conceptualization of his character as just another smug, venal suburbanite selling houses out of a sense of superiority and a desire to amass more money than is necessary to live a worthwhile life. For Frank, realty is akin to counselling. On the Friday before the Independence Day holiday weekend, Frank narrates that he has an appointment with some clients, Joe and Phyllis Markham, lower-middle-class naifs who are looking to move to the area from Vermont. Frank relates the tortured history of their house search – he has been showing them houses in the Haddam area since March – yet he does so in sympathetic, if slightly wearied, terms. Part of his service to the Markhams is to address 'that feeling of not knowing' the 'fears' that 'come quaking and quivering into clients' hearts' in this sort of scenario (Ford, 2003, p. 43).

Frank sees himself, then, as not just a real estate agent, but an agent of social change: he just wants to get on with the job of 'lifting sagging spirits, opening fresh, unexpected choices, and offering much-needed assistance toward life's betterment' (ibid., p. 47). Later on, during a phone conversation with Frank, Phyllis, using a malapropism that is highly suggestive of how she, at least, views his efforts, refers to Frank as a 'relator' rather than a realtor (189). It needs to be noted, though, that Frank is not merely a dispenser of easy platitudes; there is a distinctly spatial aspect to his optimism. He is eager to avoid a scenario where the Markhams 'dribble off elsewhere' to another agent, but the reason he gives is not solely to do with the fear of a lost sale, although that is a factor. Frank is equally keen that the Markhams, clearly feeling 'the need for an unattainable fresh start', avoid a situation where they just 'end up buying the first shitty split-level they see' (ibid., p. 47). Frank's hope that the Markhams open their minds to the possibilities on offer in the changing suburban spaces of the Haddam area is buttressed by a concern that they don't misapprehend what is available on the basis of an unattainable, clichéd fantasy. Thus, as far as Frank is concerned, the Markhams are experiencing problems of perception. While in Frank's mind house-buying should 'easily be one of life's most hopeful optional experiences', Joe is fearful of ending up 'just like the other schmo' (ibid., p. 57), a tension Frank understands but is dismissive of. For Frank, the hope that should be attendant on buying a house in the Haddam area is a direct result of the realization that space is produced through a negotiation between people and place; unlike the Markhams, Frank does not believe that space can ever be perfectly realized, or that it remains fixed in its aspect. Instead he has learned that space is constructed through provisionality, through a series of 'optional experiences'.

While Frank and Joe are debating the merits of the Penns Neck neighbourhood, Ford scripts an amusing yet highly revealing episode which questions the whole notion of a stereotypical spatiality. In the course of his conversation with Joe, Frank spots 'across the picture-window space' of the house across the way the confounding sight of a woman walking 'totally in the buff, a big protuberant pair of white breasts leading the way, her arms out Isadora Duncan style, her good, muscular legs leaping and striding like a painting on an antique urn' (ibid., p. 66). Of course, in some post-war analyses of the suburban lifestyle (e.g. Keats, 1957; Gordon et al., 1960) the picture window became a resonant symbol of the empty promise and stifling oppression of suburban life, functioning metonymically as a key to understanding the entirety of mass experience. But in this instance the picture window throws up for Frank 'mystery and the unexpected', suggesting (with pun no doubt intended) that Penns Neck has 'hidden assets' (ibid., p. 66). Tellingly, however, Joe misses the display having grumpily and incredulously departed for the front door of his prospective new house. Although Frank is taken with this strange occurrence, and sees it as a promising sign of what Penns Neck has to offer, fundamentally his outlook differs from the Markhams in the way that he views space as perpetually in process; as he remarks to Phyllis, 'You *are* best off . . . trying to bring life to a place, not just depending on the place to supply it for you' (ibid., p. 76).

As the third Bascombe novel, *The Lay of the Land*, opens in 2000, 12 years after the events of *Independence Day*, we find Frank's circumstances greatly changed. He is now living in Sea-Clift on the Jersey Shore and has set up his own firm, Realty-Wise, with a Tibetan-American called Mike Mahoney. Most significantly in terms of the bearing it has on his narrative, Frank is suffering from prostate cancer and has recently undergone a course of treatment.

Frank perceives a 'malign force' in the turn-of-the century economy, a market that seems to be 'in full control of every bit of real property on the seaboard . . . holding property hostage and away from the very people who wanted and often badly needed it' (Ford, 2006, p. 85). Thus, in *The Lay of the Land*, the 'redemptive theme in the civic drama' of renting or acquiring a home (ibid., p. 90) – a theme so evident in the way Frank personally practises real estate in *Independence Day* – has been lost. As far as Frank is concerned, the attitude that pervades socio-spatial relations in twenty-first-century New Jersey means that resistance to the dominating force of the market is faltering: instead of recognizing what Frank acknowledges as the 'transitory essence of everything' (ibid., p. 207) or that 'belonging and fitting in, of making a claim and settling down is at best ephemeral' and that being ephemeral 'relieves us of stodgy house-holder officialdom and renders us free to be our own most current selves' (ibid., p. 209), Frank sees a bewildering urge in the population at large to relent to the market and to pay for a sense of permanence which can never truly be bestowed.

Ford emphasizes the corrupting influence of the market's role in the production of space by inserting into Sea-Clift an embittered couple Frank refers to as the 'Toxic Feensters' (ibid.). Newly rich following a state lottery win, the Feensters have moved down to Sea-Clift from Connecticut. However, their dedication to property as a mark of status has meant that, as far as Frank is concerned, they 'got detached from their sense of useful longing' and that 'They only know they paid enough to expect to feel right, but for some reason don't feel right, and so get mad as hell when they can't bring all into line' (ibid., p. 210). When, in a finale to the novel that functions almost as a *deus ex machina*, the Feensters are both shot by Russian gangsters (and Frank is unwittingly caught in the crossfire), Ford strains the limits of novelistic technique to condemn the couple's implication in a way of life that privileges money over all else.

Despite his sense that society in New Jersey is more in thrall to the market than it should be, Frank nevertheless still seeks to enrich himself through pragmatic, optimistic choice. He declares that 'a lot of life is just plain wrong' but that 'all you can do about it . . . is just start getting used to it, start selecting amazement over bewilderment' (ibid., p. 141). Frank describes himself as a 'lifelong practitioner of choices' (ibid., p. 144) and he remains convinced that the changed suburban topography and the 'multi-use society', as he terms it, does offer scope for contentment. It is precisely this landscape that offers what Frank sees as the positivist principle that best defines American culture: the idea that one can 'leave, and then . . . arrive in a better state' (ibid., p. 337). 'Sometimes', Frank proclaims, 'a new vista, a new house number, a new place of employ, a new set of streets to navigate and master are all you need to [paradoxically] simplify life and take a new lease out on it' (ibid., p. 336).

This attitude towards the market economy means that Frank offers the reader a nuanced view of commercial development which 'involves not just what something *ought* to cost . . . but what something *can* cost in a world still usable by human beings' (ibid., p. 86). In other words, Frank disdains 'the millennial free-enterprise canon in which the customer's a bit-part player to the larger drama of gross accumulation' (ibid., p. 327); instead, he sees the prospect of 'commerce with no likelihood of significant growth or sky-rocketing appreciation' as a 'precious bounty' (ibid., p. 399).

In *The Lay of the Land*, then, real estate becomes a vocation for Frank, not a profession, and one with a responsibility to 'leave the client better than I found him – or her'. Indeed, Frank sees his role as having 'a lay therapist's fiduciary responsibility' and believes a 'version' of the 'perfect real estate experience' would be one in which 'Everyone does his part, but no house changes hands' (ibid., p. 270). In *The Illusions of Postmodernism* Terry Eagleton argues that socialism and postmodernism 'Both believe in a history which would be one of plurality, free play, plasticity, open-endedness', but that socialism aims 'to release the sensuous particularity of use-value from the metaphysical prison of exchange value' (Eagleton 1996, p. 64). In many respects, this is precisely the balance that Frank seeks in the suburban spatiality he inhabits. Reflecting on a contractor's offer to Mike to get involved with the development of a cornfield site, Frank states baldly that flattening such places 'for seven-figure mega-mansions isn't after all, really *helping* people in the way that assisting them to find a modest home they want – and that's already there – helps them' (ibid., p. 198).

If *The Lay of the Land* – set as it is over the Thanksgiving holiday – is a novel organized around the idea of understanding what a person should be thankful for, its conclusion leaves the reader in no doubt that the production of a spatiality that is more mindful of people than capitalist economic dictates is of paramount importance. In the novel's final scene Frank descends from the sky on-board a flight to Rochester where his cancer clinic is located, and sees 'the bundled figures of the other humans coming into clear focus . . . Some are watching, gaping up, some are waving. Some turn their backs to us. Some do not notice us as we touch the ground.' Then, with 'A bump, a roar, a heavy thrust forward into life again . . . we resume our human scale upon the land' (ibid., p. 485). For Frank, at the end of a 17-year immersion in the changing New Jersey landscapes he has called home, nothing is more important than the understanding that the true measurement of any particular geography has to incorporate human needs, weaknesses and desires. Frank's narrative in *The Lay of the Land* is bittersweet in tone: largely in agreement with his colleague Mike's Buddhist-inflected wisdom that 'we're all fathers of ourselves and the world's the result of our doing' (ibid., p. 20), Frank laments the fact that so much of the New Jersey suburban environment is an empty reflection of society's acquiescence to the forces of the late-capitalist economy. But, finally, he retains hope that 'our doing' might yet result in a different world. Frank's tone here is consistent with the voice in which he relays the lessons learned in the course of *The Sportswriter* and *Independence Day*: despite the concerns he harbours from the vantage point of the year 2000, he is still convinced that an imaginative engagement with space can generate a spatiality – a nexus of society's spatial practices – that is more than a reflection of acquisitiveness. From the perspective of someone who has been close to death, he allows himself a certain measure of contentment that, through his work as a realtor, he has embraced an ethical stance that enables him to understand his surroundings on a 'human scale'.

11

Ordinary Geographies: Trajectories of Affect in the Work of Kathleen Stewart and D. J. Waldie

Neil Campbell

Human beings are tied together by a certain sensory fabric, a certain distribution of the sensible, which defines their way of being together; and politics is about the transformation of the sensory fabric of 'being together'. (Rancière, 2009, p. 56)

The life of country and city is moving and present: moving in time, through the history of a family and a people; moving in feeling and ideas, through a network of relationships and decisions. (Williams, 1993 [1973], p. 8)

In section 49 of D. J. Waldie's *Holy Land* (1996, pp. 24–5) he describes his father's death in the bathroom of their suburban house on Graywood Avenue, Lakewood, California. The description meditates on the door behind which he dies, 'a well-made, wooden bathroom door', 'a three-panel door' wherein 'Each panel is nearly square, twenty-one inches wide by nineteen inches high. From edge to edge, the door is twenty-eight inches wide.' This strangely unsettling juxtaposition of intense personal tragedy and extraordinary, material detail speaks to Waldie's remarkably affective relationship with space and objects in space. We all live amid such quotidian moments bridging the gulf between the unnoticed ephemera of our ordinary lives and their intersection with such momentous events of intimacy and calamity, but too often they are simply overlooked. In such details, however, we uncover, I would suggest, what Kathleen Stewart calls 'the charge of an unfolding' (2007, p. 19) as one experience or everyday event gives rise to a set of thoughts, feelings and intensities that cannot be foreseen or fully defined. From the immediate and local material of the ordinary, therefore, worlds unfold. They *touch* and, in turn, touch us.[1]

'All the original doors in the house' in Waldie's Lakewood home, he continues, 'are the same – grids of three rectangles surrounded by raised framework'. (Waldie, 1996,

---

[1] The British writer Paul Barker takes a similar view: 'Suburbia's enemies mock such places as uniform, dull, conformist. When were they last there? As rebellious teenagers? Suburbs are libertarian, eccentric, humane. By comparison with a city street, a leafy avenue, with its rampant hedges, has an appealing openness. Even a fruitful sense of anarchy.' (Barker, 2009a; see also Barker, 2009b).

p. 24) This 'thing', this ordinary door in an ordinary suburban tract home tells its own story as the material assemblage of post-war American suburbia, of Lakewood and Levittown, with their endless repetitions of form and 'sameness'; its factory-made precision, and its absolute utilitarian purpose. The inside of Waldie's house mirrors its outside, as the gridded door panels reflect the grid pattern that stretches for miles in all directions from his tree-lined street in Lakewood. As he stares ever more intently at the seemingly banal landscape that constitutes his everyday life and specifically at the door behind which his father dies, he records that 'Painted white, as they are now, each square of each door is molded in the light by a right angle of shadow'. (ibid., p. 25) Thus, the apparently ordinary and known, the ignored and standardized features of the cookie-cutter suburban home, transformed subtly over time by coats of paint on the original wood, suddenly and astonishingly becomes altered by light and shadow into new, abstracted and engagingly poetic forms: 'molded in the light by a right angle of shadow'. The grid of the door, precise and regular, *inside* the house reflects the grid of Lakewood *outside* – itself also layered with the patina of time and human use – and, indeed, like the grid of all suburbs, as Waldie is at pains to remind us throughout his writings, never defines its absolute meaning nor contains everything within its 'framework'. Likewise as we interact with the familiar landscapes of the everyday there are moments of revelation and beauty, of surprise and enchantment, 'charge[s] of an unfolding', acting to re-connect us with what Waldie would express as the 'holy'.[2]

In the remembering of his father's death, it is the abstract pattern of light and shadow cast on the ordinariness and taken-for-granted qualities of the commonplace door that he also recalls. Through the strange 'shadow' of light, death arrives into the gridded sameness of suburbia, reminding us all of its ubiquity and presence, its inevitability, and, perhaps reassuringly and simultaneously, of our capacity for continuance.

Waldie concludes this section: 'The doors in my house are abstract and ordinary. The bathroom door is now forty-seven years old. My father was sixty-nine.' (Waldie, 1996, p. 25) There is something telling and strangely heartening in his sense of the 'abstract and ordinary' working together in our lives, challenging us to engage with and sense mystery, enchantment, and intensities through the everyday. In part, it is Waldie's Catholicism, 'ground in the material world', as he puts it (Campbell and Waldie, 2011, p. 242), which engenders such a sensibility towards the ordinary since, according to writer and priest Andrew Greeley, such an imagination is defined as an inclination 'to see the Holy lurking in creation' by existing in an everyday world 'haunted by a sense that objects, events, and persons of daily life are revelations of Grace' (qtd. in Waldie, 2007, p. 60). Rather than Transcendentalism in the American tradition, with its desire to transcend the material, Waldie asserts its 'antithesis' because for him 'Catholicism is mired in the everyday' (Campbell and Waldie, 2011, p. 242).

Thus as we read across and between the sections of *Holy Land*, we are drawn into 'a meditation on the fate of ordinary things – the things we touch and the lingering

---

[2] Waldie's attention to the 'ordinary' landscape and to the details of 'structures of feeling' connect his approach to suburbia with Raymond Williams's work both as a critic and a novelist. See, for example, his novel *Border Country* (1960) with its slow uncovering of a type of history from below, of, as he put it, culture as ordinary. Stewart in turn quotes from Williams in her *Ordinary Affects* (2007).

effects of their touch on us' (Waldie, 2007, p. 61). For as Waldie admitted to me in an interview, *Holy Land* is partly a 'meditation on the way habits become beliefs (or perhaps the other way around)' and operates as 'alternately constructed and dispersed in the experience of reading it.' (Campbell and Waldie, 2011, p. 233) As a result of such tension and motion, it is, as such, Waldie claims, an 'impure' book, 'more mixed, it's hybrid, it's unclean . . . it's about impurities' (ibid., p. 242). Thus the suburb, often defined by its sameness and uniformity, in Waldie's version becomes instead an alive and varied heteroglossic space.

This sense of the 'constructed *and* dispersed' Waldie finds in the structured, connected and lived spatiality of the suburbs which he contrasts dramatically with its conventional aerial view; an outlook that for so long has provided the standard cultural knowledge and definition of suburbia. The aerial view provides a distanced, removed and inhuman perspective constituted by remote, gridded imagery that literally and metaphorically 'looks down' on where many people live out their lives. As David Beers noted in his own memoir of suburbia *Blue Sky Dream* (1996) as he flies over his neighbourhood in California, it was like looking at 'some immense, far too complicated board game. The sensed design to it all is what vaguely terrifies' because this is an 'unsentimental schema without our home, my family, me, at its center. Down there, we could be anywhere' (Beers, 1996, p. 16). Rather like Waldie, however, Beers gazes onto the gridded landscape of apparent anonymity below and thinks differently: 'I wonder whether all these people living just like me might be my people – all of us, perhaps, with a mass of connections joining me to some whole' (ibid., p. 17). Suddenly, when one bothers to look and to see through the presupposed already-defined portrait of suburban life, there are in fact an array of stories to unravel in 'the landscape people rarely notice' (Waldie, 1996, p. 154). Kathleen Stewart poses a question that both her own work and Waldie's answers: 'What happens if we approach worlds not as the dead or reeling effects of distant systems but as lived affects with tempos, sensory knowledges, orientations, transmutations, habits, rogue force fields . . . ?' (Stewart, 2011, p. 226).

Similarly, Waldie writes of a 'joining of interests' (1996, p. 6) in the streets of suburbia through which the distanced aerial or panoptic sense of suburbia might be re-thought and undone by its 'lived affects'. Georges Bataille, although an unlikely ally of Waldie, famously referred to this viewpoint from above as eagle-like and 'Icarian' – related to Icarus – in contrast with 'the "old mole"' working down below 'in the bowels of the earth . . . where bodies rot' as opposed to 'the purity of lofty space' (Bataille, 1985, pp. 34–5). Waldie's 'impure' and 'hybrid' suburban point of view is that of the lowly old mole (Waldie has poor vision due to a long-term eye disease and walks everywhere in Los Angeles) feeling and sensing the tactility of the streets and through them, living within them, building a new suburban civics, a 'muddled notion of the Greek *polis*', as he puts it; of the 'citizen of your place . . . enmeshed in its life' (Campbell and Waldie, 2011, p. 243).

It is only then, as the old mole, that he notices the panels in the bathroom door, or the 'house frames precise as cells in a hive and stucco walls fragile as an unearthed bone', alongside the multiplicity and intensity of living that goes on layered inside these apparently anonymous dwellings (Waldie, 1996, p. 5). Through these organic, 'earthy', breathing images of cells, hives, bones and his extraordinary capacity for detailed, nuanced readings of everyday space and experiences Waldie creates his phenomenological, affective landscape vision of suburbia, which far from sterile and standardized, is 'like the illustration of a fold of skin in a high school biology book' (ibid., p. 125), never motionless or lifeless but always already engaged in the multiple processes of embodied living in the world. As he has written elsewhere, 'It's only the skin I won't slough off, the story I want to hear told, my carnal house and the body into which I welcome myself' (Waldie, 2004, p. 108). In the suburban streets of Lakewood, Waldie sees, in David Crouch's words, 'possibility and activation; opening and becoming; the "making" of space and the kinds of knowledge of the world in everyday life' (Crouch, 2010, p. 7).

Most importantly, Waldie's Lakewood suburb refuses the reductionist view of a parochial enclosure battling with events existing outside its lawned boundaries. In truth, Lakewood 'worlds' for Waldie; meaning, following Martin Heidegger and Kathleen Stewart, 'dwelling in places that bears, gestures, gestates, worlds', a living space of 'qualities, rhythms, forces, relations, and movements' (Stewart, 2011, p. 445). As Rob Wilson explains, '"Worlding" as an active force gerund, would turn nouns (world) to verbs (worlding), thus shifting the taken-for-granted and normal life-forms . . . into the to-be-generated and remade' (Wilson, in Wilson and Connery, 2007, p. 212). It is a 'de-distancing' process which refuses to dwell in the local or the 'world' uncritically but is 'active and vigilant' in its efforts to comprehend the interrelatedness of what we might term, more conventionally, the global and local (ibid., p. 213). It's about 'listening to and caring for one's own life-world as well as the related and emergent species being of others . . . a world outside' (ibid., p. 214). Waldie's *Holy Land*, with its careful attention to 'the everyday actualities of' . . . inhabiting' suburbia tells multiple and connected stories of 'worlding': of war and trauma, conquest and loss, racism, fear and nuclear paranoia; of water, geology and time; of sales pitch and salvation (Steiner, 1978, p. 83). As we read *Holy Land,* appropriately perhaps, journeying through its asides and divergences, Waldie demonstrates how the most local story is always somehow also global, connected by space and time to the wider intensities of 'worlding'. It is as if Waldie is in agreement with George Steiner's assessment of Heidegger, that 'To be at all is to be worldly' (ibid.).

Thus the nuns in Waldie's 1950s grade school who told stories of the Red Threat, taught him to hate Communists, then to hate 'intolerance' and finally made him 'want to keep everything that I could' and, as he puts it, 'First, I would keep my faith. Much later, I would keep our regard for each other, and the ways in which we revealed ourselves in these small houses' (Waldie, 1996, p. 60). *Holy Land* enacts this 'keeping' of everything, of 'faith' and 'regard for each other' and shows that even living within maligned suburban space, one might be a part of some revelation of worlding, a form of 'compelled . . . conviviality', as he calls it, flowing outward from the material detail of his house on Graywood Avenue to reveal 'ourselves' *in-the-world* through 'these small houses'. From noticing the particulars of the everyday, from the care, concern and apprehension one demonstrates to the very minutiae of ordinary existence, one connects outward to the politics of something larger but related, 'a concern with, a caring for, an answerability to, the presentness and mystery of Being itself, of Being as it transfigures beings' (Steiner, 1978, p. 97). This relation between 'being' and 'Being' derived from Heidegger, is not necessarily religious (although it has those connotations for Waldie), but stands for the intrinsic 'ethic of concernedness' (ibid.)

that might forge a greater social care and communal regionality from local affects and actions to global interests and decisions; a genuine process of worlding.

As we have seen, this might begin at home, for as Gaston Bachelard puts it: 'A house that has been experienced is not an inert box. Inhabited space transcends geometrical space' (Bachelard, 1969, p. 47). The apparent 'geometrical object' of Waldie's house set out within its grid of other houses, streets and boundaries makes its 'prime reality . . . visible and tangible', 'marked . . . with its discipline and balance' (ibid., p. 48), and yet for Waldie the geometric patterns of the grid-plan and the aerial view are never sufficient to tell the complex stories of the suburbs since, as we have seen, through his sense of 'worlding' the 'universe comes to inhabit this house' (ibid., p. 51) with its human interactions, dreams and disappointments, the intimate experiences and the mutual moments of vulnerability that form the worlding suburb. 'Worldings', after all, as Kathleen Stewart argues are part of the attunements and attachments thrown together in the everyday; a multiplicity of trajectories, forces, intensities like a 'nexus of worlds' prismatically refracted and reflected in the lives we live and our 'ways of going on' (Stewart, 2012).

> All of these little worlds that some people immerse themselves in, or dip in and out of, or make fun of, or build a light or temporary link to before they move on to something else. (Stewart, 2011, p. 452)

Stewart's words enable us to understand what Waldie achieves in reflecting upon Lakewood lives and 'these little worlds . . . people immerse themselves in': of Mrs R whose dying child was baptized by Waldie's mother, or Mr H who dug a fallout shelter under his suburban home, or Mr L who returned his mail to city hall 'unopened and stamped with a bewildering number of biblical and political exhortations' (Waldie, 1996, p. 128). Ultimately, *Holy Land* is not his individual memoir of Lakewood at all, but rather its 'distributed biography': an attuned, rhizomatic life history of suburban timespace drawing together its various lines and layers intersecting there. So rather than reduce or summarize his approach, understood through Stewart's terms, we trace becomings and trajectories, 'interleavings' (as Waldie terms them), because 'Only when lives are placed side by side do they seem larger' (ibid., p. 94).[3] The book as memoir is always already, as Waldie told me, a self-conscious combination

---

[3] 'Distributed Biography is a web 2.0-based application created to support groups of individuals in their efforts to narrate shared experiences about people, events or locations in ways which interrupt monolithic conceptualizations of identity . . . Our tool centers on the periphery of identity in constructing assemblages of short to medium length experiential narratives linked to one another via temporal, geographical, emotional and other loosely coupled folksonomies or lines of flight. The periphery places the banal on similar footing with the quintessential, exposing it even for the damage it does to the biographed. Within Deleuze and Guattari's construct of the rhizome, several principles are outlined, these served as guides for DB. They suggested that we create tools and containers that encouraged heterogeneity; make multiple and overlapping connections possible; support multiplicity; create an asignifying environment in the face of rupture; lean on cartographic notions which privilege no sequence or starting point over others; and present trajectories that allow for flexibility and adaptability which rise to the level of decalcomania.' Perhaps the best way to summarize this is via an artistic metaphor: 'Distributed Biography is like a post-1988 Chuck Close painting. Each story is like a square/pixel. Together they bring the subject into view' (Digital Spaces Working Group, n. d.).

of movements and trajectories: 'turning to myself and away from myself, [and] of turning toward the reader' (Campbell and Waldie, 2011, p. 232). In these various 'turnings' Waldie explains the spiralling rhythms of the book; 'to myself' as a source of the memoir and experience of living in Lakewood and then 'away from myself', as the personal and local 'worlds' and connects, refusing to remain only a private and parochial story, while simultaneously always being this, yet finding ways to 'turn' outward to the reader to record all the patterns and threads that loosely assemble together a community made up of diverse and complex lives-in-the-world. Through this narrative process of self, not-self, reader Waldie creates in the 316 sections of *Holy Land* his 'distributed biography' of Lakewood, 'like a post-1988 Chuck Close painting. Each story . . . like a square/pixel. Together they bring the subject into view' (Digital Spaces Working Group, n. d.).

Thus *Holy Land* works from the base ground of the ordinary to engage us in what Waldie has called 'affective history', 'a history that discourses on a sensibility as the means to integrating a useful life' (Campbell and Waldie, 2011, p. 236). From the design blueprints to the wood and nails that constructed the frame of the houses, to the plaster on their walls, the grass on their front lawns and the deep geology upon which it all sits he writes an earthy poetics of space that understands also that such real, material places are also already imbued with memories and dreams cast in the very fabric of their construction. 'When I walk to work, thinking of these stories, they seem insignificant', Waldie writes, 'At Mass on Sunday, I remember them as prayers' (Waldie, 1996, p. 111).

Following Bachelard, we might indeed think of Waldie's memoirs of the suburb of Lakewood as about 'felicitous space' – 'space that may be grasped, that may be defended against adverse forces, the space we love' (Bachelard, 1969, p. xxxi). Indeed Bachelard is a writer admired by Waldie and when one considers the 'protected intimacy' revealed in *The Poetics of Space* (1969, p. 3) one begins to comprehend the closely observed connections Waldie has to his suburban home. 'An entire past comes to dwell in a new house' writes Bachelard (ibid., p. 5) and for Waldie that house is the one bought by his parents in 1948 in Lakewood and that he still lives in today. A house whose details become the cadences of Waldie's prose poetics, his intimate and collective histories of a suburban place usually regarded as without history: 'Past, present and future give the house different dynamisms, which often interfere, at times opposing, at others, stimulating one another' (ibid., p. 60). Bachelard comments 'we are never historians, but always near poets, and our emotion is perhaps nothing but an expression of a poetry that was lost' (ibid., p. 6).

And so we return full circle to the bathroom door. To death and life; to a strange continuing in the encounter with everything and nothing. With the door and what's behind the door. As Juhani Pallasmaa has written, a door is 'a sign to halt and an invitation to enter', it 'silences' and also 'concealed voices' and yet for Waldie it also becomes the stimulus to his doubts, memories and meanderings (Pallasmaa, 2011, p. 131). Through this process, the intimate always relates, always journeys outward to the very public histories of suburbia, for as Waldie writes, 'The grid on which my city is built opens outward without limits. It's the antithesis of a ghetto' (Waldie, 1996, p. 118).

Anthropologist Kathleen Stewart, as if responding to Waldie, states that:

My work is an experiment that writes from the intensities in things. It asks what potential modes of knowing, relating or attending to things are already being lived in ordinary rhythms, labors, and the sensory materiality of forms of attunement to worlds. (Stewart, 2009)

More specifically, she suggests how regional writing 'worlds':

It follows leads, sidesteps, and delays, and it piles things up, creating layers on layers, in an effort to drag things into view, to follow trajectories in motion, and to scope out the shape and shadows and traces of assemblages that solidify and grow entrenched, perhaps doing real damage or holding real hope, and then dissipate, morph, rot, or give way to something new. (Stewart, 2005, p. 1028)

Stewart refers directly to Waldie's work in her *Ordinary Affects* as 'surreally realist', describing *Holy Land* as 'constructed out of tiny bits of personal narrative, hometown tales, and moments in the history of real estate development, all held together with the mortar of a singular though widespread form of ordinariness' (Stewart, 2007, p. 7). In reading their work together, through their correspondences and echoes so as 'to follow [their] trajectories in motion', is to begin to see how one might think differently about what Stewart calls 'regionality' – her 'edgy composite' or 'prismatic ecology' of circulations and 'tactile compositions' (Stewart, 2012).

Affective critical regionalism, as I have termed it elsewhere, worlds the immediate landscapes of the local and the proximate, tracing a 'force field' in 'the generative precarity of ordinary sensibilities' (Stewart, 2011, p. 452; see also Campbell, 2011). It, therefore, becomes a form of uncanny and grounded globalism sensed through Waldie's layered prose poetics and paralleled in Stewart's experimental, speculative thinking and writing through which lived, 'concrete' theory is recognized and utilized (Stewart, 2007, p. 1). For Stewart, that is often found in the 'descriptive detours' (2011, p. 452) of the suburban everyday, 'imagined and inhabited . . . a sensory connection. A jump.' Suddenly, therefore, the suburb becomes 'a world of affinities and impacts that takes place in the moves of intensity across things that seem solid and dead' (Stewart, 2007, p. 127). The apparently 'solid and dead' environment of suburbia, like the one seen from 3,000 feet above in the Lakewood aerial photography of William Garnett that Waldie so often condemns, is interfered with by Stewart's 'cabinet of curiosities designed to incite curiosity' rather than 'to characterize things once and for all' (Stewart, 2005, p. 1041). We cannot know or fix the meaning of the suburbs either despite the efforts of many sociologists and urban historians, for what is required are stories in forms of writing that 'tracks the pulses of things as they cross each other, come together, fragment, and recombine in some new surge . . . as the promise or threat, that something is happening – something capable of impact' (ibid.). As we have traced in Waldie's *Holy Land*, such a distributed biography of place attuned to the very minute activities of ordinary lives can begin this process. Stewart's work, as Ben Highmore, explains, is like a 'field diary of someone sensitized to a range of emotional ecologies as they are played out in the localised encounters of individuals, couples, and small groups' (Highmore, 2011, p. 8).

And so her suburban narrative emerges to put alongside Waldie's:

> She walks the neighbourhood with Ariana in the very early morning, laying down imaginaries.
>
> The yards are vulnerable in the predawn.
>
> The mist rises in a yard full of playful and scary cement statues of giant bunny rabbits and gargoyles. What are these people doing with all these statues? . . . Up the street a large plastic ball is lodged in a tree . . .
>
> The vagueness or the unfinished quality of the ordinary is not so much a deficiency as a resource, like a fog of immanent forces still moving even though so much has already happened and there seems to be plenty that's set in stone.
>
> This is no utopia. Not a challenge to be achieved or an ideal to be realized, but a mode of attunement, a continuous responding to something not quite already given and yet somehow happening. (Stewart, 2007, p. 127)[4]

What Stewart conveys here is an intense sense of 'regionality' registered through the same kinds of 'turnings' discussed earlier in Waldie's *Holy Land*; from self to not-self to reader and the world. For the 'she' in *Ordinary Affects* is Stewart herself turning in and out of identities (her daughter is called Ariana), just as the 'he' in *Holy Land* is Waldie. Stewart explains that 'she' is 'not so much a subject position or an agent in hot pursuit of something definitive as a point of contact; instead, she gazes, imagines, senses, takes on, performs and asserts not a flat and finished truth but some possibilities (and threats) that have come into view in the effort to become attuned to what a particular scene might offer' (ibid., p. 5). Her walk in the predawn suburb with its whole way of life exposed is both reassuring and perplexing; 'a fog of immanent forces still moving', always tantalizing and surreal. Stewart's descriptive style, in short sections like Waldie's, is a gathering-up of invisible fragments to remind us of their significance. 'This is', she writes, 'the ordinary affect in the textured, roughened surface of the everyday. It permeates politics of all kinds with the demand that some kind of intimate public of onlookers recognize something in a space of shared impact' (ibid., 39). In noticing and sharing these details and events of the everyday, Stewart creates a 'relay' of sense to spark the reader into a re-engagement, or possibly an astonishment or enchantment, with what is present, but so often ignored, in the world around us. Through this, to follow Jacques Rancière who I quoted at the opening of this chapter, Stewart's 'politics' is concerned with 'the transformation of the sensory fabric of "being together"' through a recognition of affect in the everyday. This, she admits is 'a kind of involuntary and powerful learning and participation', which, I would argue, has the potential for a shift in perception, a re-attuning of our senses to self, region and world (Stewart, 2007, p. 40).

---

[4] Some of the atmosphere of this suburban gothic can be found in David Searcy's *Ordinary Horror* (New York: Viking), 2001, a book admired by Stewart.

Of course, Stewart is not a suburban writer exclusively, but my point is that her attention to the regional worldings of suburbia when placed alongside D. J. Waldie's *Holy Land*, help us reframe how we might engage with these misrepresented spaces. Their combined works read in dialogue remind us of our relations to the everyday regionalisms of ordinary places, like suburbia, with their multiple impacts and traces. It is in this turning, stopping and starting, looking, pausing and even avoiding that we mark our sensual engagements with place and space. Mark Paterson in *Senses of Touch* (2007) refers to 'an "intensive" spatiality of affects . . . between built space and individual resonances', where '[i]n touching and affecting the spaces we move within, we are correspondingly touched and affected' (Paterson, 2007, p. 101). Similarly, for Ben Highmore in *Ordinary Lives* it is the 'pulsings of affect: the risings and fallings of hope, love, hatred and irritation; the minor and major disturbances of life set against and within a world of day-to-day habits, routines and collective sentiments' that are vital expressions of culture (Highmore, 2011, p. xii). It is these 'pulsings' Highmore responds to and describes so well in Stewart's work, and that I would similarly feel in Waldie's work, for, as he puts it, 'As you read the book you become more and more alert to your surroundings. Your skin begins to prickle with the apprehensions of the lives of others, of resonances of care and indifference, of anxiety and ease' (ibid., p. 8). In Stewart's work, as in Waldie's, these feelings emerge most often through stories of suburban life, riffing on the American Dream images of 'home is where the heart is' (Stewart, 2007, pp. 52, 55) only to remind us that like Waldie's aerial view, such ideals are simply a 'still life' made up of myths and dreams awaiting the intrusion of 'everything the heart drags home' and, therefore, always at risk of turning into 'horror stories' that 'take one foot out of the frame' until what one confronts is a very different reality where the 'home cocoon' is no longer a 'still life', but rather 'open, emergent, vulnerable, and jumpy' (ibid.). In the end her affect-narratives are 'about how moving forces are immanent in scenes, subjects, and encounters, or in blocked opportunities or the banality of built environments' (ibid., p. 128). For her, as for Waldie, 'thought' (as she calls it) does not flow naturally from a given and fixed 'way of life', like the still life suburban American Dream, 'but [is] rather something that takes off with the potential trajectories in which it finds itself in the middle' (ibid.).[5] Through all these stories in both *Holy Land* and *Ordinary Affects*, one feels not a sense of suburban inertia or irrelevance, but rather 'tendrils stretching into things I can barely, or not quite imagine' (ibid.). As we journey through the everyday regionalism of Waldie and Stewart suburbia is re-envisioned as a 'world . . . still tentative, charged, overwhelming, and alive'. As Stewart comments on this point of view, 'This is not a good thing or a bad thing. It is not my view that things are going well but that they *are* going' and it is the job of her writing, as it is in Waldie's, to capture this imprecise yet intense feeling (ibid.).

The affective critical regionalism I see in both Waldie and Stewart understands and includes this intense layering of senses and apprehensions in what Lauren Berlant calls the 'zone of convergence of many histories' (Berlant, 2011, p. 10), wherein our

---

[5]   Nigel Thrift argues that affect is 'a form of thinking, often indirect and non-reflective . . . but thinking all the same. . . . Affect is a kind of intelligence about the world . . . attempts to either relegate affect to the irrational or raise it up to the level of the sublime are both equally mistaken.' (2008, p. 175).

production of space is always multiple and complex as it simultaneously and dialogically produces us. In Stewart's words from the passage quoted earlier, 'the ordinary is not so much a deficiency as a resource': suburbs re-thought as (critical) regionality deepen and include, encouraging a kind of expansive inwardness, redolent of Waldie's grid not as a limitation but as a 'compass of possibilities' (Waldie, 1996, p. 4). The regionality of suburbia, in the terms Stewart introduces and which we can trace in the diverse stories of *Holy Land*, connects and crosses over, spreads and intensifies, commingles and flows, shifting from 'public feelings' to 'intimate lives' (Stewart, 2007, p. 2), from daydream to trauma; it 'worlds' even when it begins from an unpromising but 'well-made, wooden bathroom door' in suburban Graywood Avenue, Lakewood, California.

Part IV

Suburban Communities and Cultural Production

12

'A chicken ain't nothin' but a bird': Animals, Suburbia and the Evolving Terrain of Production, Consumption and Representation

Hugh Bartling

As discourses of sustainability and the awareness of the environmental and health impacts of factory farming have become more widespread in the United States in recent years, many residents of urban and suburban communities have become interested in producing their own food. Spurred by popular writers like Michael Pollan and Barbara Kingsolver, celebrity chefs like Jamie Oliver and First Lady Michelle Obama who planted an organic garden at the White House in 2009, gardening and food production has gained in popularity in recent years. While much of this activity is allowable (and encouraged) by local governments, some urban agricultural activity falls outside the limits of permissibility in local zoning codes and land-use ordinances.

While 'urban farming' is multifaceted and international in scope, this chapter looks at the phenomenon in the United States from the standpoint of the political conflict that arises when land-use policy changes are required to accommodate urban agricultural production. On the basis of the analysis of primary documents and interviews, I will specifically look at the conflict around the desire to introduce ordinances allowing micro-scale poultry-keeping in cities and, in particular, suburban communities.

Suburbs are an important site for understanding this emergent conflict for several reasons. First, the bulk of municipal governments that are engaging in debates around changing poultry ordinances are considered 'suburban'. Although the phenomenon of urban chicken-keeping in the United States is prevalent in large cities, many of these older metropolises have never had prohibitions against the practice. Many of the suburbs investigated in this study developed formal restrictions against poultry-keeping during the post-World War Two era of metropolitan expansion as a way to mediate between the interests of new residents attracted to suburbs for a decidedly residential character and older, commercial agricultural enterprises whose practices were perceived as incompatible with residential land uses.

In the intervening years, commercial agriculture has largely disappeared from the suburbs, impacting perceptions of the 'place' of certain types of agriculture in residential settings. Market pressures favouring residential, retail and office land uses as well as consolidation in commercial agriculture has made commercial agriculture infeasible in older suburbs. In these suburbs, however, the laws prohibiting chicken-keeping remain on the books. Given that the motivation of current advocates for urban chicken-keeping is explicitly non-commercial, the ways in which communities negotiate the efficacy of prohibitions written to address a fundamentally different set of circumstances exposes a fundamental conflict about what sorts of practices and behaviours are 'appropriate' for urban life.

A second reason for focusing on suburban settings in this chapter lies in exploring the nature of this cultural conflict. Although there is a long and important literature concerned with interrogating the notion of an urban-suburban divide as well as exploring the heterogeneity of what constitutes 'suburbia', there still persists a set of dominant cultural referents defining acceptable activities in a suburb (e.g. Pack, 2002; Hanlon, Short and Vicino, 2010; Hanlon, 2012). As the realities of suburban heterogeneity become more visible and suburban residents engage in vigorous reconceptualization of suburban norms, conflict is sure to emerge around particular policy decisions. By exploring the rhetorical texture that is manifest in the debates surrounding pressures for a policy shift in the domain of something like chicken-keeping, we can highlight the shifting nature of suburban life and governance which could point to a host of new areas of policy change.

In the remainder of this chapter I will first provide a historical context for the shifting terrain governing animals in the city. Urban food production and animal husbandry have been around as long as cities themselves. For the purposes of this study, I will discuss how processes of industrialization shaped the expectations for agriculture and the city with a specific emphasis on animals. The expansion of the industrial city of the late nineteenth and early twentieth centuries was marked by a changing conception of the relationship between humans and nature. This change has been multifaceted, but of particular import for an understanding of current policy debates, I will briefly look at the literature of suburbanization and the human–animal relationship. While on the surface the connections between these two domains (and their relationship to contemporary policy debates) may appear opaque, I argue that they are essential for understanding the motivations behind the push in many communities to allow chicken-keeping as well as for comprehending the resistance towards such proposals in many quarters. In a sense, the debates over urban chicken-keeping are reflective of a larger ambiguity that characterizes the human relationship to the environment in an era of climate change and concern about the sustainability of the dominant practices of consumption and production.

In the subsequent part of this chapter, I will analyse several contemporary conflicts surrounding efforts to allow suburban chicken-keeping. In particular, I will look at how the policy reform agendas have been articulated and how policy conflict has been framed. I look at a variety of cases in order to generate rich data. No large-n studies have been done on this policy conflict given its relatively recent and rapid resurgence. However, it has been possible to identify a variety of cases in the different geographic regions of the United States. Although the cases emerge within particular, localized contexts, they are similar in the quality of issue framing and rationalization.

I will conclude the chapter with a discussion of how the issue of local policies regulating suburban and urban poultry raising are enmeshed within a larger set of concerns relating to environmental constraints and evolving conceptions about what it means to live in a metropolitan setting. The early part of the twenty-first century has been marked by a whole host of policy problems reflecting the tenuous nature of metropolitan life in North America. From a planning regime that has separated land-use functions making mobility via automobile a necessity to the homogenization of suburban consumption reflected in the proliferation of corporate-owned big boxes, suburbanization – as the dominant mode of metropolitan development – is failing to fulfil a host of social ends for a growing number of people. I will argue that the debate over raising poultry in these settings is an indicator (albeit a rather small one) of this ennui and that efforts to legalize chicken-keeping should be thought as a step towards realizing a new type of urbanism.

Animals and the city

Early in his majestic tome, *The City in History*, the commentator of cities Lewis Mumford (1961) identifies the domestication of plants and animals in the Neolithic period 10,000 years ago as laying the groundwork for urbanism. Being able to manipulate nature through cultivation and husbandry made the nomadic life less urgent and by literally 'putting down roots', humans – accompanied by their plants and animals – began constructing durable edifices, developing infrastructure and creating technologies that expanded the capacity of humanity to manipulate their environment. In the words of Mumford, 'the shaping of the earth was an integral part of the shaping of the city – and preceded it. That intimate biotechnic relationship is one that modern man, with his plans for replacing complex earth-forms and ecological associations with saleable artificial substitutes, disrupts at his peril' (Mumford, 1961, p. 17).

'Modern man's' [sic] 'biotechnic relationship' with the earth and its non-human flora and fauna took on a qualitatively different character during the nineteenth century as capitalism and industrialization began to radically reshape cities. William Cronon, in his environmental history of Chicago, *Nature's Metropolis* (1991), describes how the confluence of a new transportation and communications technology and Chicago's particular geography helped to revolutionize regional agricultural production. Rail lines and grain elevators allowed grain ownership to be fungible and the product itself to be a speculative commodity. The massive stockyards that were erected in the southern part of the city in the 1860s had a similar impact. Cattle and pigs transported on trains could swiftly reach slaughtering facilities in Chicago where they were processed for national and global consumption on an unparalleled scale.

As the latter half of the nineteenth century progressed, these slaughterhouses were increasingly organized around methods of production that would be deployed on a wide scale via Taylor's 'scientific management' practices. In a reverse of the industrial factory's assembly line where disparate component parts were *assembled* in a logical and endlessly repetitive manner, the stockyards and packing plants of cities like

Chicago *disassembled* animal bodies to standardize and increase the pace of producing meat products.

Disassembly lines created a less expensive product and the development of refrigerated train cars allowed meat to be processed and dressed in large centralized facilities and then efficiently distributed throughout the United States. Cronon discusses the contentious nature of this transformation. He recounts that there were significant cultural and economic obstacles that needed to be overcome by the large urban meat packers in order for centrally processed meat to be accepted by consumers and local butchers. Prior to the ascendancy of urban consolidated meat production, live animals were transported directly to the places where they would ultimately be consumed. Local butchers would slaughter the animals and sell the product immediately after butchering.

With the development of refrigerated rail cars and rapid distribution systems spoilage could more easily be avoided making local slaughter less of a necessity from the standpoint of food safety and product viability. Cronon discusses how butchers in smaller midwestern and eastern United States cities initially resisted selling dressed meat, claiming that customers preferred a locally slaughtered product. In response, the large urban meat packers established their own, competing affiliate networks that directly sold and marketed the dressed product. Cronon argues that the combination of this aggressive marketing and lower prices was successful in overcoming consumer hesitancy, marking a significant change in the geography of food consumption and production.

If it was the economic imperative of centralized meat packers to actively create demand for non-locally produced meat, they were assisted by shifting norms relating to acceptable animal behaviour in cities. Geographer Chris Philo (1998) draws comparisons between mid-nineteenth-century London and Chicago and suggests that the urbanization of meat processing and distribution was accompanied by an emergent hostility towards livestock in the city. In the context of rapidly growing cities, livestock contributed to polluted streets and congestion. Speaking of London, Philo charts contemporaneous efforts to link livestock with other urban 'ills' such as prostitution and gambling. Objections towards livestock in the case of London's Smithfield market were justified on the grounds that their unrestrained sexuality and the brutality with which they were treated by drovers was incompatible with refined urban life. In this interpretation, the combination of new demands on scarce urban space and a sense of a new 'urban' sensibility led to the justification for excluding livestock from urban settings.

The development of an urban sensibility was tied to general changes in the labour market and industrialization. Food production as a whole became more mechanized, centralized and globalized restricting farming as a legitimate economic activity to a shrinking number of individuals with access to the capital necessary in order to compete in a geographically dispersed market (Lipman, 1935).

By the twentieth century, as operations for processing large animals such as pigs and cattle were confined to distinct (sub)urban districts, smaller animals like chickens remained a presence in cities. In some locales, chicken-keeping was presented as a part-time endeavour that could supplement wage work and simultaneously be a leisurely diversion from the stress of urban life (Farrington, 1912). This presence, however, was contested. There were two major arenas of conflict related to poultry-raising in the growing metropolis during the early twentieth century that will be revisited in the discussion of contemporary disputes below.

The first is the issue of residential growth encountering commercial poultry operations on the exurban fringe. As the industrial city experienced population growth, new transportation technologies such as the streetcar and the automobile allowed urban expansion to grow in a low-density fashion further from the urban core. One of the major selling points of the new suburbia was that it provided neighbourhoods with single-use land planning so as to physically segregate residential activity from other 'incompatible' uses. This desire would be the impetus for municipal zoning ordinances that proliferated following the landmark 1926 Supreme Court decision in *Euclid v. Ambler* which solidified the constitutionality of zoning. In exurban areas of the rapidly growing metropolis it was not uncommon for new residents to object to the smell and neighbourhood impact of agricultural enterprises like poultry operations and demand action from municipal authorities. In cases when the agricultural businesses predated residential development, new residents argued that the urban engulfment of contested areas was inevitable and that agricultural operations that created nuisances should be closed ('Geese and goats jostle citizens', 1907; 'Suburb wants chicken law', 1908).

Secondly, there was increasing tension between urban residents and neighbourhood butchers and residents who often raised poultry in shop basements or in the yards of mixed-use neighbourhoods. The *Chicago Tribune*, for example, ran a column called 'The legal friend of the people' where readers would ask the newspaper's advice on how to resolve local problems through the municipality and the courts. Every few months readers would write with complaints about the noise and smell emanating from small-scale poultry raising. The response from the *Tribune*'s columnist was consistent – in the absence of any ordinance prohibiting chicken-keeping in Chicago, residents had to rely on the city enforcing general nuisance provisions to resolve problems between neighbours.[1] Although there is no census of chicken-keeping in the early twentieth-century industrial city, there is evidence to suggest that some of the objections to the practice were likely bound up with scepticism of immigrant populations as in a 1909 *Chicago Daily Tribune* article that asserted 'in short, wherever immigrants who stand on the lowest scale of industry live, thousands of chickens are being raised. Many a family in these districts may live in two basement rooms only – it may have no room for its children to play in, but it has a bit of space, a two by four coop, wherein chickens are kept' ('Many chicken farms in Chicago slums', 1909, p. H2). In this case, objections towards chicken-keeping must be understood within the context of increasing heterogeneity, class biases and the insufficient housing conditions characteristic of the industrial city.

Conflict over the use of urban space was not exclusive to issues involving agriculture or animals. Rather this conflict should be thought of within the context of a wide variety

---

[1]   For examples of tension between neighbours see the 'Legal friend of the people' columns published in the *Chicago Daily Tribune*: 11 May 1914, p. 6; 2 July 1917, p. 8; 14 June 1917; 23 May 1921, p. 8; for examples of tension involving grocers and butchers see: 3 January 1916, p. 8; 7 May 1921, p. 6.

of differences related to the nature of urban life that accompanied industrialization and massive population growth. Concern over pollution, housing and working conditions revealed a growing discontent for the dominant social, economic and ecological practices of the industrial city. While the manifestations of and responses to this conflict were multifaceted, for the purposes of this discussion, I will focus on suburbanization and the use of municipal regulatory power as an important response to urban conflict.

There is an ample literature in US urban history that explores the idea of the industrial city as disorderly and socially unsustainable and examines the various responses to resolve these perceived social ills (Boyer, 1978; Smith, 1996; Pile, Brook and Mooney, 1999). Of these responses, suburbanization was probably one of the most dramatic. While suburbanization has a long history (Bruegmann, 2005), the post-Civil War expansion of suburbia took on a particular character. As mentioned above, new transportation technologies allowed for greater geographic dispersion of population in metropolitan areas allowing the value associated with proximity to urban centres to be re-evaluated.

The historian Carl Smith (1995), in his study of nineteenth-century Chicago, focuses on the 'disorderly' nature of the city and situates responses like railroad magnate George Pullman's eponymous planned community outside of the boundaries of the industrial city as an effort to reform existing urbanism by literally constructing a new city. In place of Chicago's chaotic land use that mixed residences, factories and saloons in incompatible ways, Pullman invented the city anew where order and separation of land functions were privileged. Pullman was tied to the orbit of Chicago (upon which it relied for its economic viability), but was physically and socially separate, allowing for greater control of the social and physical conditions.

Although Pullman's rather utopian visions for urbanism were unable to function within the confines of his requirements for corporate profit (Lindsey, 1942), the idea of a functional space in proximity to but separate from the city was compelling in many quarters. Perhaps most influential in this regard was the idea of the 'garden city', developed by Ebeneezer Howard in 1898. Howard argued for a middle landscape between the country and the city. This garden city would include the employment, recreational and cultural opportunities offered by the city, but be built on a small scale and planned in such a way as to afford residents with a salubrious, manageable environment. Like Pullman's town, districts in the garden city are segregated by function in a rational and efficient way in order to maximize social gain in the community.

The concept of segregating function through deliberate planning animated the effort to develop municipal 'districting' or zoning laws. While New York was the first US city to establish zoning in the first decade of the twentieth century, the policy instrument was quickly adopted by suburban municipalities. Owing to the suburb's nascent nature, zoning therein created a better opportunity than in the city for rationally configuring land use. Zoning was firmly established as a tool for municipal land-use policy by the mid-twentieth century, just as the middle-class suburban 'revolution' commenced.

Much of the criticism of post-war zoning practice tends to be focused on its exclusionary nature, which created homogeneous municipalities and segregated economic, educational and housing opportunities for people based on race and class (Babcock, 1966; Downs, 1973; Jackson, 1987). Processes of suburbanization also served a cultural function helping to define what social, economic and ecological practices are 'acceptable' in suburban space. Beauregard (2006), for example, connects suburbia with an ethic of consumption that began to dominate post-war metropolitan development. Suburbs were planned to accommodate consumption through the laying out of streets, the particularities of zoning and land-use restrictions. While 'suburban culture' was articulated in a diversity of forms (e.g. media representations, socialization pressures, advertising), the planned environment (and the land-use policies that shaped its contours) provided the space for actively engaging in suburban life. The policies and practices experienced in suburban settings help to formulate the norms and land-use policy expectations that have been called into question by the contemporary efforts to modify land-use laws to allow chicken-keeping.

Rethinking suburbia: A Chicken Ain't Nothing But a Bird

In this part, I will discuss the current movement in many areas of the United States to reform laws restricting poultry-keeping in urban and suburban settings. I will focus in particular on the factors motivating reformers and the resistance experienced in many communities to these new initiatives. I will conclude by linking these efforts within the context of the historical development informing the shifting terrain of acceptable suburban practice. Chicken-keeping, I will argue, is a modest – but important – reflection of a larger dissatisfaction with the dominant practices that frame modern metropolitan life. In a world marked by the uncertainties of the global ecology and economy and the social ramifications generated by such uncertainties, these localized movements can be thought of as an effort to reassert a different and, perhaps, more sustainable mode of political, economic and ecological action.

Over the past decade there have been numerous studies of the phenomenon of small-scale urban agriculture and gardening in the United States and elsewhere. While in some cases, like Cuba, the impetus for urban agriculture projects has been a product of immediate economic necessity, in the context of countries like the United States and Canada urban agricultural projects have been undertaken for a variety of reasons. In many cities non-profit organizations have developed innovative projects using under-valued land in distressed neighbourhoods to provide local jobs and healthy food to neighbourhood residents (Feenstra, 1997). Others have emerged to link commercial chefs and a wider range of consumers with fresh and local ingredients, while simultaneously linking ecological concerns for soil fertility into the larger discussion of food insecurity (Broadway, 2009). Urban agriculture has also experienced a renaissance on a more micro-scale in the form of the rise of community gardens and garden-sharing projects as engines of neighbourhood community-building (Blake and Cloutier-Fisher, 2009) and regeneration (Zukin, 2010).

Urban agriculture's expansion has occurred within the context of a simultaneous emphasis in environmental thought and practice on the advantages of 'local thinking'. The Local Agenda 21 movement stemming from the 1992 Earth Summit in Rio put the city and metropolitan region in a prominent place for forging policies purporting to be environmentally sustainable. Along with improvements in transportation and building performance, enhancing green space, gardening and food production began to be taken seriously in municipal policy and planning circles (Beatley and Manning, 1997; Nordahl, 2010). Along with more interest in 'sustainable cities', there has been a parallel effort over the past ten years to closely examine the ecological consequences of the dominant industrial food supply (Kloppenburg et al., 1996). Journalists writing to a large audience like Eric Schlosser (2001) and Michael Pollan (2006) have given mainstream audiences compelling critiques of the industrial food system. In turn, this greater awareness has led to consumer demand for organic and local foods (Starr et al., 2002).

Along with the expansion of farmers markets and the corporate deployment of 'local' sourcing of food, the late part of the first decade of the twenty-first century also saw a renaissance in gardening, with major seed companies seeing record demand for their product (Reimer, 2010). With all of these factors appearing concomitantly – sustainable cities discourse, popular critiques of globalization and the industrial production of food, an increase in the popularity of gardening – localized movements to allow urban poultry appeared as well.

Because of the nascent, rapid and decentralized nature of urban poultry legalization efforts, there is little in the way of systematic research to draw upon in order to understand the movement. Governmental agencies in the United States such as the US Department of Agriculture collect no data on micro-poultry flocks. Because the efforts to change poultry laws are at the municipal level where local officials have the authority to regulate land-use, developing a comprehensive data set on local poultry laws and debates surrounding them has not been undertaken.

This chapter represents an initial effort to develop a general understanding of this new phenomenon. The data analysed herein are primary documents from city council meetings and other municipal advisory boards that advise local officials in the area of planning, land-use and health and secondary documents garnered from news reports and websites created by groups seeking to change local ordinances. Cities were selected through a two-year period of monitoring internet news aggregators for relevant reports.

In most of the cities examined, the movements to amend restrictive ordinances were initiated by citizen activists who connected through neighbourhood interactions or social networking internet sites. Consequently, advocates were well organized and in many cases they have developed research and educational materials to bolster their case for reform. Opponents tended to be isolated individuals or sceptical elected officials who were not necessarily convinced that reform would be in the best interests of their respective cities.

The variety of arguments made by advocates of chicken-keeping can be broken down into several categories involving ecology, education, health and alternative models of consumption. Opponents to revising laws prohibiting poultry deploy arguments pertaining to a desire to maintain a particular vision and meaning of urban space, a concern over perceived health risks, and a modernist ecological conception.

The ecology of chicken-keeping

A consistent refrain from advocates is that urban chicken-keeping is an ecologically beneficial endeavour. In a public hearing before the city council of Gresham, Oregon, an advocate argued that chicken waste's properties as a fertilizer will militate against the use of artificial fertilizer in citizens' gardens resulting in less fuel being used to transport fertilizer in to town from afar. Other advocates extolled chickens' ability to eat kitchen scraps and other waste normally destined to be dumped in landfills, thus potentially reducing the city's waste stream (City of Gresham, 2009).

The issue of chicken-keeping as a response to climate change also was brought up as beneficial in debates. After the city council of Missoula, Montana voted to reject an urban chicken ordinance, a state-wide environmental group, the Montana Conservation Voters, highlighted how each city councillor voted on the ordinance in their annual 'scorecard' of Missoula elected officials. Along with more traditional environmentalist concerns like open-lands preservation and municipal shifts to renewable energy, the group felt that the chicken ordinance was important since '85–90% of Missoula's food comes from elsewhere, relying on fossil fuel dependent transportation. So as residents become increasingly concerned with climate change . . . they gravitate toward greater self-reliance' (Montana Conservation Voters, 2009). Relatedly, during the public comment period at a city meeting in New Haven, Connecticut, one citizen 'associated hen keeping with a response to climate change, high energy costs and re-localization' (Legislation Committee, 2009).

Rethinking consumption

In many locales, advocates for chicken-keeping assert that structural obstacles outlawing the practice are either outdated or insufficient for addressing contemporary concerns about the perceived fragility of economic opportunities during a prolonged period of stagnant wages and increasing prices for many essential commodities. These obstacles are manifest in many ways. One way is in the 'framing' of chickens and their relationship to human owners. A common refrain in many public deliberations regarding poultry-keeping is what 'kind' of animals are chickens: pets, livestock or some hybrid?

The 'existential ambiguity' of chickens serves as a significant point of disagreement between reformers and defenders of the status quo. A debate from a city council meeting in Bingen, Washington is exemplary. At the behest of a citizen who kept a duck without knowing that poultry was forbidden in the town, the council deliberated about what constitutes 'livestock'. After members of the public and council members spoke positively about the citizen's illegal duck suggesting that illegal poultry was posing no problem, one council member is described as saying 'she thinks there are reasons why the ordinance exists'. This prompted an intervention from the Mayor who thought 'that a definition separating an animal as a pet versus an animal used for another purposes such as for food might be appropriate' (City of Bingen, 2009).

Poultry ordinance reformers often contribute to this ambiguity, describing hens as both pets and sources of food; although in talking of the food potential of chickens, emphasis is usually placed on their egg-producing capacity, rather than their meat. While some chicken owners are unabashedly raising hens for both eggs and meat, there is little evidence of active enthusiasm for permitting on-site butchering in reform efforts. In fact, in most of the cases analysed in this study where ordinances have been reformed, butchering of birds is prohibited.

Nevertheless, the potential of eggs and their place in a mode of consumption outside of the market model is given great prominence in the pleas by ordinance reformers. For example, in the case of Sanford, North Carolina an advocate who had been keeping chickens illegally for 16 years before being found out by the city, argued that Sanford's ordinance should be changed because 'in a typical week, his chickens lay five to eight dozen fresh eggs. The eggs are used by his family, his wife's daycare, and he gives the eggs away to the homeless shelter run by Pastor Donald Kivett' (City of Sanford, 2009, p. 2). The advocate was also supported by testimony from representatives of food banks and homeless shelters all of whom argued that they are serving poor populations in need of assistance and that eggs are a valuable commodity that they are unable to afford on the limited budgets of non-profit agencies (City of Sanford, 2009).

From the standpoint of rethinking consumption, on the one hand advocates for allowing chicken-keeping are facing resistance due to the unique (metropolitan) nature of the request. Unlike a dog or a cat, which are common animals for people to own and which have a prominent infrastructure supporting ownership (in the guise of pet stores, their place in advertising and popular culture, etc.), owning live chickens is unusual. The 'normal' presence of the animal in the urban and suburban landscape is in its inanimate form, safely ensconced in grocery store refrigerators. Under the dominant logic of urban zoning policy animals are either pets (accepted and regulated), wild (managed) or livestock (prohibited). Chickens do not conform to this typology and in this sense their hybridic nature is difficult for non-enthusiasts to embrace.

Education and health

Many of the debates for chicken ordinance reform are focused on health and education. Much of this discourse is directly critical of the dominant industrial food system. Advocates for reform often assert that many people are unaware of the practices of industrial agriculture and want to use chicken-keeping as a way to show (especially children) the actual origin of food. In some cases, advocates also extol locally grown eggs as having nutritional benefits exceeding those of industrial eggs. Within the context of an industrial food system that many perceive as insufficiently regulated, backyard poultry advocates argue that they feel safer by having more control over their food supply.

While health concerns are a major rationale deployed on the part of reformers, health issues are also mentioned by opponents and sceptics as a reason to maintain urban poultry prohibitions. Most of these objections are related to a concern about salmonella, avian flu and the potential for an increase in the community of rodents or predators that might be attracted to the chicken coops.

Criticisms and conclusions

Interestingly, arguments of opponents surrounding a fear of avian flu and of contaminated food supply suggest a possible point of convergence with reform advocates. These maladies also motivate those who want to be able to keep backyard chickens as well. Both express a recognition that dominant practices of industrial agricultural production are potentially problematic. The two sides diverge in their explanation for the causes of the problems with the former equating maladies with the animals themselves and the latter questioning more directly the social practices of industrial agriculture.

In some sense the divergences could be explained by differences in understanding the nature of food production and are reflective of the disconnect between urban communities and their food supply which reformers are trying to bridge. Because the prohibitions in many communities were put in place within a cultural and ideological context whereby the industrial food system was becoming a 'natural' component of a consumptive landscape which segregated production from consumption, their seeming permanence presents a challenge for reformers. While there is a legitimate concern about the possibility of nuisance and impacts on neighbouring properties generated by chicken-keeping, much of the response on the part of elected officials is marked by an incredulity as to why anyone would want to spend the time raising chickens.

In College Township, Pennsylvania, for example, an individual appeared before the planning commission to advocate for an overturn of the ordinance prohibiting chicken-keeping. Armed with blueprints of the proposed coop and affidavits from neighbours endorsing the project, one plan commissioner reacted to the presentation by saying that 'it deserved an A+ however, he still does not agree with chickens in a residential neighborhood' (College Township Planning Commission, 2009). In several cases opponents or reform sceptics were worried about chickens as a 'gateway animal'. The fear is that a precedent would be set whereby 'if we allow chickens in then what if someone asks for a pig or a lamb' (City of Pleasant Grove, 2010, p. 4).

Given the analysis presented here and the shifting cultural context of urbanism, agriculture and consumption presented above, the conflict surrounding chicken ordinance reform can be read as a modest manifestation of the contested nature of the social uncertainty around the practices of food production, economic development and environmental despoliation at this particular historical moment. By presenting the historical discussion of animals and food production in the city, I have shown that there has been a long historical precedence for particular urban agriculture practices and that the policies that prompted their disappearance and prohibition came out of a particular set of historical circumstances: namely, rapidly growth of a suburban landscape coupled with a shift in production and consumption that made localized food production a necessary casualty of modernity's 'progress'.

As the notion of the spatial segregation of consumption and production in agriculture and other sectors of the economy became normalized, the logic of forbidding production animals in urban and suburban settings followed. Food provision for metropolitan citizens became an exclusive part of the domain of market interactions. Grocery stores and restaurants provided foodstuffs for workers in the industrial or post-industrial economy who no longer had the time, need or inclination to engage in direct food production. The simultaneous industrialization and globalization of the food production system ensured that prices remained low and product selection increased in diversity.

As argued above, a change in perception as to the feasibility of this system of food provision began to be rigorously pursued in the late twentieth and early twenty-first centuries. This challenge – which is reflected at the municipal level by the poultry-keeping reform movement – is reflective of a larger uncertainty about economic and ecological sustainability. Examples provided from contributions to the public discourse by reformers suggest that urban chicken-keeping is a response to a perceived systemic dysfunction. As indicated in the examples, reformers link their desire to keep chickens with concerns about the safety of industrial food, climate change and potential economic disruptions. Efforts are informed less by solipsistic desires and more by a desire to engage in micro-practices of resistance.

In the absence of longitudinal data pertaining to local chicken-keeping reform efforts, it is difficult to definitively argue about general trends. However, the proliferation of news stories, websites and ancillary data suggests that a reform movement is underway. Since most of the opposition to reform tends to be based on impressions and preconceived perceptions – as opposed to widespread experience with the actual practice of chicken-keeping in cities – the next step in considering the significance of these localized efforts will be to see how cities' re-introduction of production animals translates into the shifting social understanding of urbanism. Although the success of reform efforts is rather nascent, the movement could act as a harbinger of a larger reconceptualization of metropolitan life that impacts other policy sectors such as zoning, transportation and economic development. To borrow from the 1930s Babe Wallace song popularized by Cab Calloway, a chicken may be 'nothin' but a bird'; or it could be a signpost on the way to a different kind of city.

13

Kvart KVART: Contemporary Art Activism in Suburban Split, Croatia

Dalibor Prančević

kvart = Part of a town which consists of several streets; neighbourhood, area; in the former Yugoslavia a district police office that had jurisdiction over a certain part of town was referred to as a 'kvart'.

KVART = Association of Contemporary Art, established in Split, Croatia in 2006; constituted of local artists involved in the promotion and development of art and who investigate contemporary society through public and community art projects; the organization's financial support comes from various sources (ranging from the city and state funds to private donors).

Peripheral space

The title of the conference 'Peripheral Visions: Suburbs, Representation and Innovation', at which an earlier version of this chapter was delivered, contains the determinant 'peripheral', which corresponds to an interesting connecting thread in a theoretical art history text from the Croatian cultural frame. The text, titled *On the Influence of Local Ambience on the Art of Croatia*, was published in 1963 and written by the distinguished art historian, conservator and cultural worker, Ljubo Karaman (1886–1971). The book was re-printed in 2001 under the title *The Problems of Peripheral Art*. In it Karaman examines the interference of different cultural spaces, primarily those which were dislocated in relation to progressive centres. While dealing exclusively with examples of artistic activity in the Croatian national context, Karaman introduces three very useful categories:

- 'Provincial society' (and, correspondingly, provincial art), which denotes a society of prevailingly 'pastoral' character, living and developing in the shadow of a larger cultural centre; its expression is inspired by that centre yet also accords with its own, often humble, economic and social circumstances.

- 'Boundary society' (and, correspondingly, boundary art), which denotes a society characterized by its position at the boundary of direct influence of at least two significantly different artistic circles, which often creates within its own artistic production a hybrid of those two cultural inputs.
- 'Peripheral society' (and, correspondingly, peripheral art), which denotes a society which is positioned at a certain distance from the dominant cultural regions and which is influenced from multiple sources. By adopting and processing these various influences, such a society develops its own independent local artistic activity. As Karaman writes: 'The most interesting characteristic of peripheral society is the independent development which such a society, unbound by authority and examples of great masters and their grand monuments, sometimes provides to the masters that work within it.' (Karaman, 1963, p. 7)

These terminological determinants suggested by Karaman should be understood not as rigid canons but as directional signs for observation and interpretation, and the borders between them should be understood as relatively fluid. In any case, it is interesting to note the freedom of activity and independence which are being imputed to the peripheral society – which is a productive frame for discussing the contemporary art situation in the town of Split.

Referring to that same theoretical platform which examines forms of 'free activity' at the periphery, architectural theorist Ivan Rupnik (2010) explains recent architectural practice in Croatia. The 1990s in Croatia were defined not only by the Homeland War but also by the transformation of its sociopolitical system. The instability that marked the period of transition towards a post-socialist condition opened up a productive space for architectural experimentation, whereby adverse conditions became stimuli for creative architectural activity. In the emergence of new architectural offices (e.g. 3LHD STUDIO UP, njiric+njiric and Randić-Turato) Rupnik recognizes innovative platforms for thinking about architecture and urban planning and provides examples of realized architecture within the municipal entity that are characterized by a strong local charge. However, political instability and creative innovation, says Rupnik, are not just characteristics of recent Croatian history: throughout its history there were many such periods, particularly the Romanesque and Renaissance, as discussed in Karaman's theoretical text. Yet, it seems that over the past few years the movement towards 'peripheral freedom' in Croatia has been overtaken by 'provincial reality'.[1] Rupnik explains this development as a delayed consequence of the rapid transformation of Croatian society in the 1990s (2010, pp. 15–16).

Much has changed since Karaman considered this subject in *On the Influence of Local Ambience on the Art of Croatia*. The flow of information in today's internet era has brought about completely different levels of interference and exchanges of experience. Here I am not so much interested in making a judgement about the originality and quality of artistic production as I am mapping the organizational structures and locations of cultural events in order to determine the politics of their distribution. It appears that the centre still continues to reserve the right to a greater concentration of

---

[1] In this context it is essential to make a clear distinction between the creative and innovative potential of 'the periphery' and the petit-bourgeois passivity of 'the province'.

cultural events, which when they move towards the periphery become more curiosities rather than stable practice. Throughout this chapter I shall try to demonstrate that outside of virtual space (i.e. the interconnectedness of virtual reality), the model of the established centre and dependent periphery is still operational.[2]

However, the city in general appears to be a pulsating organism, that is, an open system subject to change, which nonetheless retains easily recognizable historical layers. In this context, peripheral zones are actually areas of urban expansion that respond more easily to political, social and economic change. The historical city centre, although not completely immune to change, is less subject to radical architectural or urban interventions, so the focus of new neoliberal financiers and investors rather moves to the peripheral zones. Generally, the sole aim of the new business elites is to gain profit. The newly built residential facilities, as well as oversized shopping malls, both developed without adequate public space, encourage new critical positions, including in particular the growing artistic activism which will become the focal point of this chapter.

The disappearance of cultural content

Looking at contemporary art events in Croatia it is easy to track their centralist model. Many institutions that deal with contemporary artistic practices as well as the rich variety of non-institutional practice position the Croatian capital of Zagreb as the major centre of cultural events. This pattern, however, is replicated in regional contexts where major cities have supremacy over the smaller towns and finally to the urban organism itself: many peripheral parts are completely 'free' of cultural events, particularly the visual arts. In a sense it is possible to discuss the phenomenon of the disappearance of cultural content with reference to a geographic plan.

I now turn to the 'art-situation' in Split, the second-largest Croatian city that is proud of its rich cultural heritage. It is often pointed out that it is also the biggest city on the East Coast of the Adriatic, with a population of 178,192 according to the most recent data (City of Split, n. d.). The renowned Diocletian's Palace is at the heart of the city centre, out of which grew the Split of today. It is important to note that Diocletian's Palace, together with the historical city centre, is inscribed in the UNESCO World Heritage List, which affords it special protection from most architectural interpolations. Immediately following the Second World War Split experienced rapid transformation, when it was developed as the economic, industrial and transit centre of the region. These functions were proscribed in the so-called Base regulatory directive for the city of Split of 1951, which compiled the basic guidelines of 'stratigraphy' for the urban development of Split (Majić, 2011). Within the newly established socialist system, this plan positions Split as the main political, administrative and cultural centre of the entire region of Central Dalmatia, and as an important port and industrial zone. Notably there was no reference to the development of tourism, even though it would have been

---

[2] Lately there has been much discussion in Croatian society about the need to decentralize the organizational structure of cultural activity; however, all efforts remain to a large extent declarative in nature (see Bajo and Bronić, 2004; Rogić Lugarić, 2005).

justified because of the city's unusually beautiful coastline and excellent climate. The citizens of Split were unsatisfied with such a developmental plan and they objected to it. In further discussion the authorities gave them banal explanations:

> Namely, during a public debate on the Regulatory Plan Directive when the question of why it was not planned for Split to become a tourist centre was raised, the response that was given was that Split will be an industrial port, so there is no need for it to appropriate tourism as well. It is considered that the development of tourism was an earlier tendency, which was based on the commercial development of the city. Split is a transit industrial port that leads to other tourist destinations. (ibid., p. 18)

Changes which have taken place during the last two decades have significantly altered the cityscape by systematically erasing 'factory chimneys' and at the same time promoting the appearance of 'shopping mastodons'. Despite significant changes, the centralist model is largely operational in the urban structure and organization of Split. It is evident that all cultural institutions, especially those engaged in visual arts, as well as all cultural events, are grouped around the very centre of the city. Meanwhile the peripheral zones are completely devoid of them. The new urban landscapes in the peripheral areas are increasingly dominated by new commercial facilities. For example, the disproportionately large buildings of the new shopping centres (Bauhaus, Mercator, City Center), whose commercial architecture resembles boxes, feature signs positioned high on their exterior walls, signifying places exclusively for consumption.

KVART at the urban periphery and the 'politics of consciousness'

The semantic play with the term 'kvart' is here used in order to underline the 'territory of activity'. This term signifies the strategy of breaking the tissue of the city, that is, separating the city into zones that are found to be more or less in a position of subordination to the centre. Yet it seems that the significance of territorial belonging to a district becomes stronger the further away from the city centre one goes. According to the 'Dictionary of loanwords in the Croatian language' by Bratoljub Klaić, 'kvart' is defined as part of town which consists of several streets, that is, a neighbourhood or area; in the former Yugoslavia the district police office that had jurisdiction over a certain part of town was referred to as a 'kvart' (Klaić, 2007). In 2006 a group of artists from Split founded the Association of Contemporary Art KVART, choosing this particular name in order to define the specific territory on the city's edge where they live and work. Their activities centre on the promotion, development and enrichment of the contemporary art scene and researching contemporary society by means of artistic interventions in the immediate and wider community. What is most valuable about the recent efforts of the artistic collective KVART is the manner in which they break the cohesion of this centralized system in order to make visible the exploitation and misappropriation of resources situated in suburban areas.

As a matter of fact, KVART was founded as a response to the need for clear critical speech in response to the many problems faced by the local community, many of which related to the loss of public space. The actions of KVART are focused on the municipal district of Trstenik which has suffered due to the erosion of the practice of perennial domicile thanks to profiteering developers, who have been able to act so freely following Croatia's recent transition to neoliberal capitalism. Trstenik is one of Split's districts or quarters located at the south-eastern part of the city. Its name derives from a local brook and a cove into which the brook flows. According to latest data its population numbers around 7,000. Although this city district has key infrastructure such as a health clinic, primary school and a section of the city library, like many other marginal quarters of the city of Split, Trstenik is devoid of places for cultural articulation. It should not be forgotten that parts of the city district that have not been developed yet are located in the immediate vicinity of the sea, and represent a prime target for private investors whose only motive for developing public spaces is, once again, profit.

It is impossible to detail all of the actions performed by this 'artistic collective'; however, some of them have alarmed representatives of the local authority and caused some unpleasant public scandals. Artists who have actively participated in KVART events and public interventions are: Zvonimir Bakotin, Andro Banovac, Duška Boban, Milan Brkić, Luka Duplančić, Boris Cvjetanović, Rino Efendić, Marko Marković, Željko Marović, Ivan Svaguša, Boris Šitum, Šimun Šitum, Marin Zorić. All of these artists permanently reside in this particular part of town, or were invited as its guests.

As pointed out above, the Republic of Croatia entered a tumultuous period following the disintegration of Yugoslavia and the rejection of its socialist system, and during its transformation towards a new sociopolitical paradigm at the beginning of the 1990s. As a result, popular developments such as the establishment of an independent Croatian state were accompanied by other more controversial processes. One of these was the transformation of social ownership (of, for example, industrial plants, trade companies, etc.), that is privatization, the first wave of which occurred in the first half of the 1990s. During this time the Republic of Croatia was still embroiled in the Homeland War which significantly weakened the apparatus of the state. Establishing the 'rule' of private concerns over the public interest led to the usurpation of public spaces in the cities, which greatly disturbed its citizens and caused protests throughout the country. The consequences of such fundamental re-organization have become even more evident today across all segments of social life, which have led to frequent activist campaigns aimed at animating anew its citizens in order for them to be able to critically respond to the present situation, and in particular the transformation of the city. The main issue has been the exclusion of the local population from active and direct decision-making processes regarding the transformation and management of public space, stimulating a range of locally organized counter campaigns. For example, following the demilitarization of the coastal area around the historic city of Pula, buildings once used by the army found themselves taken over by private interests at the expense of the general public, prompting the 'Katarina 06' project by The Pula Group (see Jurcan et al., 2006). A similar situation transpired in Dubrovnik: a plan to construct a golf course at the Srđ hill overlooking the city, which would have significantly limited public access, spurred the civil initiative 'Srđ Is Ours'. These are only two of the recent initiatives whose number has grown exponentially in recent times.

Within this context, the aim of actions performed by the art collective KVART may be also described as 'the politics of consciousness' and are directed at provoking the local population, motivating them to look at new relationships, while also actively including them in direct artistic actions. Members of KVART mostly operate outside formal exhibition spaces. Their actions take place, for example, in playgrounds, garages and beaches, in order to foreground the public function and accessibility of such locations.

The activities of KVART are organized not only as individual projects by some of its members, but also as joint actions. The presentation of the results of the yearly fermentation of their critical thinking is especially productive. The titles of these annual events signify basic warning signals for the local community and are indicative of an responsive attitude towards the situation faced by their immediate environment, or *kvart*. The first of such yearly actions, titled 'Trstenik OPEN-END', was organized in 2007 and involved artistic interventions in local public spaces to highlight the problems of living in the housing 'mastodons' that were built during the so-called epoch of late socialist modernism (see Unfinished Modernisations, 2012). Artists intervened in public spaces of the district using textual and pictorial strategies in order to re-evaluate the present condition and essential human needs, in order to comment on the role of such spaces as sites of community and social contact, and to highlight the fact that such spaces are disappearing (Figure 13.1).

Figure 13.1 Project 'Trstenik OPEN-END', 2007; art-intervention at local playground
Photograph: Author

Fragmented insight: Questions to be asked
on the outskirts of Split

Although the art collective KVART operates at the urban periphery, and its actions refer mainly to the problems of the local community, it also seeks to highlight some of the crucial problems faced by Croatian society more widely. It is important here to emphasize its peripheral position in order to draw attention to certain freedoms which are, according to Karaman's thesis, inherent to the peripheral context. Outside of the city centre – where systems of control are often strongest – the district of Trstenik provided the artists with a significantly freer context for action. This is the first time an art collective has been established in the city of Split and, over the course of several years, it has consistently affirmed the principle of civil participation in art projects. This is certainly not an unknown practice in twentieth-century art; however, this is a new mode of artistic activity and organization in Split. It should be noted that I am not referring here to the participation of thousands of people. Nevertheless, even the minority that recognized the possibility of direct participation in the art project accomplished certain results which will be described below.

One of the main concerns of KVART is the official policy – both at the state and local authority level – of the use of public space. In this context, worthy of mention is 'Trstenik BEACH', a project organized in 2009, which deals with the transformation of urban space, with a special emphasis on the beach area. Since one part of the Trstenik beach is located near the newly renovated hotel Radisson Blu, the fear has been that it might be adapted exclusively for hotel guests thereby limiting the local community's access. Their artistic takeover of Trstenik beach as a franchise demonstrates the possibility of protecting public spaces from the intrusion of private interests. In one instance, the collective declared their aim of establishing:

> [a public] swimming zone for parents and children with developmental disabilities, creating signalization for blind persons, access and ramps for the disabled, bicycle tracks, eco-toilets for animals and people, eco-lighting, opening of the mobile UNICEF-library for children, prefabricated art-galleries for exhibition activities (exhibitions, performances, installations, body-art, lectures, video and art-park, etc.), affirmation of gay and nudist parts of the beach, installing a telescope for space observation and performing other tourist activities (renting sun umbrellas, beach-beds, beach canoes and boats, etc.).

The above is an extract from an art document, signed by Milan Brkić, which was placed alongside the beach promenade as a billboard. Besides protesting against private interests, it also tries not just to point to the issues of adapting this type of public space to people with 'special needs', but also to affirm the idea of 'difference' and 'otherness'. This work by Brkić was meant to trigger an examination of the extent to which the citizens were tolerant of 'difference' and receptive to the idea of 'choice'. It is symptomatic of the heteronormativity of contemporary Croatian society that soon after the billboard was erected, part of the poster with text referring to the 'gay' population was censored. This detail is rendered significant by the events of 11 June 2011 when the first Gay Pride in the city centre of Split was disrupted by homophobic militants, which reflects how basic human rights and freedoms are not universally upheld in contemporary Croatia. Despite the presence of security forces – because the event was deemed 'high-risk' – the programme was interrupted and participants (several of whom sustained injuries from objects hurled at them) were evacuated from the city centre to their homes (it was feared that if they were not removed from the city centre they would subsequently have been beaten). The obvious question is why were those citizens who threatened and resorted to violence not isolated instead? There is then an obvious need for cultural interventions like Brkić's which question the limits of tolerance. What though is the concrete effect of KVART's 'occupation of the beach'? Its true value is in sensitizing the public to the idea of diversity and of the right to public space – in this case the 'maritime demesne' as the common good which is the property of all (*res communis omnium*). Such heightened public awareness is evident in one recent affair. In 2012, a Saudi prince was denied his request to enclose a portion of the Trstenik beach for private use. Radisson Blu Hotel, where he stayed, was denied a concession for commercial exploitation of the maritime demesne. Plutocracy and the illegal usurpation of public space was in this case indeed prevented by articulations of public interest.

One action that testifies to the direct pressure exerted by KVART on the local authorities was called 'The Investigation'. It was concerned with the pollution of a rainfall creek inside the beach zone, caused by an illegal discharge of wastewater which happens periodically, directly endangering the health of swimmers. The collective clearly expressed its request for urgent investigation and processing of the case, by means of a billboard. The billboard clearly displayed the word 'investigation' as well as a group portrait of artists standing in the creek. This act of artistic 'advertising' together with the utilization of the word 'investigation', with its powerful performative value, achieved results. One might assume that individuals who caused the pollution realized the implications of their illegal activity and they soon desisted. Local authorities increased levels of supervision of the creek as well. In any case, following such artistic intervention, there has been no further contamination of the beach.

Several actions of the KVART art collective are focused on the right to green space such as parks, which provide opportunities for the local community to socialize, and resistance to new construction projects which fail to include such spaces. One such action was called 'The Right to Sight', in which members of the local community together with the artists wore blindfolds and stopped traffic, thus pointing to the loss of the city tailored to man (Figure 13.2). This loss is primarily manifested in the inertia of the majority of the population who seem to be blindly observing the non-transparent policy of management of public spatial resources.

Planned property development gave way to individual buildings whose sole purpose is to generate profit from their sale. Such buildings alter the urban landscape and oftentimes obstruct the view of the surroundings from extant buildings. With this action the artists point to the lack of organized urban planning and supervision, which might provide better guidance to such construction. (Notably the Urban Planning Bureau of Dalmatia – an important institution charged with taking care of development

Figure 13.2 Project 'Trstenik RIGHT TO SIGHT', 2010
Photograph: Author

in the city – was closed in 1993.) The title of the action paraphrases the title of David Harvey's 2008 book *The Right to the City*, in which he argues for that most precious, yet most neglected of human rights. The right to the city, says Harvey, involves far more than just an individual freedom; it includes a feeling of community that derives from actually and actively being part of one. It is therefore more appropriate to understand the right to the city as a common right. After identifying radical changes to the spatial forms of our cities, Harvey concludes that profit serves as the basic corrective (i.e. the trigger and basis) in the adaptation of city resources. He contends that the right to the city is usurped by the unstoppable appetite of neoliberal financial practice, and is limited exclusively to political and financial elites that administer money and power. Thus Harvey recommends the right to the city as a common working slogan and a political ideal, in order to realize a true democratization of that right.

Statements made by the protagonists of the art collective KVART during the action 'The Right to Sight' are of particular interest because they literally rest on Harvey's open critique of economists and bankers, advocates of money and power. Boris Šitum sarcastically commented on the reality of his own suburban environment which is so embroiled in murky transactions motivated by greed: 'We salute the construction of a new building in our city district. Press forward! There are several other locations nearby suitable for construction. Eyes firmly shut, this is for our own good. Long live liberal capitalism.' On the other hand, Milan Brkić detects the real strategic position of liberal capitalism, which can be summed up in the expression 'for a fistful of dollars': 'This is the most duplicitous crime committed in our city district, in collaboration

Figure 13.3 Project: 'Trstenik BEACH', 2009 ('THE FIRE': installation consisting of the emblems of the leading political parties set on fire)

between the city authority and entrepreneurs. Tenants were dispossessed of their right to see the sky, the sun and the birds. All for a fistful of dollars.'

Many of the KVART art-actions contribute to the denunciation of the empire of money that is clearly exemplified in the recent practice of public space management in Split. In a collective work titled 'Bottles', plastic bottles become a kind of decoration for streetlights. It is possible to understand them as emblems of the recently emerged practice of the collection and sale of used plastic bottles by the poor and the elderly. However, the work is not an attempt to bring about ecological enlightenment of the population but rather alludes to what is a mode of survival for some of its members. Flags, which are usually placed on lampposts during public holidays and other special occasions, were replaced by a multitude of bottles embodying the new social reality: plastic containers empty of content and thus indicative of local poverty. Another of the projects, 'Fire', involved the creation of a bonfire, which had an extremely cathartic effect (Figure 13.3). The authors used the purifying character of the fire to suggest the ultimate reform, that is the 'resetting' of Croatian society in general. Emblems of leading political parties were lined up on the 'left' and 'right', expressing the necessity for their reform or complete removal from the political scene since they were not showing any capacity to lead the country.

Articulating its actions *from* and *in* the urban periphery the art collective KVART uses art procedures to foreground social (in)tolerance and as an effective method for preserving public spaces from slowly disappearing under the governance of the new neoliberal society. But KVART goes even further: towards the city centre.

Sabotage of the centre

While KVART have largely limited their activities to the area of the city district of Trstenik, some members also ventured into the city centre. In 2010 KVART participated in DOPUST (Open Performance Days in Split), which involved activities taking place in different parts of the city. Their approach and methods are still critical and controversial. For instance, one group of KVART members visited the cramped offices of the Homeless Shelter of the association, Most. By taking the number 17 bus to their destination while wearing the figure 17, they hoped to draw attention to Most's limited 'accommodation facilities', to use the language of tourism. The shelter is only able to accommodate 16 people. The art activists' repetition of number 17 also underlines the perversity of forcing the homeless into a kind of competition in which 16 people win temporary shelter, while the seventeenth person is left out in the cold. Notably the Homeless Shelter is located in close proximity to the grandiose Bishop's Palace, immediately next to the perimeter of its back garden, which contains a recently built terrace with a lovely view. The intention of the KVART collective was to secure accommodation for one more homeless person inside the Palace, which contains a considerable amount of empty space. A voice from the entrance telephone system

Figure 13.4 Anonymous action by KVART in the Diocletian's Palace, 2010
Photograph: Author

informed them that they should come back tomorrow, confirming the absence of empathy from an institution marked with the sign of Christian 'charity'.

Furthermore, by mapping the neglected areas in the Diocletian's Palace, the monument which carries the insignia of the World Heritage Site, the KVART artists demonstrate the malfunctioning of structures that are supposed to look after its conservation and revitalization. The artists crossed out the World Heritage logo thus bringing into question the status of the UNESCO protected site (Figure 13.4). However, performed by the artists that operate from the 'periphery' this act could also be interpreted as a metaphor expressing distrust of the system of domination of the 'protected centre' in relation to its subordinated peripheral zones.

Conclusion

Most of the strategies of KVART could be said to revive Friedrich Nietzsche's philosophical postulates, namely his division of nihilism into two fractions: passive and active nihilism. Nietzsche distinguishes passive nihilism, which presupposes inertia and unconsciousness and the inability to carry out change leading necessarily to decadence, from an active nihilism that possesses historical consciousness and, thanks to the disappearance of dominant values, is capable of reaching a state of absolute negation of everything in existence to create and affirm new values. Nietzsche assigned this task to the area of culture, especially art. Such strategic positions of active nihilism are delineated in activities of the art collective KVART, especially in their project 'Fire'.

The basic strategies of this artistic collective are uncompromising activities centred on public space which insist on the active participation of the local community. These strategies help to galvanize feelings against a dehumanized urbanism motivated by profit. The collective has enjoyed some success. Trstenik beach is refurbished and open to all; the artistic activities helped to raise awareness of the value of the right to space, and also helped pose environmental questions regarding the local creek. Although this is not 'functional' art, the artists' intent is aimed at positive change. Considering Karaman's thesis about peripheral society and art, KVART – metaphorically speaking – operates from a peripheral position which is marked with a certain autonomy and is free from the rigid surveillance of the centre. It was not my intention here to define 'peripheral art' in an era which has seen the further internationalization of the artistic scene, but to emphasize those parts of the city – deprived of cultural content – which can stimulate very interesting forms of contemporary artistic expression. In this sense, following Karaman, the periphery is not a defect and it should not necessarily be viewed negatively. In colloquial discourse peripheral and provincial are often equated; however, Karaman's text clearly distinguishes them. Peripheral space is the space for free and independent activity which implies diverse creative possibilities. Therefore, the space of peripheral experience, free of a rigid control system, is the only possible locus for the collective's actions and communications. Indeed, although its activity is largely dislocated from the city centre, KVART has become one of the focal points of contemporary art practice in Split.

14

'MANS IS ON STAGE': Rappers as Disseminators of (Sub)urban Language Varieties

Nichola Smalley

'Slang Like This'[1]

'Vi representerar förortens röst med stil
berättar om vår vardag som en säkerhetsventil'
(We represent the voice of the suburbs with style,
Describing our lives like a safety valve).

(The Latin Kings, *Botkyrka Stylee*, 1997)

This chapter discusses the role played by rappers in disseminating emerging language practices from the social and geographical contexts in which they have developed to the wider world. Recently, increased attention has been directed at the language practices of young people in urban and suburban contexts across Europe as sociolinguistic studies have documented new language varieties. These 'multiethnolects' (Qvist, 2008), and 'contemporary urban vernaculars' (Rampton, 2010) are shown to have developed in areas of high linguistic and ethnic diversity. They are often described in terms of their connection to rap and other youth subcultural practices. However, few studies have looked in depth at this connection, or examined the role of rappers in promoting or disseminating language varieties.

These varieties (or practices – language use is too complex to be described solely in terms of fixed varieties, although I do so for reasons of clarity in this article) are frequently described in terms of their connection to particular locations. I examine this geographic/linguistic interplay, finding links between the physical peripherality of the suburbs and the cultural peripherality of the inner-city. In particular, I look at two forms, *multietniskt ungdomsspråk* (multiethnic youth language, or MU), a variety of Swedish that has emerged on the periphery of major Swedish cities, and *Multicultural London English* (MLE), a variety of British English that has emerged in areas of

[1] P. Money, *Slang Like This*, 2010.

London. Both of these have developed over the last 30 years among young people in areas of high ethnic and linguistic diversity. Similar phenomena have occurred across Western Europe, with the Swedish and UK studies that first identified these varieties playing a key role in shaping later research (see Clyne, 2000).

Using Swedish and UK sociolinguistic studies as a basis, I identify a few key language features, and explore the occurrence of these in hip hop and grime lyrics. I have chosen to restrict my selection to lexical, rather than, say, phonetic features, as lexical features are more clearly identifiable in lyrical contexts. The lyrics for my analysis have been taken from my own transcriptions of the songs concerned, or, in the case of the Swedish lyrics, from the fan website hiphoptexter.com. In this latter case, I have checked fans' transcriptions of lyrics for accuracy by listening back to the tracks. Unless otherwise stated, translations of lyrics and citations are my own. Attempts have been made to preserve slang terms where relevant.

'Everyone thinks to MC good, your lyrics must be about living in the hood':[2] Rappers and associations with place

My main analysis focuses on the use of MU and MLE features in the lyrical practice of rap in Swedish hip hop and UK grime. A major feature of the discourse around hip hop and, by extension, grime is the idea of marginal cultures taking their voice into the mainstream. Much has been written about hip hop's relation to marginalized cultures around the world (see Toop, 2000, Alim et al., 2009), although hip hop is now unquestionably a prominent part of mainstream entertainment culture, even if many hip hop and grime artists maintain strong connections with a perceived 'underground' (Nyberg, 2008).

Since originating in New York in the 1970s, hip hop has become a global phenomenon, recorded and performed in many languages. Bearing witness to this, H. Samy Alim refers to the '"Global Hip Hop Nation" [. . .] a multilingual, multiethnic "nation" with an international reach [and] a fluid capacity to cross borders' (Alim, 2009, p. 3). I focus here on a specific branch of Swedish hip hop that located itself in Sweden's post-war suburbs, performing a '*förortspoesi*' (suburban poetry) (Dahlstedt, 2005) that informs lyrical content and style.

The Latin Kings (TLK) are often referred to as pioneers of Swedish-language hip hop, releasing their best-selling debut album V*älkommen till förorten* (Welcome to the Suburbs) in 1994. Although Swedish hip hop was produced from 1979 onwards, commercially successful acts generally rapped in English until TLK's breakthrough (Nyberg, 2008, p. 162). TLK formed in Norra Botkyrka, a post-war suburb of southern Stockholm, where the three members, frontman Dogge, producer Chepe and DJ Salla grew up. Throughout their career, they cultivated associations with Botkyrka and with 'förorten' (the suburbs). They did this through the imagery of high-rise blocks and suburban landscapes they used in videos and album covers, through the subject matter of their songs, and the linguistic form and delivery of their lyrics. They were the first

[2] JME, *Shut up and Dance*, 2006.

Swedish rappers to articulate the social, as well as geographical, marginality of the suburbs in this way.

Sometimes referred to as the United Kingdom's answer to hip hop, grime developed from dance music genres in the early 2000s; MC is the title generally given to grime rappers. Grime is associated with the genre 'urban music', as evidenced on the music news website www.grimedaily.com: 'The Epicentre of Urban Entertainment'. According to Encyclopaedia Britannica, 'urban contemporary [music] began as an American radio format designed to appeal to advertisers who felt that "black radio" would not reach a wide enough audience'.[3] It is now standard (if not undisputed) terminology in the United Kingdom.

JME is an MC from Tottenham, north-east London, who has been prominent since around 2004. His relationship with the urban tropes that constitute much of grime's imagery is intriguing. As blogger Blackdown says:

> Though JME's long since been an independent, free thinker, his hardcore grime credentials are unquestionable: he founded BBK [Boy Better Know] alongside grime legends DJ Maximum, Jammer and his brother Skepta, and was part of Wiley [the so-called Godfather of Grime]'s Roll Deep and before that Meridian Crew (who had a serious street reputation). (Blackdown, 2012)

A good example of JME's 'critical insider' role is the track *Serious*, in which he challenges MCs to think more critically about their lyrical themes. The video for *Serious (Remix)* is especially interesting in relation to this discussion.[4] Starting out on a pleasant street lined with trees and semi-detached houses, JME is then pixelated out of the real world into an animated fantasy of grime stereotypes, framed by tower blocks bouncing in time to the beat, or a beam of endlessly reproduced handguns. The video plays with typical grime imagery, stating an awareness of this representation, but maintaining visual distance.

Welcome to the suburbs? Suburban and inner-city peripheries

In order to analyse the role music has played in disseminating features of contemporary urban vernaculars from the social and geographic contexts in which they originate, it is important to examine these social and geographic contexts in more detail.

MU is generally spoken of as a suburban phenomenon, and is often used interchangeably with terms like '*Rinkebysvenska*' (Rinkeby Swedish – referring to a Stockholm suburb), '*miljonsvenska*' ('million programme' Swedish, named after the 1965–75 urban planning scheme) and '*förortsslang*' (suburban slang). In the United Kingdom, MLE and the social environment in which it is spoken are commonly seen as inner-city phenomena, with MLE described as exclusive 'urban' or 'street' slang, as exemplified by London's *Evening Standard* newspaper: 'Often impenetrable and indecipherable to all but those in the know, street slang has become a separatist form

---

[3] www.britannica.com/EBchecked/topic/619429/urban-contemporary-music [accessed 16 February 2012].

[4] www.youtube.com/watch?v=JpLzYIgUojo [accessed 25 February 2012].

of communication' (Johns, 2010). But although these language varieties are associated with locations that differ in terms of their proximity to the urban centre, the associations have much in common: I would argue that both the Swedish *förort*, and the 'inner city' can be viewed as peripheral: socially, linguistically and culturally.

It should also be noted here that geographic peripherality is subjective. As Hinchcliffe states, '[t]he literature on suburbs is extensive, yet the subject always seems elusive. For some the suburb is a geographical space; for others, a cultural form; while for others still it is a state of mind' (Hinchcliffe, 2005, p. 899). It can also be seen that the 'inner city' is not always so 'inner'. An example can be found in the administrative division of London's boroughs into 'inner' and 'outer' London. Haringey and Newham, two boroughs central to grime and to MLE (research has shown that MLE features occurred frequently in Haringey as well as 'inner-city' Hackney (Cheshire et al., 2011)), are classed as outer London in statutory terms (see London Government Act 1963 (c. 33)). I would argue that all these areas would be viewed by a layperson as 'inner-city', due to the prevalence, for instance, of high-rise housing estates, and the proportion of disadvantaged and ethnic-minority residents, though this does not necessary reflect geographical proximity to the centre of London.

'She was the one who got me to discover my own language':[5] Research on contemporary urban vernaculars in Sweden and the United Kingdom

In the 1980s, Ulla-Britt Kotsinas highlighted a new phenomenon, which she termed *Rinkebysvenska*, after the post-war Stockholm suburb where she conducted her initial research (Kotsinas, 1988). Fraurud and Bijvoet have since argued for the use of the term '*multietniskt ungdomsspråk*' (multiethnic youth language), on the basis that this language variety is not restricted to a single geographic location (Fraurud and Bijvoet, 2004). I use the latter term throughout this chapter.

Kotsinas found that adolescents living in her research locations spoke a Swedish that sounded different to that spoken elsewhere in Stockholm (Kotsinas, 1988a; 1998). As well as having a markedly different prosody and tone, they borrowed lexical and syntactical elements from the languages spoken around them (Kotsinas, 2002, p. 56). These languages included Turkish, Arabic, Spanish and Greek.

The adolescents also created new words or meanings from existing Swedish terms through wordplay and association (an example is the use of the term *betongen* (concrete) for the suburbs where MU originated – alluding to their concrete construction). Other typical MU features include the '–isch' suffix in verbs, nouns and adjectives (e.g. *taggisch* (run away), *grymmisch* (cool) [Kotsinas, 2001, p. 12]), as well as lexical loans from American English, for example *fet* (very, or great – from the US hip-hop term *phat*) (ibid.).

Since Kotsinas conducted her studies during the 1980s and 1990s, researchers have continued to investigate suburban language practices across Sweden. The multi-institutional project 'Language and Language Use among Young People in Multilingual

---

[5] 'Det var ju hon som fick mig att upptäcka mitt eget språk' (Dogge Doggelito, in Bäckstedt, 2004).

Urban Settings', conducted between 2002 and 2006, identified features common to all areas studied, although not to the degree that had previously been assumed (see Bodén, 2011; Ekberg et al., 2004). This complicates the somewhat simplistic image of MU that had developed through media interpretations (which I discuss below) of Kotsinas's work. Nevertheless, there is general agreement that the Swedish spoken in the multilingual environment of the post-war suburb has evolved significantly in the last 30 years.

Research into urban language change in the United Kingdom over the last 30 years has indicated comparable trends. Ben Rampton coined the term 'crossing' to refer to the way young people from a variety of ethnic groups ('Anglo' and Afro-Caribbean, but also Punjabi and Bengali) 'crossed' into one another's language varieties in certain social situations (Rampton, 1995). Crossing 'focuses on code alternation by people who are not accepted members of the group associated with the second language they employ' (ibid., p. 280), indicating familiarity with the out-group variety through personal ties or popular culture.

Some types of crossing (for instance, into what Rampton calls stylized Asian English) were seen as being predominantly mocking or joking in tone, whereas others (Jamaican Creole and Punjabi) were recognized by speakers as having 'serious youth cultural' uses (ibid., p. 60), meaning than they could make their users look cool or well-informed, regardless of ethnicity. Creole's cachet was attributed partly to the continued popularity of reggae, as previously noted by Hewitt (1986, p. 112) in *White Talk Black Talk*, his examination of language change brought about by interracial friendship among young people.

In addition to their examinations of cross-group borrowing, both these authors also refer to a fledgling hybrid variety. For Hewitt, this 'local multi-racial vernacular' (ibid., p. 188) combines features of London Jamaican with the existing London vernacular (i.e. Cockney). For Rampton, there is the additional influence of 'Panjabi, Indian English or second language learner interlanguage' (Rampton, 1995, p. 127). However, neither author explores the hybrid form in detail. The focus changed in the 2000s, with two projects studying language use in London: the 2004–7 project 'Linguistic Innovators' and 2007–10 project 'Multicultural London English'.

Multicultural London English (MLE) was found to exhibit 'a range of linguistic forms that cannot necessarily, or at least can no longer, be attributed to specific ethnic groups' (Cheshire et al., 2008, p. 1). These include a characteristic accent, grammatical features and lexical innovations, and loans from a range of languages, including Jamaican Creole. Core lexical features include the discourse marker 'you get me' and the use of 'man' as an indefinite pronoun (Kerswill et al., 2007, p. 8). Significantly, the researchers classified MLE as a pool of features, rather than as a variety, arguing that its heterogeneity precluded it being referred to by the latter term. They noted, however, that both speakers and non-speakers were able to identify these features as belonging together in some way (Cheshire et al., 2011, p. 152), which is why I have chosen to refer to it as a variety, with due caution.

The UK-based studies indicate a progression over time from out-group borrowing of in-group ethnically marked forms, to a hybrid language that is more tied to location and class than to particular ethnic groups, in keeping with Marzo and Ceeleurs's statement that 'the social meaning of language variants can progressively change from a clear social category (as social class, gender and ethnicity) to a more geographic one, namely a local identity' (Marzo and Ceeleurs, 2011). Despite this, migration and ethnic diversity have a clear role in the emergence of MLE (see Cheshire et al., 2011). This resonates with the Swedish studies, as Kotsinas stated that young Swedes from diverse ethnic backgrounds used MU, with the primary common factor being the place they live, that is suburban areas with high ethnic and linguistic diversity (Kotsinas, 2001, p. 14). Many recent studies have also referred to these varieties as examples of the same phenomenon, with Cheshire et al. noting how, for MLE and equivalent varieties across Northern Europe, 'there are increasing indications that these varieties have become the unmarked Labovian "vernacular" for many speakers' (Cheshire et al., 2011, p. 153).

'The kids of the concrete are growing up. Politicians – here, have something to suck on':[6] Media representations of the 'concrete generation'

Ever since Kotsinas's work was first publicized, concerns have been voiced about the negative impact of *Rinkebysvenska*/MU. These concerns fit into a larger discourse about immigration and national identity that has centred on the suburban estates of the *miljonprogram*. These areas, despite initially being intended as the Swedish welfare state's solution to the post-war housing shortage, have come to be seen as increasingly problematic. During the last 40 years, ethnic segregation, poverty and crime have featured prominently in media discourse around the estates, as explored by Ristilammi's still pertinent 1994 study *Rosengård och den svarta poesin* (Rosengård and the Black Poetry). Ristilammi highlights the media's use of negative visual and verbal imagery to portray the Rosengård estate in Malmö, southern Sweden, analysing how this contributes to a national stigmatization, not only of Rosengård, but of all such estates throughout Sweden (see Ristilammi, 1994).

When MU has been discussed in the media, it has often been framed by concerns over the future of the Swedish language, as exemplified by the '*Blattesvenska*' debate about Swedish language teaching in schools, which raged in *Dagens Nyheter*, a major national newspaper, in 2006. In this debate, teachers, authors, journalists and academics all weighed in with comments on the nature and implications of MU, which ranged from concern that MU would damage young people's chances of integration into Swedish society (Witt-Brattström, 2006) to celebrations of the variety's role as an expressive conduit for marginalized youth (Gringoredaktionen, 2006).

A comparable discussion has taken place in the UK media over the past few years. The language used in this debate illustrates the perceived marginality of MLE. It is described as 'impenetrable' and 'secret' (Johns, 2010). 'Jafaican' is a term that appears in the discussion of youth language in multiethnic areas, clearly connoting similarities to Jamaican Patois and artificiality. Cheshire et al. remark that 'Jafaican' 'most likely

---

[6] 'Betongens barn har växt upp så politiker här får ni något o suga på' (TLK, *Välkommen till förorten*, 1997).

has media origins', and is 'not essentially a "members' concept"' (Cheshire et al., 2011, p. 152). They assert that MLE speakers refer to their way of speaking simply as 'slang' (ibid.). Adding to this perception of marginality, some media representations of MLE have featured interviews with teachers, in which young people's potential ability to use 'appropriate' language in their future workplaces is questioned (Johns, 2010).

'We represent the voice of the suburbs with style'[7] – The Latin Kings and MU

> Du vet, slangen är central för rappen, i en rapp behöver man rim, man rimmar hela tiden, och i slangen finns det massor av rim, den är en gruva av guld för mig.
>
> (Slang is central to rap, you know? In a rap, you need rhymes, you're rhyming the whole time, and in slang there's loads of rhymes, it's a goldmine for me.) (Dogge Doggelito in Bäckstedt, 2004)

In this quote, we can see how Dogge values the lyrical potential of slang. His MU 'credentials' are widely recognized: as an adolescent, he was part of a focus group in Kotsinas's sociolinguistic studies, and in 2004, he collaborated with her to produce a dictionary entitled *Förortsslang* (Suburban Slang) (Kotsinas and Doggelito, 2004). JME's use of MLE features can be witnessed in the videos he frequently posts online. In some of these he is talking to camera, or engaging in casual conversation with friends, or, in a recent example, police.[8] He also makes frequent use of MLE features on the social networking site Twitter.

These examples of Dogge's and JME's language use in a variety of situations show that not only are they everyday speakers of MU and MLE respectively, but also that they are conscious of their own language practices, choosing to implement and accentuate them in their lyrical production and promotion of themselves and their music. They hail from the multiethnic urban environments in which these varieties emerged, performing their belonging to these locations through their lyrical, verbal and visual imagery. For many grime MCs, the MLE accent is central, demonstrating an allegiance with the domestic scene. As Skepta (JME's brother and fellow MC) observed in an interview on a US hip-hop radio station, referring to how this has limited grime's popularity in the United States: 'I don't think you lot was feelin' our accents at first' (Skepta, 2010).

At this point, it may be useful to consider the significance of the different types of text I am using in my analysis. Rap lyrics differ from the spontaneous speech which makes up instances of MLE and MU in everyday personal interactions. Lyrical instances of MLE/MU features and instances of these varieties in media representation are just that – representations. Such language use 'stand[s] out from the ordinary, marked and reframed in some explicit way as "performed"' (Bell and Gibson, 2011).

---

[7] '*Vi representerar förortens röst med stil*' (The Latin Kings *Botkyrka Stylee*, 1997).
[8] www.youtube.com/watch?v=dh5pDBQ10dA [accessed 16 March 2012].

Dogge raps with a clear MU inflection, as well as using many of the typical MU lexical features identified by Kotsinas. The following lyrics are an example of TLK's use of the suffix *-isch*:

Meckisch en B, Meckisch Zutt zutt
[Meckisch (make) a joint, Meckisch a Zoot zoot (cannabis cigarette)]

(TLK, Mecka, 1994)

sooooftischhh!!
[Chiiiilll!!]

(TLK, Måla mer, 1997)

dax för gittisch, dax för taggisch
[Time to gittisch (split), time to taggisch (move)]

(TLK, Dax för Bax, 1997)

Another example is TLK's frequent use of the word *guss* in their songs, for instance in the track *Gussen* (The Girl) from 1997. *Guss* is derived from the Turkish word *kız*, (girl), despite TLK not being of Turkish descent. In 2006, the word was added to the SAOL, the Swedish Academy Glossary, which is generally seen as the most authoritative lexicon of the Swedish language (Bäckstedt, 2005). Not only had the word been acknowledged by the Swedish Academy, the body responsible for issuing the Nobel prize, but it was also rumoured to be in use in locations as distant as Kiruna, a town situated within the Arctic circle (Bäckstedt, 2004).

It is difficult to trace this usage, short of asking the Swedish Academy and the young people of Kiruna how they became acquainted with the term (perhaps a task for future research!), but the popularity of hip hop throughout Sweden (see Strage, 2001, p. 298) may be a contributing factor, as TLK themselves emphasize:

Latin Kings skakar om hela nationen
med den rätta tonen från betonggenerationen.

[Latin Kings shaking up the whole of the nation
With the right sound from the concrete generation.]

(The Latin Kings, *Passa micken*, 1997)

'Mans is on stage'[9] – JME and MLE

JME is well-known for his catchphrases and wordplay. I focus here on his use and promotion of the word 'man' as a personal pronoun, both in his lyrics and through the social networking website Twitter, where he currently has over 100,000 followers

---

[9] twitter.com/jmebbk [accessed 1 June 2011].

(twitter.com/jmebbk [accessed 20 September 2011]). In the following lyrics, two different uses of 'man' can be seen. The first two excerpts show 'man' used to refer to an unspecified third person, while in example three, JME uses 'man' to refer to himself:

Man see me and think I got P's

(JME, *Poomplex*, 2006)

Man'll go to radio on Thursday, even though it's his birthday

(JME, *Serious*, 2005)

That's how you know *man's* got bare fans

(JME, Boy Better Know, 2006)

These uses of 'man' derive from Rastafari traditions in Jamaica (Henry, 2006, p. 12). They feature among the core innovative features identified by the MLE study (Kerswill et al., 2007, p. 8).

Dramatic changes in media and distribution technologies mean that many musicians now promote themselves without the mediation of a journalist or agent. Artists are thus able to interact directly with their fans, shaping the identity they present to them, rather than being 'presented'. Perhaps because of this, they have the potential to impact upon the language of those who come into contact with them. I will now explore this briefly by looking at JME's use of Twitter.

Online social media represent an ideal opportunity for MCs to promote their work and shape their identity as lyricists. Twitter, in particular, provides a high-profile space for wordplay, with its 140-character message format, and many MCs tweet dozens of times daily. JME's engagement with this form can be demonstrated anecdotally: at a concert I recently attended, he took a photo of himself on stage with the audience in the background, and tweeted it immediately, with the tagline 'Mans is on stage'. This engagement was echoed as fans at the concert checked their Twitter feeds to see it.

An added dimension of Twitter is the 'Retweet' function, where a member can re-publish another member's tweet onto their own profile, enabling their own followers to see it. JME makes extensive use of this function, Retweeting fans' comments in which they have made use of turns of phrase associated with him. In this way, the fans whose messages he is Retweeting are affirmed in their use of this terminology.

Accurately tracing the dissemination of the language features discussed above is difficult. However, a personal observation might be of use: in a straw poll of my personal acquaintances who use MLE features in their everyday speech, the majority stated they were raised in London, and had been using MLE since adolescence. Others, who use occasional MLE features as slang, but grew up outside London and do not have pronounced MLE accents, frequently used these MLE features when talking about grime or music in general. They were all fans of grime and the majority were Twitter users who followed JME. It would be unwise to draw concrete conclusions from this, but it is interesting that the out-group users of MLE features generally acknowledged that they had acquired them from MCs and their interest in grime.

'I'm not average or decent, and it's hard to write lyrics like these':[10] Rap and subcultural capital

It might be asked why rappers are so well placed to act as disseminators of contemporary urban vernacular and slang features. A useful idea is Thornton's term 'subcultural capital', a phenomenon which is 'embodied in the form of being "in the know"' (Thornton, 1995, p. 11). Owing to their possession of subcultural capital, successful MCs and rappers are highly visible both from within, and outside of, the urban/suburban culture they are seen to represent. Therefore, they act as a sort of benchmark by which fans and others wishing to be associated with this culture can measure and mould their own practices. Thornton also mentions that 'using (but not overusing) current slang' is typical of those who possess subcultural capital. This is relevant in all subcultures, but especially a highly verbal form such as rap. Indeed, the MLE study found that prodigious users of MLE were all 'dominant characters within their friendship groups and highly regarded by their peers'; they were 'involved in activities such as rapping and MCing either as participants or consumers, and these are highly valued resources in contemporary youth culture' (Cheshire et al., 2008, p. 19).

We can look back at Rampton's analysis to see an example of how music has provided a conduit through which diverse language communities are exposed to the linguistic features represented in lyrics. Rampton gives the example of Mashuk, a young man of Bangladeshi descent who toasted in sound system performances, and, according to Rampton, 'emerged from these with considerable local prestige, and much greater licence to use Creole in ordinary talk than any other white or Asian (Rampton, 1995, p. 236).

Looking at the research of Kotsinas, Rampton and the other researchers I have mentioned, it can be seen that individuals in any given locality may pick up the language features of those they come into contact with in that locality (see also Marzo and Ceeleurs, 2011, p. 453). However, people not living in that area may come into contact with those features through their contact with prestigious cultural forms. This may explain the presence of similar features in suburban estates across Sweden, as fluency in the language of hip hop is seen as a conduit through which to express affiliation with other suburban communities, in contrast to mainstream urban Swedish culture. Although a causal relationship is difficult to prove in this context, especially so long after the event, the fact that Swedish acts such as TLK started using local MU/suburban slang features in commercially successful rap as early as 1993 may mean they helped spread these features to other suburban communities. Fans may have felt a desire to express their affinity for the rappers by picking up elements of their speech.

Hewitt highlights the interplay between music, language and identity. He talks, for example, of the 'toasting' practices of reggae Dancehall deejays in the United Kingdom during the 1980s. He defines toasting as '*the* oral form of reggae music' (Hewitt, 1986, p. 115, original emphasis). Lez Henry explores this in more depth, describing how Dancehall deejays consciously used a UK-inflected Jamaican Creole (Patwa) in their performances, in order to assert their identity as members of a

---

[10] JME, *Serious*, 2005.

universal black culture: 'Reggae Sound System culture and Deejaying gave all black youth, irrespective of where in the Afrikan Diaspora either they or their parents came from, a voice that spoke to their immediate concerns' (Henry, 2006, p. 2). According to Henry, by using Patwa, these young people were able to signal affiliation with a particular historical descent and highlight the widespread racism they faced in mainstream British society.

London deejay Smiley Culture showed how this performance can move beyond this group into popular culture, upturning Henry's view of an inward-looking practice. His 1984 hit *Cockney Translation* brought to the attention of mainstream society the linguistic and cultural changes that were taking place in Britain at that time. Paul Gilroy notes how Smiley's 'translation' of words and phrases between Creole and Cockney highlighted commonalities between black and white urban subcultures, thereby challenging the idea that there was an inherent incompatibility (Gilroy, 2002, p. 262). As journalist Dotun Adebayo put it: 'through his musical slapstick, Smiley made it OK for guys like me (i.e. a black Londoner) to chat cockney without being regarded as 'coconuts', and for white guys to speak "yardie"' without being regarded as wiggers' (Adebayo, 2011). This perspective demonstrates how young people express musical or subcultural affiliations through language without necessarily aligning themselves with the political, ideological or geographical connotations of that language use.

'Forward slash slash dot JME, Mash up the whole HTTP'[11] – Conclusion and areas for further research

In this chapter, I have argued that new language varieties, Multiethnic Youth Language (MU) and Multicultural London English (MLE) have emerged from areas of high linguistic and ethnic diversity in Sweden and the United Kingdom respectively. These varieties are characterized, as Cheshire et al. have stated, by the fact that their constitutive features are no longer attributable to specific ethnic groups (Cheshire et al., 2008, p. 1).

These varieties have been strongly associated with the environments in which they developed, that is the post-war suburban estates of the Swedish *miljonprogram* and the so-called inner-city estates of London. I have explored the complexity inherent in the portrayal of these environments and the language varieties associated with them. It is likely that the geographically peripheral location of certain of these environments has led to a physical separation of the communities in them from other urban communities, creating a fertile environment for linguistic and creative innovation. However, I have suggested that, both in areas that are geographically peripheral and those that are not, a cultural and social peripherality may persist. In many cases, this has led to linguistic communities forming, with implications for the language practices in these areas.

Furthermore, I have explored the ways in which hip hop and grime artists are among the most visible practitioners of these linguistic phenomena. They construct and perform identities, emphasizing their connection with place. In some ways, they

[11] JME *Boy Better Know*, 2006.

have become symbols of these places. Through their prominence and their possession of subcultural capital, they are key agents in the dissemination of certain language features to a wider context.

In conclusion, I would like to assert that this dissemination confirms the fluid, adaptable and adoptable nature of the language varieties I have focused on. They are not fixed to a given social or geographical environment, and are liable to flow into other receptive environments. This flow occurs via friendship links, online interactions and music culture, as in the following example of MLE use in the rapping of Virus Syndicate, a Manchester grime act. Despite their audibly Mancunian accents in interviews the MCs use distinctly MLE features in their rapping.[12] Despite this fluidity, I would argue that language varieties retain an association with their place of origin that is often difficult to shake off.

An area that is worth exploring further is the dissemination of language varieties through music blogs and online fan forums. Androutsopoulous has conducted interesting research into online language use associated with hip-hop culture in Germany (Androutsopoulous, 2011), but I have yet to encounter any such research focusing on the United Kingdom and Sweden. Rappers are, of course, not the only people who speak contemporary urban vernaculars in public or in private, and examples can commonly be seen on hip hop or grime forums (see www.grimeforum.com). Blogs and online forums play a key role in genres such as hip hop and grime, and it would be interesting to analyse the extent to which these other aspects of the hip hop and grime community are active in promoting urban vernaculars online.

---

[12] See www.youtube.com/watch?v=lqBjlTiqowk [accessed 28 January 2012].

15

The Goat Boy of Mount Seething: Heritage and Folklore in an English Suburb

Helen Wickstead

'Suburbia has no history; its archives are empty. There is no depth from which archaeology might exhume its artefacts.' (Webster, 2000, p. 2)

The assumption that suburbs lack an authentic past is deep-seated, and yet, in England, this prejudice coexists with a multitude of local museums, historical and archaeological societies, listed buildings and conservation areas in suburban locations. Relations with phenomena perceived to be 'of the past' are important in suburbia. But in what ways might pasts be constructed differently in suburbs? Is there such a thing as distinctively suburban heritage?

The Legend of Lefi Gandersen tells how a little goat-boy defeated a terrible giant, how cheese was invented, and how Mount Seething was razed to the ground, becoming part of Surbiton, a London suburb. In this chapter, I describe the activities which perpetuate this local folk tradition as interventions in suburban spacetime. I suggest that they re-appropriate stereotypes of Surbiton, particularly those derived from television comedies, which treat Surbiton as the ordinary home of the extraordinary and absurd. Celebrating a 'new', deliberately improbable tradition the 'villagers of Seething' claim the absurd as their heritage.[1]

I argue that Seething's heritage practices are significantly influenced by a 'suburban imaginary' (Silverstone, 1997). In making this argument I align myself with theorists who see heritage as 'the performance of identity, values and a sense of place' (Smith and Waterton, 2009, p. 292). Through such performances, some of that which is associated

---

[1] An enormous debt is owed to Robin Hutchinson, who acted as informant and inspiration, and to David Jeevadrampillai (currently researching Seething for his PhD at UCL) who shared ideas and commented on the draft. Prof. Bobi Robson fosters the genuinely collegiate environment of the Free University of Seething. Many villagers of Seething and residents of Surbiton have contributed to the development of this study, including Brett Alderton, Jack Bartley, Howard Benge, Fairy, Liz and Adam Lewis and Simon Tyrrell.

with the past is handed on. Heritage is not limited to the historic, nor to items designated as heritage by recognized authorities. It includes the so-called intangible heritage of customs, crafts, oral traditions, folklore, processions and performances (Smith and Akagawa, 2009). It is a form of cultural action 'produced in the present to deal with the circumstances of everyday life' (Harrison, 2010, p. 36).

In England suburbia is now a declared priority for the state heritage agency under the new National Heritage Protection Plan (English Heritage, 2007a, b). Behind this new interest in suburban heritage are concerns that listing in suburbs has lagged behind other areas and that 'heritage assets' which might be listed are subject to new threats from home extensions and the 'infilling' of green spaces (ibid.). The ageing of England's housing stock has resulted in an increasing proportion of older houses potentially suitable for listing, and many of these are found in suburbs. Houses and estates from the twentieth century are increasingly likely to be categorized as 'heritage assets'. The focus of the new interest in suburban heritage is primarily on tangible historic buildings, sites and artefacts, rather than on heritage as a form of cultural action related to the distinctive materialities of suburbia. While English Heritage's 'Conservation Principles' (2008) provide for the inclusion of 'Communal' and 'Social Value' in assessing significance, it is still difficult to take account of these values within formal procedures for designating heritage assets, especially when intangible heritage is at issue (Smith and Waterton, 2009). UK legislative measures, such as listing, 'tend to abstract buildings and settings from the context in which they were created, separating them from the people who use and interact with them' (Malpass, 2009, p. 205). This can lead to tensions over how heritage agencies and suburbanites value suburban homes and environments (Malpass, 2009; Buss, 2012). At the same time the transformation of England's planning system under the Localism Act and new National Planning Policy Framework brings to the forefront questions about which groups can influence the future of a 'neighbourhood' and define its heritage (Bowes, 2011). Provisions under the Localism Act for Neighbourhood Plans seem likely to raise questions concerning what heritage can be, how it should be enacted and whose heritage is recognized. Case studies which allow investigation into how heritage differs in suburbs are timely.

I begin by describing the representation of Surbiton in literature, politics and television, and suggest that stereotypes of Surbiton constitute a legacy that is difficult to ignore. I go on to describe the Festival of Seething as an intervention in spacetime, and I explore how parody, archaeology and mockumentary has been used to construct Seething's folk traditions as 'new'. I discuss the partial connections between Surbiton and Seething, suggesting that Seething plays with the diversification of opportunities for 'elective belonging' in suburbs, with dreams of suburban utopia, and with the longstanding notions that suburbs lack a sense of community (and therefore require community be built) and lack authentic claims over folk heritage.

The stereotyping of Surbiton

Surbiton is seen as representative of a certain kind of English suburbia (Goldsworthy, 2004, p. 104). The Anglo-Saxon 'south bereton' has become suburb-town – the place locals 'jokingly call Suburb-iton' (*London Evening Standard*, 2012). In 1995, Liverpool

City Council 'seriously considered adopting "Liverpool – it's not Surbiton" as marketing slogan' (Statham, 1996, p. xiii). John Burnside's memoir, *Waking Up in Toytown*, reports on his quest for a 'Surbiton of the mind': '. . . a normal life. Sober. Drug-free. Dreamless. In gainful employment. A householder. A taxpayer. A name on the electoral roll . . . I wanted, in short, to be comfortably numb' (2011, p. 19). Burnside's voyage through Surrey commuterlands installs Surbiton as the unconquerable peak of stifling normality, although the actual Surbiton is never reached.

Surbiton is stereotypically ordinary (see Keble Howard's 1906 novel *The Smiths of Surbiton*). Regardless of actual demography, its population is seen as representing the most middling inhabitants of 'Middle England'. The ordinariness of Surbiton has made it available for political valorization in the same way the views of the Clapham Omnibus commuter once claimed a special right to champion 'ordinary' opinion. 'While the suburbs are culturally derided, in politics – where demographic choices matter – they are often flattered and pandered to . . . uncritically' (Goldsworthy, 2004, p. 102). The political usefulness of the stereotyping of Surbiton is exemplified by the 1967–8 'I'm Backing Britain' campaign, when the plans of 'five girl typists at a factory in Surbiton' to work 'an extra half-hour a day without extra pay' (*Times*, 1968, p. 1) ballooned into a national campaign supported by the Duke of Edinburgh, by the Poet Laureate (in verse), and the Wilson government, and dubbed 'the Surbiton Revolution' (*Economist*, 1968, p. 12). At a time when the workforce was relatively highly unionized, Surbiton supplied an alternative basis for claims to represent the 'ordinary' worker, based on the imaginary ordinariness of Surbiton and with none of the inconveniences of representation through the ballot.

Paradoxically, the stereotyping of Surbiton as ordinary brings with it a latent capacity for extra-ordinariness. If the everyday of modernity, as Ben Highmore has observed, is the place where we are made ready for the revelation of the extraordinary at the heart of the ordinary (Highmore, 2002), then the more disenchanted and familiar Surbiton becomes, the greater its capacity for highlighting the enchanted and unfamiliar will be. In English suburbs associated with lower-middle-class aspiration this dynamic is usually staged as comedy (Medhurst, 1997). Surbiton has been a significant location for TV situation comedy, most famously in *The Good Life* (BBC, 1975), in which Tom and Barbara Goode struggle to attain self-sufficency, while their next-door neighbours attempt to keep up the appearance of middle-class respectability. *The Good Life* constructs Surbiton as straight man; a disenchanted 'normality' against which self-sufficiency becomes wildly improbable. However, it is also available to another reading: '*The Good Life* was one of many [television situation comedies] which presented suburbia sentimentally but positively as a place where eccentricity prospered quietly behind the privet hedge and social discord could be resolved over a cup of tea and a biscuit' (Vaughan et al., 2009, p. 9). In this reading Surbiton is the site where the lost rural idyll might potentially be reclaimed and suburbia's utopian dreams realized.

As homeland of the absurd, Surbiton has 'comedic capital'. Surbiton is often the butt of the joke, but is also available as a position for joking from – for humbling the mighty. The BBC2 sitcom *Stella Street* (1997–2001) was filmed on handheld video in documentary style, revealing the everyday lives of British and American celebrities (Marlon Brando, Mick Jagger, Al Pacino – all played by John Sessions and Phil Cornwall) in Stella Street, Surbiton. Michael Caine (Cornwall) introduces the action, speaking directly to camera. Using documentary premises of truth-in-place, 'mockumentary' grounds the extraordinary in the heart of Surbiton's ordinary. Mockumentary, and the Surbiton map used in the credits, bring celebrity culture back to earth.

Heritage can provide a means to re-enchant the ordinary. The extraordinary often erupts into modern life as an unexpected encounter with future or past. Television representations of Surbiton (mostly – like *The Good Life* and *Stella Street* – shot elsewhere), lead many to assume that it consists entirely of twentieth-century semis snuggled among assiduously manicured lawns. History supplies a powerful challenge to this caricature. Local historians often frame their accounts as attempts to dislodge stereotypes, drawing attention to Surbiton's 'italianate villas and tree-lined streets' (Statham, 1996, p. xiii), to its nineteenth-century significance as 'London's first railway suburb' (London Transport Museum, 2011), and to the vivid histories of its community life (French, 2011). Insisting that Surbiton is 'not *really* like that', is a move that requires historians to hold fast to their authority over 'what the past *was* really like', maintaining a respectable distance from the absurd eccentricity that popular culture lampoons and cherishes. Monty Python's 'Emigration from Surbiton to Hounslow' sketch (Episode 28, BBC1, 1972) uses mock-documentary with authoritative narration to satirize the heroic heritage missions of Thor Heyerdhal's Kon-Tiki and Ra expeditions, in which reconstructed ancient craft crossed the Pacific and Atlantic oceans. Mr and Mrs Brian Norris set out on an epic voyage in their Ford Popular to prove the people of Surbiton were descended from the original inhabitants of Hounslow 'who had made the great trek south'. There is no reason why the epic tale of human origins should not be discovered in the London suburbs as much as anywhere else. (As it happens, the Thames gravels really do contain some of the earliest evidence for human occupation in Britain.) However, suburbia is often presumed to be in the vanguard of recent rather than ancient colonization, a category that is forever reforming itself as inherently 'new' (Vaughan et al., 2009, p. 6).

Surbiton's popular culture profile is itself a heritage. *The Good Life* continues to exert a significant influence. Surbiton's Neighbourhood Plan, (drawn up under the provisions of the Localism Act), twice mentions *The Good Life*, both as something Surbiton has 'moved on from' and as a model for encouraging a sense of neighbourliness (Royal Borough of Kingston Upon Thames, 2011). According to Surbiton's 'Farmer's Market' Magazine (2012, p. 1) the actors who played Tom and Barbara, 'would have been first in the queue to shop at the monthly farmer's market in Maple Road'. The stereotyping of Surbiton in popular culture, and the 'comedic capital' that is its legacy, is available to Surbiton to disown, accommodate or re-appropriate, but seldom to ignore.

The Festival of Seething

Had you happened to be shopping in Surbiton on the last weekend in February in the last three years you would have seen hundreds of people processing along the road. You would have observed a mass parade or demonstration (with hand-sewn banners like those seen at mining galas, and a brass band), alongside phenomena often seen at anarchist or environmental direct action events (giant puppets, bicycle powered floats), individuals and families in costume (giant hamsters, horned figures, people wearing goat masks) and people walking with the procession, filming it on

Figure 15.1 The Festival of Seething 2011 with Lord Scroley on right
Author's Photograph

their phones or taking photographs. Unless you are very incurious, it is likely that you would have stopped along with the many others whose progress has been interrupted by the parade, to watch it pass. Possibly, you would have thrown some change into the buckets, branded with charity stickers, rattled by the marchers. Certainly, you would wonder, if you had never heard of it, what an earth was going on. This is the Festival of Seething (Figure 15.1).

Promoted as the 'revival' of a legendary festival held by the Villagers of Seething every year until 1921, the most recent festival attracted around 350 people. Marchers were organized into loose affiliations around the Ancient Guilds and Liveries of Seething – the Cheesemakers, Talcum Miners, Taxonomists, Curriers, Water-Bearers, Sardine Fishers and Cyclists. The Ancient Guild of Talcum Miners (from the now sadly defunct Seething Talcum Colliery) make a particularly notable contribution, with the Seething Colliery Brass band, along with the Ale Voice Choir. The festival weekend begins the day before, with a communal costume and goat-mask-making workshop. This is followed by the parade itself, in which the Ancient Guilds process around the 'Seething Square Mile'. (It is with some resentment that the State of Seething notes the appropriation of this concept and that of the Ancient Guilds and Liveries by the City of London.[2]) The parade culminates in an assembly with stage, bar, bands, collective renditions of Seething's traditional songs and dancing of the customary 'Maurice' Dance.

Heritage is a form of cultural reproduction often understood as 'everything that people want to save' (Howard, 2003, p. 1) or that which 'a significant group of population wishes to hand on to the future' (Hewison, 1989, p. 16). The Festival of Seething involves the conscious attempt to implant a 'new piece of folklore' – the Legend of Lefi Ganderson – and to hand this on. The festival is a vehicle for

---

[2] See the 'State of Seething' website, at which films, books and other materials connected with Seething can be viewed: www.seethingwells.org/Welcome_to_Seething_Home.html.

reproducing cultural property, including many practices which recognizably belong within England's intangible heritage of folk dance, brass bands and processional demonstrations. Children are a significant presence at the festival and an important audience. Stories connected with the festival have been published by Robin Hutchinson in a series of children's books (Hutchinson, 2010a, b; 2011; 2012) and Hutchinson works as a Seething 'ritual specialist', visiting schools and working within the Seething community.

Connecting selected aspects of the present with the past and future, heritage intervenes in a politics of time-space. Suburbs have been seen as significant in the structuring of the everyday rhythms of modernity, creating landscapes that shaped the emergence of the daily commute and the weekend (Cross, 1997). The politics of time-space in suburbs can therefore be seen as having distinctive qualities. Historically, the railway has been a significant influence on the built environment (Sampson, 2002, pp. 101–6). Time-space in Surbiton is patterned by enduring rhythms, within which the tidal flows of commuting still play a recognizable part, albeit counterpoised and cross cut with travel to other centres, home working and internal commuting.[3] The Festival of Seething both participates in and interrupts these everyday rhythms or flows, holding up the traffic and interfering with the perambulations of weekend shoppers on the main shopping street. It is an annual intervention in the weekly and diurnal rhythm which has much in common with the annual gatherings and processions (the May Day parades, Beating of Bounds, summer fetes and annual fairs) that formed part of the yearly round in many suburbs in the past and which continue to do so (Clapson, 2003, chapter 7; for a history of the wealth of communal activities in Surbiton, see French, 2011). The Festival of Seething connects the everyday rhythms coursing through Surbiton town centre with those 'eternal' rhythms often envisaged as structuring time over eons – the 'deep' pasts of myth and cosmos.

Reshaping the perceived temporal and spatial rhythms of the suburb is the explicit aim of one of the festival organizers, Robin Hutchinson:

> Surbiton has an interesting challenge because, effectively, it's a dormitory town. The vast majority of people just get on a train, go to London, do their work and then come back, and if they want a night out they stay in London and kind of just treat Surbiton as a place to sleep. And I was fascinated about – were there ways in which you can get people to sort of work together to get a real sense that they love where they live? And also what the impact of that would be? . . . Whether people's behavior patterns begin to change. So . . . the most logical way to do that was to create a half-man half-child . . . to create a new folk-tale, a legend. (RH, 11 March 2011)[4]

---

[3] The 2001 census returns for Surbiton record 26 per cent commuted to work by rail and underground, 9 per cent by bus, 42 per cent by car and 21 per cent worked from home or travelled by bicycle or walking (Royal Borough of Kingston of Thames n.d.). In the borough of Kingston as a whole, people were around 10 per cent more likely to travel to work by car or train than the average London resident (Kingston Data Observatory, 2012, p. 35). I am indebted to David Jeevadrampillai for the idea of time-space 'rhythm'.

[4] Quotes from interviews with Robin Hutchinson are listed as 'RH' followed by the date of the interview in brackets.

Folk heritage can shake people out of established rhythms, entangling them in forms of creative expression and collective participation that, Hutchinson suggests, transform the patterns of space-time that constitute place.

The Festival of Seething has complex and changing economic entanglements. The festival benefits businesses hosting the festival and related events, performers, crew, barstaff, along with a range of cultural producers including photographers, bloggers, local journalists and academics. The festival 'started from a Cheese Club' (RH, 11 March 2011) dedicated to cheese tasting and the creation of cheese-based art taking place at The Lamb, an independently owned and run pub which maintains social networking sites essential to the festival's promotion and growth. The club compere, Lord Scroley (aka Robin Hutchinson), also presides over the Festival of Seething. The 'Villagers of Seething' include cheese club regulars who organized a series of events based around the construction and playing of gigantic board games in the Lamb pub garden. Along with the Festival these and other events raise money for charity (£60,000 for various charities in the last four years, according to the State of Seething website). Fundraising is an important factor in Seething heritage but, like the business interests involved, it is not a rationale to which it can be reduced.[5] The festival does not just exist to make money; it also exists to lose money productively. Interrupting suburban space-time rhythms causes (some) businesses and individuals to lose money, diverting economic flows from well-worn into alternative channels – towards charity buckets, and the potlatch of free labour the State of Seething demands.

The 'Newness' of Seething folklore

A distinctive aspect of Seething folklore is the effort that has gone into advertising its 'newness'. The foundational story – the Legend of Lefi Ganderson – contains archaic features, yet Robin Hutchinson and the Villagers of Seething have gone to remarkable lengths to insist on its novelty. The first Festival was promoted under the title: 'Lefi Ganderson – The Legend Begins'. It is in the nature of folk tradition to be both brand new and ancient at the same time, as it is continually recreated: 'Contemporary folklorists recognize that folklore is the active and creative aspect of tradition, and that change is important in the creation of folklore' (Gavin-Schwartz and Holtorf, 1999, p. 11). How then has the emphasis on newness been achieved? And why has it been so important?

The legend of Lefi Ganderson is a variant of the well-known type 'lone boy defeats the ogre', (AT 327B within the Aarne-Thompson International Tale Type Index). Motifs within the tale include 'eating contest with a giant' (ATU 1088), 'magical ring' (AT 560) and 'ogre's pitfall' (ATU 1117) (Ashliman, 1987). Lefi Ganderson is an ancient hybrid, prefigured by Pan, (who had the legs, hindquarters and horns of a goat), and by the satyr who accompanied Dionysus. Lefi can be associated with drinking, pleasure, priapism and the wild, hedonistic properties that make him appropriate for a festival. Since Lefi is a goat-boy rather than a man, the potential threat he represents (the devil is also a goat hybrid) is tamed; he is playful rather than sinister. Popular in the arts

---

[5] Figure from State of Seething, www.seethingwells.org/Welcome_to_Seething_Home.html. On the 'About' page Lord Scroley describes fund-raising as a 'byproduct' of the 'madness'.

since the Romantics, the satyr suggests hybridity, including ethnic hybridity (as in Defoe's 1701 poem 'The True-born Englishman: A Satyr'). A less dangerous version exists in children's literature and film (Mr Tumnus from *The Lion the Witch and the Wardrobe* is one example). Lefi's fight with the Mount Seething giant is a retelling of Jack the Giant Slayer. The pairing of giant and mountain is fabulously old. King Arthur tackles a giant who inhabits St Michael's Mount in Malory's *Morte d'Arthur. The Epic of Gilgamesh* tells of a fight with a giant born and reared by a mountain.

The usefulness of folklore is not its historical accuracy, but what it implies about the meaning of entities understood as belonging to the past: 'Ancient elements . . . may or may not be of any great age, but this does not affect their social and cultural significance' as 'meaningful and functioning' aspects of the present (Gavin-Schwartz and Holtorf, 1999, p. 6). Seething's heritage practice introduces the eternal 'once upon a time' of fairy stories alongside history's linear time and the time rhythms of contemporary capitalisms. The capacity of folklore to be outside and inside contemporary spacetime is significant: 'For a lot of people, community is something that was wonderful but happened at a time they don't really remember. And it is trying to create this time that never was. To me it's trying to, not model itself on something that wasn't, but trying, through these tales, [to ask] could we define what community could be?' (RH, 11 March 2011). Seething folk tradition is not constructed around the premise of a return to the past, or the survival of a relict past, but on the projection of a possible future past that is efficacious in the present. Insisting on its 'newness' is one way of emphasizing this. However, 'newness' is also important to the antiquarian hoax and archaeological parody that allowed the legend to become implanted in Surbiton.

Archaeology, authenticity and absurdity

In 2009, the obscure British Society of Antiquarians and Archaeologists (BSAA) announced that it had obtained funding from Google to add a new layer of ley-lines onto Google Earth.[6] They had discovered several sites of ley-line intersection. One of these, they announced, was the former site of Mount Seething, where they intended to carry out a ley-line survey and archaeological excavation. These became occasions for the filming of two mockumentaries, produced on handheld camera, with voice-over, interviews to camera and subtitling.

The film 'BSAA Seething Project 2010' documents the BSAA investigation of the Seething ley-line intersection, using dowsing rods and pioneering 'geophys' to trace the convergence of 15 ley-lines in The Lamb beer garden, the 'highest convergence of any location in the UK'. 'BSAA Seething Project 2010' was not only a film, but a means of summoning Seething into being. The event was promoted through social networks and websites as a community happening. Both the performance of ley-line location, which involved costumed people behaving oddly on the streets of Surbiton (Figure 15.2), and the social networks through which the event was organized, emphasized the spatially extensive nature of Seething – a 'place' which is also a network extending outwards to

---

[6] The British Society of Antiquarians and Archaeologists (BSAA) has since changed its name to The British Antiquarian and Archeological Society (BAAS). The earlier name is retained here in the interests of historical accuracy (which BAAS zealously champions).

Dr Ian Best and Professor Simon Clegg
Ministry of Safety and Research

Figure 15.2 Film still from 'BSAA Seething Project 2010'
Reproduced with permission of Lord Scroley and the villagers of Seething

other places. The State of Seething website stressed that BSAA events were 'open to everyone in the community, wherever you live, to join in'.

The BSAA archaeological excavation produced another mockumentary, 'The Dig'. An enthusiastic team, many of them children, assembled at the ley-line convergence under the leadership of Professor Brett Alderton (presenter of the Cable TV documentary *Dead Boring*). In the film, the method appears unstratigraphic, and interviews with participants confirm that little was adduced about the archaeological sequence. However, the finds were spectacular. An iron object was interpreted as the stirrup of the famous White Horse of Seething (Hutchinson, 2010b). A key with an ornate head represented the head of Lefi – with two 'eye holes' and 'horns'. The excavation was not only an occasion for filming, but also a community-building activity in preparation for the first 'revived' festival a few days later. Excavation was valuable, not as a way of finding out what 'really happened' in the past, but because of the capacity it had for creating new kinds of interaction (Smith and Waterton, 2009b): '[we thought] wouldn't it be great, actually, if we could have kids and digging, and just the joy of discovery, and . . . two odd things come out of that, one is the joy of play, and also letting them use their imagination to take something and work it out . . .' (RH, 11 March 2011). Archaeological excavation could create community among people who did not necessarily know each other, or live in Surbiton.

Much in Seething folk tradition has been excavated from the earth of Surbiton. In the film 'Lefi Ganderson's Maurice Dance' the 'the world's oldest footprints' have been unearthed during the digging of a Surbiton water main. Analysis of the footprints by the Museum of Humanity's Choreographic Archaeologist, Janet Lake, leads to reconstruction of 'the world's oldest dance', the Maurice Dance. Analysis of a fossilized cheese, thought to be of the same period as the footprints, reveals musical notation, encoded in the holes of the cheese, allowing the forensic reconstruction of music which may have accompanied dancing of this type. Another Seething legend – Jack and the Golden Egg – has been translated from an ancient text unearthed in 1938 (Figure 15.3).

Excavation grounds Seething in the earth of Surbiton, while also highlighting the 'newness' of Seething's heritage. The Maurice Dance is within the English folk dance tradition with linking arms, hitting sticks, circling in star formation, etc., all set to a piece of folk music. 'Jack and the Golden Egg' contains magical items also found in Aesop's fable 'The Goose that Laid the Golden Egg', and a bowl that never empties (folk tale type AT 565). These productions are, in a sense, genuinely ancient, but archaeological parody is used to deny their antiquity.

Behind the patently falsified pedigrees of Seething lies a concern for factual truth. In advance of the 'revival' of a public festival that might expose the villagers to accusations of 'lying', archaeology supplied Seething with a language of proofs and mechanism of authentification that could be used to safely reveal the invention of tradition:

> We had a lot of discussions in a small group to start with about how people would feel if they thought they had been used or a joke was being made at their expense. So how do you do it so that when they find out they don't feel angry they just go 'yeah'? . . . The essential element was nobody should feel tricked. They can make the discovery in their own time, but they must discover it in such a way that makes them smile and makes them think this is fun. (RH, 11 March 2011)

It is obvious to those who watch the films or follow the links on the State of Seething website and associated sites that the 'archaeological' interpretations put forward are preposterous. The Earth Energies and archaeological investigations are jokes, but they are not hoaxes or Piltdown Man-style forgeries. The archaeology of Seething falls mostly within the category of what Roscoe and Hight (2001) classify as 'degree 1' mock-documentaries: using parody to gradually let everyone feel in on the joke, thereby encouraging them to feel part of an in-crowd. Factuality is not subverted here, on the contrary it is reinforced, as the 'untruthfulness' and 'newness' of Lefi folklore are highlighted and advertised. This calculated non-discovery preserves the existence of Lefi as purely dependent on acts of faith, allowing Lefi mythology to embrace continual manufacture as its origin (Latour and Weibel, 2002).

Seething heritage practices, despite their refusal to take archaeology and the 'Authorised Heritage Discourse' (Smith, 2006) seriously, support their legitimacy. During the excavation the 'ethics' of archaeology were observed – despite the temptation, nothing was planted in the trench. Furthermore, the excavation turned up some material that, off camera, provoked genuine interpretation. Brick paths connected to earlier buildings were uncovered, setting off historical researches into the

The Surbiton Herald

Saturday 21st M

Three Local Men Find Box Whilst Digging for Drainage

Three local men have found a box whilst digging for a new drainage ditch in Brighton Rd.
The men, Mr A Lewis, Mr T Foot and Mr G Leen had been digging for nearly two hours when they unearthed the box.
Mr A Lewis said, "We were very surprised and thought it must be something important.
The box has subsequently been examined by the local Heritage service who have

DENTISTS RECOMMEND DAILY GU

VIBRA-
GUM MASSAGER

FINGER

• STIMULATES GUM TISSUE
• INCREASES and IMPROVES CIRCUL
• SANITARY — FITS IN YOUR HAND
• CLEANSING and REFRESHING

On Thursday 19th May in 1938 three workmen who were digging for a new drainage trench in Surbiton unearthed a wooden box. Although the wood was rotting away the box had been lined with lead.

This was taken to the Kingston Heritage Museum where, on opening, it revealed an ancient book. The script was unrecognizable and so the book was sent to the Ancient Language Department of the Epigraphy and Papyrology Society where work on a translation and dating commenced.

International events overtook the project and it was only in 1948 that the full translation was completed. It was published to great acclaim in 1951 but fell from print in 1966.

This is the first publication of the found story since then.

Figure 15.3 Frontispiece for 'Jack and the Golden Egg, or, How the Seething Community Sports Day started' by Robin Hutchinson (2011)
Reproduced with permission

Lamb Brewery thought to have once been nearby. Far from challenging archaeology's authority then, a kind of homage, a longing, can be detected:

> 'the other [reason they didn't plant anything] was . . . I thought we might just stumble on the actual cave. I think we might just have been slightly out. Some of our ley-lines might be slightly off . . .' (RH, 11 March 2011)

The Legend of Lefi Ganderson needed archaeology, not to authenticate it, but to deny the legend's antiquity. The mockumentaries undermine Lefi's pretension to great age, but there is a real sense in which archaeology nonetheless 'proved' the Lefi Ganderson Legend to be 'true'. The ultimate 'proofs' of the legend's meaning and power are not in its links to factual history so much as in its effects in the present; that is, its effects in creating a community. The excavation really did create the kind of community feeling that allowed the last weekend in February to become the occasion of the 'special day' that, in the legend, reminds the villagers of Seething to 'help others in their community' (Hutchinson, 2010, p. 19). This may be Lefi's legacy and ultimate 'proof'.

Seething and Surbiton

Lefi-related folk traditions take place somewhere both inside and outside Surbiton – the semi-mythical village of Seething. Seething, until recently, was remembered mainly in the name of Kingston University's Seething Wells Halls and in several street names around The Lamb. Rather than occupying a recognizable territory, it was an administratively liminal location; the boundary between the boroughs of Kingston and Elmbridge runs right through the places where Seething's name is preserved. 'The whole point of going onto the Seething bit was to pick on a place that is historically accurate and relevant but not in the language anymore' (RH, 11 March 2011). Neither entirely real nor absolutely fictitious, Seething is the perfect location to nurture a hoax that can grow into parody.

The Legend of Lefi Ganderson transposes the enchanted time-space of Seething onto Surbiton's topography. Place names are reinterpreted as deriving from the legend, and thereby 'confirming' the legend's veracity (while also denying it, depending on how one chooses to read the parody). The occasion of the 'revived' festival (on or near 29 February) becomes its 'proof', as Lefi's words 'twenty-nine fed you and me', are transposed into calendrical time. Yet Seething is not Surbiton, but rather, somewhere where people can express something repressed by Surbiton: 'It's really nice now that we've got a lot of people for whom Seething is a place they come to be; even if it's in sort of a spiritual sense . . .' (RH, 11 March 2011).

The villagers of Seething can 'go to' Seething, but they are also involved in events in Surbiton. In the annual national 'Suburban Skiing Championship', participants ski down one of Surbiton's main shopping streets with blocks of ice strapped to their feet. The Surbiton Escalator Choral Society gathers without prior warning, reciting 'Stairway to Paradise' on shopping centre escalators. Both these events look outwards from Surbiton towards Kingston (the nearest large shopping centre) and the nation (thorough a 'national' sporting event), exporting Surbiton's 'comic capital' as home of the improbable.

Seething's alternative reality expresses something already part of Surbiton's identity, and that which can also be found in the history of suburbia – Utopia. In the time of legend Seething contains all the elements of a lost rural idyll: green fields, tall trees, a sparkling river and before its destruction by Thamas Deeton, the purple mountain of Mount Seething. The suburban dream from the garden city to the present has been built on visions of a similar arcadia (Fishman, 1985). Seething contains something of the Goodes' dream of going back to the land. In the legend, Thamas Deeton the giant returns to Mount Seething every four years until Lefi commands him to leave 'so that the villagers of Seething can have the good life they deserve' (ibid., p. 8). Television sitcom and folk tradition intersect in a rereading of *The Good Life* that seeks to re-appropriate its utopian potential: '*The Good Life* has been the absolute lead weight hung round Surbiton's neck. I think it's interesting because everybody goes "it's Jerry and Margot", but actually, the underpinning of what we're doing is saying . . . it's actually Tom and Barbara; it's actually that sense of adventure and creating' (RH, 11 March 2011). The heritage of Seething reworks the – to some extent unwanted – heritage bequeathed to Surbiton by television.

Suburbs often diversify the opportunities individuals have to exercise 'elective belonging'. Residents articulate 'senses of spatial attachment, social position, and forms of connectivity to other places' that are 'critically dependent on people's relational sense of place, [and] their ability to relate their area of residence against other possible areas, so that the meaning of place is critically judged in terms of its relational meanings' (Bagnall et al., 2005, p. 29). Those who live within the administrative boundaries of Surbiton may identify themselves with many different places across the globe, which might include London, Kingston, Surbiton (and its many internal differentiations) and also Seething. The creation of Seething is part of a play of identification which further diversifies opportunities for 'elective belonging' in suburban life. Furthermore, Seething emerges from place without being place-bound. The socially networked villagers of Seething live in many different places inside and outside the United Kingdom. Just as we may speak of an 'elective belonging' that works in space, so we might also consider one that operates in time. In fact, since places must be defined in terms of time at the same that they are defined in terms of space (Massey, 1995) to identify with a place is also to identify with a past. The villagers of Seething may read parts of Seething tradition as 'false' fiction, as faction (containing elements of truth), or even elect to receive it against the intentions of some creators, as historical truth; Hutchinson reports that he knows people who 'believe that the legend of Lefi Ganderson has existed for generations *emphatically*' (RH, 11 March 2011, his emphasis) – and, as I have argued above, parts of it have.

Seething heritage practices have characteristics that can be described as distinctively suburban. The Seething festival interrupts everyday rhythms of space-time in the suburb, connecting them to a cosmological and mythic timespace, re-directing social and economic flows, and allowing money to be 'lost' in a way that is nonetheless productive for certain groups. In keeping with the widespread assumption that 'suburbia has no history' (Webster, 2000, p. 2) and that authentic folk tradition does not belong there, great emphasis has been placed on underlining the 'newness' of Seething folklore, including the use of archaeological mockumentary as a means of denying its ancient elements. The notion that suburbs lack authentic communities makes community-building, rather than authoritative factual discourse, the focus of archaeological activities. Finally, it can be argued that Seething heritage is a creative re-working of a heritage that Surbiton can seldom ignore – the heritage of its stereotyping as the 'suburban' home of the extraordinary and improbable.

Bibliography

Adebayo, D. (2011), 'Smiley Culture Made Us Proud to be Black and British'. www.guardian.co.uk/commentisfree/2011/mar/15/smiley-culture-reggae-star-died. Accessed 24 September 2009.

Adelson, L. A. (2003), 'Against between: A Manifesto', in Zafer Şenocak (ed.), *Contemporary German Writers*. Cardiff: University of Wales Press, pp. 130–43.

The Age Newspaper (1964), 'Memorial Recalls Seaside Settlers', 28 January.

Ahlfeldt, G., Holman, N. and Wendland, N. (2012), *An Assessment of the Effects of Conservation Areas on Value*. Swindon: English Heritage.

Alim, H. S. (2006), *Roc the Mic Right: The Language of Hip Hop Culture*. New York; London: Routledge.

— (2009), 'Straight Outta Compton, Straight aus München: Global Linguistic Flows, Identities, and the Politics of Language in a Global Hip Hop Nation', in H. S. Alim, A. Ibrahim and A. Pennycook (eds), *Global Linguistic Flows: Hip Hop Cultures, Youth Identities, and the Politics of Language*. London: Routledge, pp. 1–22.

Androutsopoulos, J. (2011), 'Language Change and Digital Media: A Review of Conceptions and Evidence', in K. Tore and N. Coupland (eds), *Standard Languages and Language Standards in a Changing Europe*. Oslo: Novus, pp. 145–61.

Archer, J. (2009), 'Representing Suburbia: From Little Boxes to Everyday Practices', Unpublished Conference Paper.

— (2010), 'The Place We Love to Hate: The Critics Confront Suburbia, 1920–1960', in K. Stierstorfer (ed.), *Constructions of Home: Interdisciplinary Studies in Architecture, Law, and Literature*. New York: AMS Press, pp. 45–82.

Ashliman, D. L. (1987), *A Guide to Folktales in the English Language: Based on the Aarne-Thompson Classification System*. New York: Greenwood Press.

Augé, M. (1995), *Non-Places: Introduction to an Anthropology of Supermodernity*. London: Verso.

Babcock, R. (1966), *The Zoning Game*. Madison: University of Wisconsin Press.

Bachelard, G. (1969 [1958]), *The Poetics of Space*. Boston: Beacon Press.

Bäckstedt, E. (2004), 'Betongen fick egen ordbok'. *Svenska Dagbladet*, 17 September.

— (2005), 'Hajp, keff och guss nytillskott i ordlista'. *Svenska Dagbladet*, 24 September.

Bagnall, G., Savage, M. and Longhurst, B. (2005), *Globalization and Belonging*. London: Sage.

Bajo, A. and Bronić, M. (2004), 'Fiskalna decentralizacija u Hrvatskoj: problemi fiskalnog izravnavanja' [Fiscal Decentralization in Croatia: Problems of Fiscal Equalization], *Financijska teorija i praksa*, no. 28, 445–67.

Ballard, J. G. (1973), 'How to Face Doomsday without Really Dying – Interview with Carol Orr'. [Online] Available at: www.jgballard.ca/interviews/jgb_cbc_ideas_interview.html. Accessed 25 September 2009. Unpublished transcript for the Canadian Broadcasting Corporation, c. 1973–4.

— (1978), *The Crystal World*. St Albans: Triad/Panther Books.

— (1981), *The Unlimited Dream Company*. Reading: Triad/Granada.

— (1985), *Vermilion Sands*. London: J. M. Dent & Sons.

— (1995), *Crash*. London: Vintage.

— (1996), *Cocaine Nights*. London: Flamingo.

— (1997), 'Airports'. *The Observer*, 14 September.

— (1999), 'Despite Huge Advances in Science and Technology, the 20th Century Will Strike Us as a Barbarous Time', *New Statesman*, 20 December.

— (2000), *Super-Cannes*. London: Flamingo.

— (2001), 'Welcome to the Virtual City', *Tate, the Art Magazine*, 24.

— (2002), *Running Wild*. London: Harper Collins.

— (2003), *Millennium People*. London: Harper Collins.

— (2005), *High-Rise*. London: Harper Perennial.

— (2006), *The Drowned World*. London: Harper Perennial.

— (2007), *Kingdom Come*. London: Harper Perennial.

Ballent, A. (2005), *Las Huellas de la Política: Vivienda, Ciudad, Peronismo en Buenos Aires, 1843–1955*. Bernal, Provincia de Buenos Aires: Universidad Nacional de Quilmes.

Banco Hipotecario Nacional (1958), *Plan de Emergencia: Eliminación de las Villas Miseria de la Capital Federal*. Buenos Aires.

Barker, P. (2009a), 'Let Us Treasure the Suburbs, Our Landscape's String of Pearls', *The Independent*, 1 November. http://www.independent.co.uk/opinion/commentators/paul-barker-let-us-treasure-the-suburbs-our-landscapes-string-of-pearls-1812761.html. Accessed 12 January 2012.

— (2009b), *The Freedoms of Suburbia*. London: Frances Lincoln Limited.

Botoillo, G. (1985), *Visions of Excess: Selected Writings, 1927–1939*. Minneapolis: University of Minnesota Press.

Bean, C. E. W. (1969), speaking at the *John Murtagh Macrossen Lecture*. Brisbane: Queensland University.

Beatley, T. and Manning, K. (1997), *The Ecology of Place: Planning for Environment, Economy, and Community*. Washington, DC: Island Press.

Beauregard, R. (2006), *When America became Suburban*. Minneapolis: University of Minnesota Press.

de Beauvoir, S. (1997), *The Second Sex*. Translated by H. M. Parshley. London: Vintage.

Beck, U. (1992), *Risk Society: Towards a New Modernity*. Translated by M. Ritter. London: Sage Publications, 1986.

Beers, D. (1996), *Blue Sky Dream*. New York: Doubleday.

Bell, A. and Gibson, A. (2011), 'Staging Language: An Introduction to the Sociolinguistics of Performance', *Journal of Sociolinguistics*, 15 (5): 555–72.

Benjamin, J. (n.d.), 'How Cosmo Changed the World'. *Cosmopolitan*. [Online] Available from: www.cosmopolitan.com/magazine/about/about-us_how-cosmo-changed-the-world. Accessed 31 January 2012.

Berger, B. M. (1968), *Working-Class Suburb: A Study of Auto Workers in Suburbia*. Berkeley and Los Angeles: University of California Press.

Berlant, L. (2011), *Cruel Optimism*. Durham: Duke University Press.

Berni, A. (1999), *Antonio Berni: Escritos y papeles privados*. Buenos Aires: Temas Grupo Editorial.

Beugnet, M. (2004), *Claire Denis*. Manchester: Manchester University Press.

Beuka, R. (2004), *SuburbiaNation: Reading Suburban Landscape in Twentieth-Century American Fiction and Film*. New York: Palgrave Macmillan.

Bijvoet, E. (2003), 'Attitudes Towards "Rinkeby Swedish", a Group Variety among Adolescents in Multilingual Suburbs' in K. Fraurud and K. Hyltenstam (eds), *Multilingualism in Global and Local Perspectives. Selected Papers from the 8th Nordic Conference on Bilingualism, November 1–3,* Stockholm: Centre for Research on Bilingualism/Rinkeby Institute of Multilingual Research, pp. 307–18.

Blackdown (2012), '96 Reasons to Rate JME', 20 February. http://blackdownsoundboy. blogspot.com/2012/02/96-reasons-to-rate-jme.html. Accessed 28 February 2012.

Blake, A. and Cloutier-Fisher, D. (2009), 'Backyard Bounty: Exploring the Benefits and Challenges of Backyard Garden Sharing Projects', *Local Environment*,14(9): 797–807.

Blunt, A. (2003), 'Collective Memory and Productive Nostalgia: Anglo-Indian Homemaking at McCluskieganj', *Environment and Planning D: Society and Space,* 21: 717–38.

Bodén, P. (2011), 'Adolescents' Pronunciation in Multilingual Malmö, Gothenburg and Stockholm', in R. Källström and I. Lindberg (eds), *Young Urban Swedish: Variation and Change in Multilingual Settings.* Gothenburg: University of Gothenburg, pp. 35–48.

Bolt, A. (2005), 'Our Racism in Bronze', *Herald-Sun,* 18 May, http://ilovestkilda.julieshiels. com.au. Accessed 15 January 2012.

Bone, M. (2005), *The Postsouthern Sense of Place in Contemporary Fiction.* Baton Rouge: Louisiana State University Press.

Bonetti, K. (2001), 'An Interview with Richard Ford', in H. Guagliardo (ed.), *Conversations with Richard Ford.* Jackson: University Press of Mississippi, pp. 21–38.

Bowes, A. (2011), 'The Rise of the Neighbourhood Triffids', *Journal of Planning and Environment Law,* 4: 386–91.

Boyd, R. (1961), *The Australian Ugliness.* Melbourne: Cheshire Press.

Boyer, P. (1978), *Urban Masses and Moral Order in America.* Cambridge, MA: Harvard University Press.

Boym, S. (2001), *The Future of Nostalgia.* New York: Basic Books.

Bridge, G. (2006), 'It's Not Just a Question of Taste: Gentrification, the Neighbourhood, and Cultural Capital', *Environment and Planning A,* 38 (10): 1965–78.

Broadway, M. (2009), 'Growing Urban Agriculture in North American Cities: The Example of Milwaukee', *Focus on Geography,* 52 (3–4): 23–30.

Brooks, K. (2009), 'Life Is Not a Game: Reworking the Metaphor in Richard Ford's Fiction', in *The Journal of Popular Culture,* 42, 844–8.

Brown, N. (1995), *Governing Prosperity: Social Change and Analysis in Australia in the 1950s.* Cambridge: Cambridge University Press.

Bruegmann, R. (2005), *Sprawl: A Compact History.* Chicago: University of Chicago Press.

Bulbeck, C. (1988), 'The Stone Laurel: Of Race, Gender and Class in Australian Memorials', *Cultural Policy Studies Occasional Paper* no. 5. Brisbane: Griffith University.

Burnside, J. (2011), *Waking up in Toytown.* Vintage: London.

Buss, B. (2012), '"Let the Punishment Fit the Crime": The Case of No. 6 Trafalgar Road, London', *The Historic Environment: Policy and Practice,* 3 (2): 116–26.

Butler, J. (1997), Excitable Speech: A Politics of the Performative. New York: Routledge.

Calvino, I. (1979), *Invisible Cities.* Translated by Harcourt Brace Jovanovich Inc. London: Pan Books.

Campbell, N. (2011), 'Affective Critical Regionalism in D. J. Waldie's Suburban West', in D. Rio, A. Ibarraran and M. Simonson (eds), *Beyond the Myth: New Perspectives on Western Texts.* Vitoria-Gasteiz: Portal Education, pp. 87–106.

Campbell, N. and Waldie, D. J. (2011), '"An Assemblage of Habits": D. J. Waldie and Neil Campbell – A Suburban Conversation', *Western American Literature,* 46 (3): 228–49.

de Certeau, M. (1984), *The Practice of Everyday Life*. Berkeley: University of California Press.

Chadwick, V. (2011), 'Skating over Bali Bombing Remembrance', *Eureka Street,* 11 October.

Cheesman, T. (2004), 'Talking "Kanak": Zaimoğlu contra Leitkultur', *New German Critique*, 92, 82–99.

Cheshire, J., Fox, S., Kerswill, P. and Torgersen, E. (2008), 'Ethnicity, Friendship Network and Social Practices as the Motor of Dialect Change: Linguistic Innovation in London'. *Sociolinguistica*, 22, 1–23.

Cheshire, J., Kerswill, P., Fox, S. and Torgersen, E. (2011), 'Contact, the Feature Pool and the Speech Community: The Emergence of Multicultural London English', *Journal of Sociolinguistics*, 15 (2): 151–96.

Chicago Daily Tribune (1907), 'Geese and Goats Jostle Citizens', 25 September, p. 4.

— (1908), 'Suburb Wants Chicken Law', 3 February, p. 3.

— (1909), 'Many Chicken Farms in Chicago Slums', 9 May, p. H2.

City of Bingen, Washington (2009), Bingen city council minutes, September 15. www.bingenwashington.org/minutes%202009.09.15.pdf. Accessed 8 November 2010.

City of Gresham, Oregon (2009), Gresham city council minutes. 1 December.

City of Pleasant Grove, Utah (2010), Pleasant Grove city council work session minutes. 29 June.

City of Sanford, North Carolina (2009), Minutes of meeting of the City Council of the city of Sanford.

Clapson, M. (1998), *Invincible Green Suburbs, Brave New Towns: Social Change and Urban Dispersal in Post-War England*. Manchester: Manchester University Press.

— (2003) *Suburban Century: Social Change and Urban Growth in England and the USA*. Oxford: Berg Publishers.

Clyne, M. (2000), 'Lingua Franca and Ethnolects in Europe and beyond', *Sociolinguistica*, 14: 83–9.

College Township Planning Commission (2009), Planning Commission minutes, 21 July.

Collier, J. (1967), *Visual Anthropology: Photography as a Research Method*. New York: Holt, Rinehart and Winston.

Comisión de Afirmación de la Revolución Libertadora (1985), *A 30 Años de la Revolución Libertadora: Sucedió una Vez. . . y Sucedió Para Siempre*. Buenos Aires.

Comisión Nacional de la Vivienda (1956), *Plan de Emergencia: Informe elevado el Poder Ejecutivo Nacional*. Buenos Aires: Departamento de publicaciones y biblioteca, Ministerio de Trabajo y Previsión, República Argentina.

Corey, M. F. (1999), *The World through a Monocle: The New Yorker at Mid-Century*. Cambridge, MA and London: Harvard University Press.

Corner, M. (2006) 'Opening the Literal: Spirituality in Updike and Ford', in M. Knight and T. Woodman (eds), *Biblical Religion and the Novel*. London: Ashgate, pp. 137–52.

Cronon, W. (1991), *Nature's Metropolis: Chicago and the Great West*. New York: Norton.

Cross, G. (1997), 'The Suburban Weekend: Perspectives on a Vanishing Twentieth-Century Dream', in R. Silverstone (ed.), *Visions of Suburbia*. London: Routledge, pp. 108–31.

Crouch, D. (2010), *Flirting with Space: Journeys and Creativity*. Farnham: Ashgate.

Cruzvillegas, A. (2010), 'Thomas Hirshhorn', *Bomb*, 113, Fall. http://bombsite.com/issues/113/articles/3621. Accessed 18 January 2013.

d'Angiolillo, J., Dimentstein, M., Di Peco, M., Guérin, A. I., Massidda, A. L., Molíns, M. C., Muñoa, N., Scarfi, J. P. and Torroja, P. (2010), 'Feria La Salada: una centralidad periférica intermitente en el Gran Buenos Aires', in M. Gutman (ed.), *Argentina:*

Persistencia y Diversificación, Contrastes e Imaginarios en las Centralidades Urbanas. Quito: Olacchi, pp. 169–206.

Dahlstedt, M. (2005), 'Betongen slår tillbaks', *Häften för Kritiska Studier,* 191/192: 72–89.

Darebin Historical Encyclopedia (no date), http://dhe.darebin-libraries.vic.gov.au/. Accessed January 2012.

Dart, G. (2010), 'Daydreaming', in M. Beaumont and G. Dart (eds), *Restless Cities.* London: Verso, pp. 79–97.

Davidson, M. and Lees, L. (2005), 'New-Build "Gentrification" and London's Riverside Renaissance'. *Environment and Planning A,* 37 (7): 1165–90.

Davison, G. (1978), *The Rise and Fall of Marvelous Melbourne.* Melbourne: Melbourne University Press.

Deleuze, G. (1989), *The Logic of Sense.* Translated by M. Lester and C. Stivale. London: Athlone.

— (1994), *Difference and Repetition.* Translated by P. Power. New York: Columbia University Press.

Dibbell, J. (1989), 'Weird Science', *Spin,* February, 51–2: 75.

Digital Spaces Working Group (n.d.), 'Distributed Biography', http://distributedbiography. org/about_html. Accessed 4 September 2012.

Dines, M. (2010), *Gay Suburban Narratives in American and British Culture: Homecoming Queens.* Basingstoke: Palgrave.

Downs, A. (1973), *Opening up the Suburbs: An Urban Strategy for America.* New Haven: Yale University Press.

Duffy, B. (2008), *Morality, Identity and Narrative in the Fiction of Richard Ford.* Amsterdam and New York: Rodopi.

Duncan, J. S. and Duncan, N. G. (2001), 'Sense of Place as a Positional Good, Locating Bradford in Time and Space', in P. C. Adams, S. Hoelscher and K. E. Till (eds), *Texture of Place: Exploring Humanist Geographies.* Minneapolis: University of Minnesota Press, pp. 41–54.

Dunham-Jones, E. and Williamson, J. (2009), *Retrofitting Suburbia.* New York: Wiley.

Dupuy, E. (2000), 'The Confessions of an Ex-Suicide: Relenting and Recovering in Richard Ford's *The Sportswriter*', in H. Guagliardo (ed.), *Perspectives on Richard Ford.* Jackson: University Press of Mississippi, pp. 71–82.

Durant, R. (1939), *Watling: A Survey of Social Life on a New Housing Estate.* London: P. S. King.

Dyos, H. (1966), *Victorian Suburb: A Study of the Growth of Camberwell.* Leicester: University Press.

Eagleton, T. (1996), *The Illusions of Postmodernism.* Oxford: Blackwell.

Echchaïbi, N. (2007), 'Republican Betrayal: Beur FM and the Suburban Riots in France', *Journal of Intercultural Studies,* 28 (3), www.nabilechchaibi.com/resources/ Republican%20Betrayal.doc.

The Economist (1968), 'The Surbiton Revolution', 6 January, p. 12.

Eisinger, J. (1995), *Trace and Transformation: American Criticism of Photography in the Modernist Period.* Albuquerque: University of New Mexico Press.

Ekberg, L., Ganuza, N. and Utrzén, M. (2004), 'Language and Language Use among Adolescents in Multilingual Urban Areas in Stockholm, Malmö and Gothenburg'. Paper presented at Second International Symposium on Bilingualism, Vigo.

English Heritage (2007), *Suburbs and the Historic Environment.* Swindon: English Heritage.

— (2008), *Conservation Principles.* Swindon: English Heritage.

Farmer's Market Magazine (2012), 'The Good Life Just Got Better', 17 March.

Farrington, E. (1912), 'Hens That Cut the Cost of Living', *Chicago Daily Tribune*, 22 December, p. J8.

Feenstra, G. (1997), 'Local Food Systems and Sustainable Communities', *American Journal of Alternative Agriculture*, 12: 28–36.

Feldt, L. (2006), 'Dis/orientations: Fantastic Memory in the Exodus Narrative', in Ansgar Nünning (ed.), *Literature and Memory: Theoretical Paradigms – Genres – Functions*. Tübingen: Francke, pp. 95–112.

Ferber, S., Healy, C. and McAuliffe, C. (eds) (1994), *Beasts of Suburbia: Reinterpreting Cultures in Australian Suburbs*. Melbourne: Melbourne University Press.

Feuer, J. (1993), *The Hollywood Musical*. 2nd edn. Bloomington: Indiana University Press.

Fishman, R. (1987), *Bourgeois Utopias: The Rise and Fall of Suburbia*. New York: Basic Books.

Flagge, I. (ed.) (1999), *Geschichte des Wohnens*. Band 5: 1945 bis heute. Aufbau Neubau Umbau. Stuttgart: Dt. Verl.-Anst.

Ford, R. (1996), *The Sportswriter*. London: Collins Harvill.

— (2001), 'Introduction', in R. Yates, *Revolutionary Road*. London: Methuen, pp. xiii–xxiv.

— (2003), *Independence Day*. London: Vintage.

— (2006), *The Lay of the Land*. London: Bloomsbury.

Forsyth, A. (2012), 'Defining Suburbs', *Journal of Planning Literature*, 27 (3), 270–81.

Foucault, M. (1967), 'Of Other Spaces', available at http://foucault.info/documents/heteroTopia/foucault.heteroTopia.en.html. Accessed 3 September 2012.

— (1979), *Discipline and Punish: The Birth of the Prison*. Harmondsworth: Penguin Books.

— (2007), *Security, Territory, Population: Lectures at the Collège de France, 1977–78*. Basingstoke: Palgrave Macmillan.

Fox, S., Khan, A. and Torgersen, E. (2011), 'The Emergence and Diffusion of Multicultural London English', in F. Kern and M. Selting (eds), *Ethnic Styles of Speaking in European Metropolitan Areas*. Amsterdam: John Benjamins, pp. 19–44.

Fraurud, K. and Bijvoet, E. (2004), 'Multietniskt ungdomsspråk och andra varianter av svenska i flerspråkiga miljöer', in K. Hyltenstam and I. Lindberg (eds), *Svenska som Andraspråk: i Forskning, Undervisning och Samhälle*. Lund: Studentlitteratur, pp. 389–417.

French, C. (2011), 'The Good Life in Victorian and Edwardian Surbiton: Creating a Community Before 1914', *Family and Community History*, 14 (2): 105–20.

Freud, S. (1937), 'Konstruktionen in der Analyse', in *Gesammelte Werke*, chronologisch geordnet. Edited by Anna Freud et al. Vol. XVI, 1950. Frankfurt/Main: Fischer, pp. 41–56. (Fifth edition printed 1978).

Friedman, A. T. (2006), *Women and the Making of the Modern House: A Social and Architectural History*. New Haven and London: Yale University Press.

Gallagher, J. (1958), 'After Hours: That Lived in Look'. *Harper's Magazine*, February, 80–1.

Gans, H. J. (1967), *The Levittowners: Ways of Life and Politics in a New Suburban Community*. London: Random House.

Garreau, J. (1991), *Edge City: Life on the New Frontier*. New York: Doubleday.

Gasiorek, A. (2005), *J. G. Ballard*. Manchester: Manchester University Press.

Gavin-Schwartz, A. and Holtorf, C. (1999), '"As Long as Ever I've Known It . . .": On Folklore and Archaeology', in A. Gavin-Schwartz and C. Holtorf (eds), *Archaeology and Folklore*. London: Routledge, pp. 3–25.

Geesey, P. (2011), 'A Space of Their Own? Women in Maghrebi-French Filmmaking', in S. Durmelat and V. Swamy (eds), *Screening Integration: Recasting Maghrebi Immigration in Contemporary France*. Lincoln and London: University of Nebraska Press, pp. 161–77.

Germani, G. [n.d.], *El proceso de urbanización en la Argentina. Trabajos e investigaciones del Instituto de Sociología, Publicación interna n°4*. Buenos Aires: Servicio de documentación de sociología, Facultad de Filosofía y Letras, Universidad de Buenos Aires.

Giddens, A. (1991), *Modernity and Self-Identity: Self and Society in the Late Modern Age*. Oxford: Polity.

Gilbert, D. and Preston, R. (2003), '"Stop Being So English": Suburban Modernity and National Identity in the Twentieth Century', in D. Gilbert, D. Matless and B. Short (eds), *Geographies of British Modernity: Space and Society in the Twentieth Century*. Oxford: Wiley-Blackwell, pp. 187–203.

Gillespie, N. (1996), 'Bye-Bye American Pie', in *Reason*, December. http://reason.com/archives/1996/12/01/bye-bye-american-pie. Accessed 27 June 2010.

Gilroy, P. (2002), *There Ain't No Black in the Union Jack*. London: Routledge.

Goldsworthy, V. (2004), 'The Love That Dares Not Speak Its Name: Englishness and Suburbia', in D. Rogers and J. McLeod (eds), *The Revision of Englishness*. Manchester: Manchester University Press, pp. 95–106.

Gordon, A., Gordon, A. F. and Radway, J. (2008), *Ghostly Matters: Haunting and the Sociological Imagination*. Minneapolis: University of Minnesota Press.

Gordon, J. and Gordon, C. (1933), *The London Roundabout*. Edinburgh: Harrap.

Gordon, R. E., Gordon, K. E. and Gunther, M. (1960), *The Split-Level Trap*. New York: Bernard Geis Associates.

Gorelik, A. (1998), *La Grilla y el Parque. Espacio Público y Cultura Urbana en Buenos Aires, 1887–1936*. Bernal, Provincia de Buenos Aires: Universidad Nacional de Quilmes.

Gray, J. (2009), 'Appreciation: J. G. Ballard', *New Statesman*, 23 April.

Green, O. (2009), *Transformed by the Tube*. Presentation at the London Transport Museum, 17 November.

Griffiths, S., Vaughan, L., Haklay, M. and Jones, C. E. (2008), 'The Sustainable Suburban High Street: A Review of Themes and Approaches', *Geography Compass*, 2 (4): 1155–88.

Gringoredaktionen (2006), '"Miljonsvenska" är språkglädje', *Dagens Nyheter*, 2 May.

Guinn, M. (2002), 'Into the Suburbs: Richard Ford's Sportswriter Novels and the Place of Southern Fiction', in Suzanne W. Jones and Sharon Monteith (eds), *South to a New Place: Region, Literature, Culture*. Baton Rouge: Louisiana State University Press, pp. 196–207.

Günter, M. (1999), '"Wir sind bastarde, freund . . ." – Feridun Zaimoglus Kanak Sprak und die performative Struktur von Identität', *Sprache und Literatur*, 83/30 (1): 15–28.

Hagan, K. (2005), 'Crates Shrine to "Parkies"', *Port Phillip Leader Newspaper*, 7 July, http://ilovestkilda.julieshiels.com.au. Accessed January 2012.

Hall, P. and Pain, K. (2006), *The Polycentric Metropolis: Learning from Mega-City Regions in Europe*. London: Earthscan Ltd.

Halsall, R. (2004), 'Phenomenology of the Suburb: Peter Handke's Mein Jahr in der Niemandsbucht', in J. Preece and O. Durrani (eds), *Cityscapes and Countryside in Contemporary German Literature*. Bern: Peter Lang, pp. 159–78.

Handke, P. (1974), 'Die offenen Geheimnisse der Technokratie', in *Als das Wünschen noch geholfen hat*. Frankfurt/M.: Suhrkamp, pp. 31–54.

Hanlon, B. (2012), *Once the American Dream: Inner-Ring Suburbs of the United States*. Philadelphia: Temple University Press.

Hanlon, B., Short, J. and Vicino, T. (2010), *Cities and Suburbs: New Metropolitan Realities in the United States*. New York: Routledge.

Hapgood, L. (2005), *Margins of Desire: The Suburbs in Fiction and Culture 1880–1925.* Manchester: Manchester University Press.

Hardiman, K. G. (1975), 'Owens, Arbus, and Wisconsin Death Trip', *Creative Camera*, 134 (August): 260–1.

Hargreaves, A. G. (2007), *Multi-Ethnic France: Immigration, Politics, Culture and Society* (2nd edn). New York: Routledge.

Harris R. and Larkham, P. (eds) (1999), *Changing Suburbs: Foundation, Form and Function.* London: Spon.

Harrison, R. (2010), 'What is Heritage?', in R. Harrison (ed.), *Understanding the Politics of Global Heritage.* Manchester: Manchester University Press, pp. 5–42.

Hartwig, I. (2010), 'Die schlimme, schlimme Sucht. Georg Klein erzählt fulminant von der Zeit, als die Mädchenschlüpfer noch Gummibänder hatten', *Die Zeit*, 17 March.

Harvey, D. (1989), 'From Managerialism to Entrepreneurialism: The Transformation in Urban Governance in Late Capitalism', *Geografiska Annaler*, 71 (1): 3–17.

— (2000), *Spaces of Hope.* Edinburgh: University Press.

— (2001), *Spaces of Capital: Towards a Critical Geography.* New York: Routledge.

— (2008), 'The Right to the City', *New Left Review*, 53, September–October: 23–40.

— (2012), *Rebel Cities: From the Right to the City to the Urban Revolution.* New York: Verso, 2012.

Hayden, D. (1984), *Redesigning the American Dream: The Future of Housing, Work, and Family Life.* New York: W. W. Norton.

— (2003), *Building Suburbia: Green Fields and Urban Growth, 1820–2000.* New York: Vintage.

Henderson, H. (1953), 'Rugged American Collectivism: The Mass-Produced Suburbs, Part II', *Harper's Magazine*, December, 80–6.

Henry, W. (2006), *What the Deejay Said.* London: Nu-Beyond Ltd.

Heritage Victoria (2012), *Victorian Heritage Database*, http://vhd.heritage.vic.gov.au/places/result_detail/15142. Accessed January 2012.

Hewison, R. (1989), 'Heritage: An Interpretation', in D. Uzzell (ed.), *Heritage Interpretation*, vol. 1. London: Belhaven, pp. 15–23.

Hewitt, R. (1986), *White Talk Black Talk: Inter-Racial Friendship and Communication Amongst Adolescents.* Cambridge: Cambridge University Press.

Highmore, B. (2002), *Everyday Life and Cultural Theory: An Introduction.* London: Routledge.

— (2011), *Ordinary Lives: Studies in the Everyday.* London: Routledge.

Hinchcliffe, T. (2005), 'Elusive Suburbs, Endless Variation', *Journal of Urban History*, 31, (6): 899–906.

Hine, T. (1986), *Populuxe.* New York: Knopf.

Hobson, F. (2005a), 'Post-Faulkner, Post-southern: Richard Ford's *The Sportswriter*', in F. Hobson, *The Silencing of Emily Mullen and Other Essays.* Baton Rouge: Louisiana State University Press, pp. 165–78.

— (2005b), *The Silencing of Emily Mullen and Other Essays.* Baton Rouge: Louisiana State University Press.

Housing Development Board (2012a), 'HDB history', www.hdb.gov.sg/fi10/fi10320p.nsf/w/AboutUsHDBHistory?OpenDocument. Accessed 6 December 2012.

— (2012b), 'Home – Where the Heart Is', http://heartland.hdb.gov.sg/. Accessed 6 December 2012.

Howard, E. (1965), *Garden Cities of To-morrow.* Cambridge: MIT Press.

Howard, K. (1906), *The Smiths of Surbiton: A Comedy without a Plot*. London: Chapman & Hall.

Howard, P. (2003), *Heritage: Management, Interpretation, Identity*. London: Continuum.

Hutchinson, R. (2010a), *The Legend of Lefi Ganderson*. Seething: Homage Publishing.

— (2010b), *The King's Soup*. Seething: Homage Publishing.

— (2011), *Jack and the Golden Egg, or, How the Seething Community Sports Day Started*. Seething: Homage Publishing.

— (2012), *The Last Sardines*. Seething: Homage Publishing.

Inglis, K. (2008), *Sacred Places: War Memorials in the Australian Landscape*. Melbourne: Melbourne University Press.

Ingold, T. (2007), *Lines. A Brief History*. London: Routledge.

Jackson, K. (1985), *Crabgrass Frontier: The Suburbanization of the United States*. Oxford: Oxford University Press.

James, S. (2000), 'From Photography to Brewing and Back', *RPS Journal*, 140 (6): 269–71.

Jamoussi, Z. (2011), *Primogeniture and Entail in England: A Survey of their History and Representation in Literature*. Cambridge: Cambridge Scholars Publishing

Jarvis, H., Pratt, A. C. and Wu, P. C. (2001), *The Secret Life of Cities: The Social Reproduction of Everyday Life*. Harlow: Prentice Hall.

Johns, L. (2010), 'The Secret World of Gang Slang', *Evening Standard*, 1 November.

Jurca, C. (2001), *White Diaspora: The Suburb and the Twentieth-Century American Novel*. Princeton: Princeton University Press.

— (2009), 'Tales of the Suburb', in D. Rubey (ed.), *Redefining Suburban Studies: Searching for New Paradigms*. Hofstra: National Center for Suburban Studies, pp. 171–9.

Karaman, L. (1963), *O djelovanju domaće sredine u umjetnosti hrvatskih krajeva* ['On the Influence of Local Ambience on the Art of Croatia']. Zagreb: Društvo historičara umjetnosti [Society of Art Historians]. Republished 2001 as *Problem periferijske umjetnosti*, (The Problems of Peripheral Art). Zagreb: Društvo povjesničara umjetnosti.

Kastner, J. (2000), 'A Vision of Suburban Bliss Edged with Irony'. *The New York Times* (March 19). [Online] Available from: http://query.nytimes.com/gst/fullpage.html?r es=940CE6DC113BF93AA25750C0A9669C8B63&sec=&spon=&pagewanted=all. Accessed 31 January 2012.

Keats, J. (1956), *The Crack in the Picture Window*. Boston: Houghton Mifflin.

Kelly, B. M. (1993), *Expanding the American Dream: Building and Rebuilding Levittown*. Albany: State University of New York Press.

Kerstan, T. (2011), 'Keine Wut im Bauch. Im Ausland rebelliert die Jugend, hierzulande nicht', *Die Zeit*, 1 September.

Kerswill, P. (2011), *Multicultural London English* (PowerPoint presentation for talk given at British Library in March 2011), www.lancs.ac.uk/staff/kerswill/ Multicultural%20London%20English%20BL%2022%20Mar%2011.ppt. Accessed 20 September 2011.

Kerswill, P., Cheshire, J., Fox, S. and Torgerson, E. (2007), Linguistic Innovators: The English of Adolescents in London: Full Research Report ESRC End of Award Report, RES-000–23–0680. Swindon: ESRC.

Kingston Data Observatory (2012), 'Borough Profile 2012', www.kingston.gov.uk/ information/nhoodhome/kdo.htm. Accessed 21 October 2012.

Klaić, B. (2007), *Rječnik stranih riječi* ('Dictionary of Loanwords in the Croatian Language'), Zagreb: Školska knjiga.

Klein, G. (2010), *Roman unserer Kindheit*. Reinbek bei Hamburg: Rowohlt.

Klingst, M. (2005), 'Raus aus dem Ghetto: Deutschland hat noch keine französischen Verhältnisse. Aber viele Einwanderer grenzen sich selbst aus', *Die Zeit*, 10 November.

Kloppenburg, J., Hendrickson, J. and Stevenson, G. W. (1996), 'Coming in to the Foodshed', *Agriculture and Human Values*, 14 (3): 33–42.

Knipp, C. (2011), 'Bas-Fonds', CineScene, www.cinescene.com/knipp/bas-fonds.html.

Kohon, D. J. (1958), *Buenos Aires*. Buenos Aires.

Koolhaas, R. (2000), 'Singapore Songlines: Portrait of a Potemkin Metropolis . . . or Thirty Years of Tabula Rasa', in M. Miles, T. Hall and I. Borden (eds), *The City Cultures Reader*. London; New York: Routledge, pp. 22–5 (excerpts).

Kotsinas, U. B. (1988), 'Rinkebysvenska – en dialekt?' in P. Linell, V. Adelswärd, T. Nilsson and P. A. Petersson (eds), *Svenskans beskrivning 16*, Linköping: Linköping University, pp. 264–78.

— (1998), 'Language Contact in Rinkeby, an Immigrant Suburb', in J. Androutsopoulous and A. Scholz (eds), *Jugendsprache Langue de Jeunes Youth Language*. Frankfurt am Main: Peter Lang, pp. 125–48.

— (2001), 'Från Ekensnack till Rinkebyska', *Pedagogiska Magasinet*, 2 (1): 8–14.

Kotsinas, U. B. and Dogge Doggelito (2004), *Förortsslang*. Stockholm: Norstedts Akademiska Förlag.

Kröncke, G. (2010), 'Wie man es nicht machen sollte', *Süddeutsche Zeitung*, 17 May.

Kruse K. M. and Sugrue T. J. (2006), 'Introduction', in K. M. Kruse and T. J. Sugrue, *The New Suburban History*. Chicago: Chicago University Press, pp. 1–10.

Kuchenbuch, D. (2010), *Geordnete Gemeinschaft. Architekten als Sozialingenieure – Deutschland und Schweden im 20. Jahrhundert*. Bielefeld: transcript.

Kureishi, H. (1990), *The Buddha of Suburbia*. London: Faber and Faber.

Lachmann, R. (1997), *Memory and Literature: Intertextuality in Russian Modernism*. Minneapolis, MN: University of Minnesota Press.

— (2002), *Erzählte Phantastik: zu Phantasiegeschichte und Semantik phantastischer Texte*. Frankfurt a. M.: Suhrkamp.

Lang, R. E. (2003), *Edgeless Cities: Exploring the Elusive Metropolis*. Washington, DC: Brookings Institution Press.

Lang, R. E. and LeFurgy, J. (2007), *Boomburbs: The Rise of America's Accidental Cities*. Washington, DC: Brookings Institution Press.

Latour, B. (1978), *Science in Action*. Cambridge, MA: Harvard University.

Lee, G. (2010), 'On Identity: Singapore's Auditory Thumbprint'. 4 September. www.civiclife.sg/blog/?cat=8.

Lefebvre, H. (1991), *The Production of Space*. Translated by D. Nicholson-Smith. Oxford: Basil Blackwell.

— (2003), *The Urban Revolution* (1970). Translated by R. Bononno. Minneapolis: University of Minnesota Press.

Legislative Committee (2009), City of New Haven Journal of the Board of Aldermen Legislation Committee. 8 June.

Leinberger C. B. and Lockwood, C. (1986), 'How Business is Reshaping America'. *The Atlantic*, October, 43–52.

Levine, P. (1984), *Selected Poems*. London: Secker and Warburg.

Lewi, H. and Jordan, C. (2010), 'Commemorating and Enhancing the Everyday', in H. Lewi, and D. Nichols (ed.), *Community: Building Modern Australia*. Sydney: UNSW Press.

Li, W. (1998), 'Anatomy of a New Ethnic Settlement: The Chinese Ethnoburb in Los Angeles', *Urban Studies*, 35 (3): 479–501.

Lindsey, A. (1942), *The Pullman Strike*. Chicago: University of Chicago Press.

Lipman, J. (1935), 'Social and Economic Factors in Land-Use Planning in the Northeastern States', *Economic Geography,* 11 (3): 217–26.

London Evening Standard (2012), 'Spotlight on Surbiton', Homes and Property Supplement, 7 November.

London Government Act (1963) (c. 33), www.legislation.gov.uk/ ukpga/1963/33. Accessed 29 February 2012.

London Transport Museum (2011), *Kingston: The Growth of London through Transport.* London: Transport for London

Longenbach, J. (1997), *Modern Poetry after Modernism.* Oxford: Oxford University Press.

Lotman, Y. M. (2001), *Universe of the Mind: A Semiotic Theory of Culture.* London: I.B. Tauris.

— (2005), 'On the Semiosphere', in *Sign Systems Studies,* 33 (1): 205–29.

Lunn, M. (2007), *Street Art Uncut.* Fisherman's Bend: Craftsman House.

Majić, M. (2011), *Arhitektura Splita 1945–1960.* (Architecture of Split, 1945–60), Split: Društvo arhitekata Split (The Association of Architects Split).

Malpass, P. (2009), 'Whose Housing Heritage?', in L. Gibson and J. Pendlebury (eds), *Valuing Historic Environments.* Farnham: Ashgate, pp. 201–14.

Marc, D. (1989), *Comic Visions: Television Comedy and American Culture.* Boston: Unwin Hyman, 1989.

Marcuse, P. (1997), 'Walls of Fear and Walls of Support', in N. Ellin (ed.), *Architecture of Fear.* New York: Princeton Architectural Press, pp. 101–14.

Marks, L. U. (2000), *The Skin of the Film: Intercultural Cinema, Embodiment, and the Senses.* Durham, NC: Duke University Press.

Maroondah Tourism and Heritage Advisory Board (2009), *Maroondah Walks and Trails.* Victoria: Maroondah City Council.

Martinson, T. (2000), *American Dreamscape: The Pursuit of Happiness in Post-War Suburbia.* New York: Carroll and Graf.

Marx, L. (1964), *The Machine in the Garden: Technology and the Pastoral Ideal in America.* New York: Oxford University Press.

Marzo, S. and Ceuleers, E. (2011), 'The Use of Citétaal among Adolescents in Limburg: The Role of Space Appropriation in Language Variation and Change', *Journal of Multilingual and Multicultural Development,* 32 (5): 451–64.

Massey, D. (1993), 'Politics and Space/Time', in M. Keith and S. Pile (eds), *Place and the Politics of Identity.* London: Routledge, pp. 141–61.

— (1995), 'Places and Their Pasts', *History Workshop Journal,* 39, 182–92.

Massidda, A. (2011), 'Urban Planning and Undertakings upon Informal Settlements in Buenos Aires: A 1955–1959 Review'. University of Cambridge, MPhil dissertation, unpublished.

— (2012), 'The Plan de Emergencia (1956): The Argentine Debate about Housing Shortage Then and Now', *Scroope,* 21, 42–51.

McGinley, P. (1951), *A Short Walk from the Station.* New York: Viking.

McManus, R. and Ethington, P. J. (2007), 'Suburbs in Transition: New Approaches to Suburban History', *Urban History,* 34 (2): 317–37.

Medhurst, A. (1997), 'Negotiating the Gnome Zone: Versions of Suburbia in British Popular Culture', in R. Silverstone (ed.), *Visions of Suburbia.* London: Routledge, pp. 240–68.

Mintzer, J. (2010), 'All That Glitters, Tout ce qui brille (France)', *Variety,* 30 April, www.variety.com/review/VE1117942668?refcatid=31.

Mirams, S. (2011), *Darebin Parklands: Escaping the Claws of the Machine*. Melbourne: Melbourne Books.

Mitchell, J. (1961), 'Sprinkler in the Suburbs', *The Sewanee Review*, 69 (2): 269–70.

Mitscherlich, A. (1965), *Die Unwirtlichkeit unserer Städte. Anstiftung zum Unfrieden*. Frankfurt/M.: Suhrkamp.

Montana Conservation Voters (2009), Montana Conservation Voters – 2009 Missoula City scorecard.www.mtvoters.org/system/files/MissoulaCityScorecard_0.pdf. Accessed 6 November 2010.

Mora, G. (2007), *The Last Photographic Heroes: American Photographers of the Sixties and Seventies*. New York: Abrams.

Moraldo, S. M. (2007), 'Kanak Sprak: The Linguistic Features of Turkish Migrants' Communicative Style in Feridun Zaimoğlu's Works', in D. Miller and M. Turci (eds), *Language and Verbal Art Revisited: Linguistic Approaches to the Study of Literature*. London: Equinox, pp. 234–52.

Moretti, F. (2007), *Atlas of the European Novel 1800–1900*. London: Verso.

Mumford, L. (1961), *The City in History: Its Origins, Its Transformations, and Its Prospects*. San Diego: Harcourt, Brace and Company.

— (1966), *The City in History: Its Origins, Its Transformations, and Its Prospects*. London: Pelican.

Murray, S. (2003), *The Progressive Housewife: Community Activism in Suburban Queens, 1945–1965*. Philadelphia: University of Pennsylvania Press.

Myers, J. A. (1963), 'Death in the Suburbs', *English Journal*, 52 (5): 377–9.

The National Heritage Protection Plan (2012), Activity 4A1 'Historic Towns and Suburbs', pp. 58–61.

Nemerov, H. (1958), *Mirrors and Windows: Poems*. Chicago: University of Chicago Press.

— (1977), *The Collected Poems of Howard Nemerov*. Chicago and London. University of Chicago Press.

Ng, Y. S. (2011), 'Old Places Out Now on DVD', Civic Life Tiong Bahru.com, 5 August. http://civiclifetiongbahru.com/2011/05/08/old-places-out-now-on-dvd/. Accessed 26 August, 2011.

Nicolaides, B. M. (2002), *My Blue Heaven: Life and Politics in the Working-Class Suburbs of Los Angeles, 1920–1965*. Chicago: Chicago University Press.

— (2006), 'How Hell Moved from the City to the Suburbs: Urban Scholars and Changing Perceptions of Authentic Community', in K. Kruse and T. Sugrue (eds), *The New Suburban History*. Chicago: University of Chicago Press, pp. 80–98.

Nordahl, D. (2010), *Public Produce: The New Urban Agriculture*. Washington, DC: Island Press.

Nyberg, L. (2008), 'Från underjorden till öffentligheten – eller tvärtom?', in M. Krogh and B. Stougaard Pedersen (eds), *Hiphop i Skandinavien*, Århus: Århus Universitetsförlag, 155–80.

O'Reilly, N. (2012), *Exploring Suburbia: The Suburbs in the Contemporary Australian Novel*. Amherst, NY: Teneo Press.

Oldenburg, R. (1989), *The Great Good Place: Cafes, Coffee Shops, Bookstores, Bars, Hair Salons and Other Hangouts at the Heart of a Community*. New York: Marlowe & Co.

Orwell, G. (2001), *Coming up for Air*. London: Penguin.

Owens, B. (1972), *Suburbia*. San Francisco: Straight Arrow Books.

— (1978), *Documentary Photography: A Personal View*. Danbury: Addison House.

— (1979), *Publish Your Photo Book: A Guide to Self-Publishing*. Dobbs Ferry: Morgan and Morgan.

— (1999), *Suburbia* (revised edn). New York: Fotofolio.
— (2000), Interviewed by D. Lang, 'Photographer, Brew Master, Publisher: Bill Owens Comes Full Circle'. *Art a Gogo*. [Online] Available from: www.artagogo.com/interview/owensinterview/owensinterview.htm. Accessed 30 January 2012.
— (2007), 'The Altamont Story', in A. M. Holmes, B. Owens and C. Zanfi, *Bill Owens. Photographs 1967–2007*. Bologna: Damiani, pp. 209–10.
— (2008), Interviewed by R. Hirsch, 'Bill Owens: Photographing the Suburban Soul'. *Fotofile* 49 (May), 7–13.
— (2011), Interviewed by B. Gilman. Hayward, California, 14 April 2011.
Pack, J. (2002), *Growth and Convergence in Metropolitan America*. Washington, DC: Brookings Institution.
Pallasmaa, J. (2011), *The Embodied Image: Imagination and Image in Architecture*. Chichester: John Wiley.
Paterson, M. (2007), *The Senses of Touch*. Oxford: Berg.
Perec, G. (1998), *Species of Spaces and Other Pieces*. New York: Penguin.
Phelps, N. A. and Woo, F. (2011), *International Perspectives on Suburbanization: A Post-Suburban World?* Basingstoke: Palgrave.
Philo, C. (1998), 'Animals, Geography and the City: Notes on Inclusions and Exclusions', in J. Wolch and J. Emel (eds), *Animal Geographies: Place, Politics, and Identity in the Nature-Culture Borderlands*. London: Verso, pp. 51–71.
Pike, B. (1981), *The Image of the City in Modern Literature*. New Jersey: Princeton University Press.
Pile, S. (2004), 'Ghosts and the City of Hope', in L. Lees (ed.), *The Emancipatory City? Paradoxes and Possibilities*. London: Sage, pp. 210–28.
— (2005), 'Spectral Cities: Where the Repressed Returns and Other Short Stories', in J. Hillier and E. Rooksby (eds), *Habitus, A Sense of Place*. Farnham: Ashgate, pp. 235–57.
— (2005b), *Real Cities: Modernity, Space and the Phantasmagorias of City Life*. London: Sage.
Pile, S., Brook, C. and Mooney, G. (1999), *Unruly Cities?* London: Routledge.
Podalsky, L. (2004), *Specular City: Transforming Culture, Consumption, and Space in Buenos Aires, 1955–1973*. Philadelphia: Temple University Press.
Pollan, M. (2006), *The Omnivore's Dilemma: A Natural History of Four Meals*. New York: Penguin Press.
Porter, R. (1994), *London: A Social History*. London: Penguin.
Pratt, M. L. (1991), 'Arts of the Contact Zone', *Profession* 91. New York: MLA, 33–40.
Pratt, R. (1945), 'Easy to Live in', *Ladies Home Journal*, January, 116.
Qvist, P. (2008), 'Sociolinguistic Approaches to Multiethnolect: Language Variety and Stylistic Practice', *International Journal of Bilingualism*, 12 (1–2): 43–61.
Qvist, P. and Svendsen, B. (2010), *Multilingual Urban Scandinavia: New Linguistic Practices*. Bristol: Multilingual Matters.
Rampton, B. (1995), *Crossing: Language and Ethnicity among Adolescents*. London: Longman.
— (2010), 'From "Multi-Ethnic Urban Heteroglossia" to "Contemporary Urban Vernacular"', *Working Papers in Urban Language and Literacies* (61).
Rancière, J. (2009), *The Emancipated Spectator*. London: Verso.
Reimer, S. (2010), 'A Seed Shortage May Come in 2010', *Houston Chronicle*, 11 January. www.chron.com/disp/story.mpl/gardening/features/6809275.html. Accessed 6 November 2010.

Riesman, D. (1957), 'The Suburban Dislocation', *Annals of the American Academy of Political and Social Science*, 314, 123–46.

Ristilammi, P. M. (1994), *Rosengård och den svarta poesin: En studie av modern annorlundahet*. Stockholm: Symposion.

Rodaway, P. (2002), *Sensuous Geographies: Body, Sense and Place*. New York: Routledge.

Rogić Lugarić, T. (1985), 'Normativna decentralizacija u Hrvatskoj i njezine granice' (Normative Decentralisation in Croatia and Its Boundaries), *Društvena istraživanja*, 6 (80): 1175–98.

Roscoe, J. and Hight, C. (2001), *Faking It: Mock-Documentary and the Subversion of Factuality*. Manchester: Manchester University Press.

Royal Borough of Kingston Upon Thames (2011), 'Surbiton Neighbourhood Community Plan', www.kingston.gov.uk/draft_surbiton_community_plan.pdf.

Rupnik, I. (2010), *A Peripheral Moment: Experiments in Architectural Agency (Croatia 1999-2010)*. Barcelona: Actar.

Sa'at, A. (2001), *A History of Amnesia: Poems*. Singapore: Ethos Books.

Saint, A. (ed.) (1999), *London Suburbs*. London: Merrell.

Sampson, J. (1997), *Kingston Past*. London: Historical Publications.

Sandercock, L. (2005), 'Difference Fear and Habitus: A Political Economy of Urban Fears', in J. Hillier and E. Rooksby (eds), *Habitus, A Sense of Place*. Farnham: Ashgate, pp. 219–34.

Savage, P. M., Bagnall, D. G. and Longhurst, D. B. (2005), *Globalization and Belonging*. London: Sage.

Scates, B. (2009), *A Place to Remember: A History of the Shrine of Remembrance*. Melbourne: Cambridge University Press.

Schetzer, A. (2011), 'Supporters Speak up on "Ugly" Garden', *The Melbourne Times*, 20 December.

Schlosser, E. (2001), *Fast Food Nation: The Dark Side of the All-American Meal*. New York. Houghton Mifflin Harcourt.

Scott, A. J. (2001), *Global City-Regions: Trends, Theory, Policy*. Oxford: Oxford University Press.

Sekula, A. (1984), *Photography against the Grain: Essays and Photo Works 1973–1983*. Halifax: Press of the Nova Scotia College of Art and Design.

Self, R. O. (2003), *American Babylon: Race and the Struggle for Postwar Oakland*. Princeton: Princeton University Press.

Self, W. (2000), *Sore Sites*. London: Ellipsis.

Shane, D. G. (2011), *Urban Design Since 1945: A Global Perspective*. Chichester: Wiley.

Shanken, A. M. (2002), 'Planning Memory: Living Memorials in the United States During World War II', *The Art Bulletin*, March, 130–47.

Sharpe, W. C. (1990), *Unreal Cities: Urban Figuration in Wordsworth, Baudelaire, Whitman, Eliot, and Williams*. Baltimore: John Hopkins University Press.

Shermer, E. T. (2011), 'Sunbelt Boosterism: Industrial Recruitment, Economic Development, and Growth Politics in the Developing Sunbelt', in M. Nickerson and D. Dochuk (eds), *Sunbelt Rising: The Politics of Place, Space, and Region*. Philadelphia: University of Pennsylvania Press, pp. 31–57.

Shields, R. (2003), *The Virtual*. London: Routledge.

Sholis, B. (2005), 'Bill Owens', *Artforum*, 44 (2): 274.

Sieverts, T. (2003), *Cities without Cities: An interpretation of the Zwischenstadt*. London/ New York: Spon Press.

Silverstone, R. (1997), 'Introduction', in R. Silverstone (ed.), *Visions of Suburbia*. London: Routledge, pp. 1–25.

Sinclair, I. (1999), *Crash: David Cronenberg's Post-Mortem on J. G. Ballard's 'Trajectory of Fate'*. London: British Film Institute.

— (2003), *London Orbital*. London: Penguin.

SINdie: Singapore Films Only (2010), 'Production Talk – "The Impossibility of Knowing" by Tan Pin Pin', 11 October, http://sindieonly.blogspot.com/2010/10/production-talk-impossibility-of.html. Accessed 26 August, 2011.

Skepta (2010), Interview: www.radioplanet.tv/skepta-shade-45-interview/. Accessed 24 September 2011.

Skiba, D. (2004), 'Ethnolektale und literarisierte Hybridität in Feridun Zaimoglu Kanak Sprak', in K. Schenk, A. Todorow and M. Tvrdik (eds), *Migrationsliteratur: Schreibweisen einer interkulturellen Moderne*. Tübingen: Francke, pp. 183–204.

Smith, C. (1995). *Urban Disorder and the Shape of Belief*. Chicago: University of Chicago Press.

Smith, L. and Waterton, E. (2009a), 'The Envy of the World? Intangible Heritage in England', in L. Smith and N. Akagawa (eds), *Intangible Heritage*. London: Routledge, pp. 289–302.

— (2009b), *Heritage, Communities and Archaeology*. London: Duckworth.

Smith, M. and Associates (2011), *Hughes Park, Croydon. Landscape Master Plan*. Maroondah City Council.

Smith, R. (1999), 'Bill Owens – Suburban Folk Tales', *The New York Times* (November 12). [Online] Available from: http://query.nytimes.com/gst/fullpage.html?res=9B01E0D 8163DF931A25752C1A96F958260&scp=4&sq=bill%20owens&st=cse. Accessed 30 January 2012.

Smith, W. (2000), 'The Life of the Writer: Lunch with Richard Ford', in H. Guagliardo (ed.), *Perspectives on Richard Ford* (Jackson: University Press of Mississippi), pp. 49–57.

Spectorsky, A. C. (1955), *The Exurbanites*. New York: J. B. Lippincott.

Spliid Høgsbro, C. and Wischmann, A. (2010) (eds), *Nortopia. Nordic Modern Architecture and Post War Germany*. Berlin: Jovis.

Stafford, W. (1962), *Traveling through the Dark*. New York: Harper and Row.

Starr, A., Card, A., Benepe, C., Auld, G., Lamm, D., Smith, K. and Wilken, K. (2002), 'Sustaining Local Agriculture: Barriers and Opportunities to Direct Marketing between Farms and Restaurants in Colorado', *Agriculture and Human Values*, 20 (3): 301–21.

Statham, R. (1996), *Surbiton Past*. Guildford: Phillimore.

Steinberg, T. (2007), *American Green: The Obsessive Quest for the Perfect Lawn*. New York: Norton.

Steiner, G. (1978), *Heidegger*. London: Fontana.

Stephens, J. (2007), 'Memory, Commemoration and the Meaning of a Suburban War Memorial', in *Journal of Material Culture*, 12 (3): 241–61.

Stewart, K. (2005), 'Cultural Poesis: The Generativity of Emergent Things', in N. Denzin and Y. S. Lincoln (eds), *The Sage Handbook of Qualitative Research* (Third Edition), London: Sage, pp. 1027–42.

— (2007), *Ordinary Affects*. Durham: Duke University Press.

— (2009), 'Kathleen C. Stewart'. https://webspace.utexas.edu/kcs/stewart/index.html.

— (2010), 'Worlding Refrains', in M. Gregg and G. Siegworth (eds), *The Affect Theory Reader*. Durham: Duke University Press, pp. 339–53.

— (2011), 'Atmospheric Attunements', *Environment and Planning D: Society and Space*, 29 (3): 445–53.

— (2012), 'Worldings', University of Derby, 26 May 2012, Affective Landscapes Conference, Derby, 25–26 May.

Stilgoe, J. R. (1988), *Borderland: Origins of the American Suburb, 1820–1939*. New Haven: Yale University Press.

Stone, L. (1977), *Family, Sex and Marriage in England, 1500–1800*. Durrington: Littlehampton Book Services.

Stretton, H. (1971), *Ideas for Australian Cities*. Melbourne: Georgian House.

Summers, H. (1954), 'The Lawnmower', *Poetry*, 83 (6): 319.

Swamy, V. (2011), 'Repackaging the *banlieues*: Malik Chibane's *La trilogie urbaine*', in S. Durmelat and V. Swamy (eds), *Screening Integration: Recasting Maghrebi Immigration in Contemporary France*. Lincoln and London: University of Nebraska Press, pp. 211–27.

Swenarton, M. (2002), 'Tudor Walters and Tudorbethan: Reassessing Britain's Inter-War Suburbs', *Planning Perspectives*, 17 (3): 267–86.

Tan, K. P. (2008), *Cinema and Television in Singapore: Resistance in One Dimension*. Leiden; Boston: Brill.

Tan, S. and Yeoh, B. S. A. (2006), 'Negotiating Cosmopolitanism in Singapore's Fiction', in J. Binnie, J. Holloway, S. Millington and C. Young (eds), *Cosmopolitan Urbanism*. New York: Routledge, pp. 146–67.

Tarr, C. (2005), *Reframing Difference: Beur and Banlieue Filmmaking in France*. Manchester and New York: Manchester University Press, 2005.

— (2007), 'Reassessing French Popular Culture: *L'Esquive*', in I. Vanderschelden and D. Waldron (eds), *France at the Flicks: Trends in Contemporary French Popular Cinema*. Newcastle: Cambridge Scholars Press, pp. 130–41.

— (2009), 'Community, identity and the dynamics of borders in Yasmina Yahiaoui's *Rue des Figuiers* (2005) and Karin Albou's *La Petite Jérusalem* (2006)', *International Journal of Francophone Studies*, 12 (1): 77–90.

Taylor, G. (1919), *The Building Journal*. 12 June, 45–50.

Teaford, J. (2008), *The American Suburb: The Basics*. New York: Routledge

— (2011), 'Suburbia and Post-suburbia: A Brief History', in N. A. Phelps and F. Wu (eds), *International Perspectives on Suburbanization: A Post-Suburban World?* Basingstoke: Palgrave.

Teoalida (2010), http://teoalida.webs.com/singapore.htm. Accessed 26 August 2011.

Thompson, G. and Ellis, D. (1996), 'Interview with Richard Ford', in *OVERhere: A European Journal of American Culture*, 16 (2): 105–25.

Thornton, S. (1995), *Club Cultures: Music, Media and Subcultural Capital*. Cambridge: Polity Press.

— (2005), 'The Social Logic of Subcultural Capital', in K. Gelder (ed.), *The Subcultures Reader* (2nd edn), London: Routledge.

Thrift, N. (2008), *Non-Representational Theory: Space, Politics, Affect*. London: Routledge.

Thwaites, T. Davis, L. and Mules, W. (eds) (1994), *Tools For Cultural Studies*. South Melbourne: Macmillan Education Australia, pp. 25–43.

The Times, (1968), 'Half Hour Extra Plan Snowballs', 1 January, p. 1.

Timms, E. (1985), 'Introduction: Unreal City – Theme and Variations', in E. Timms and D. Kelley (eds), *Unreal City: Urban Experience in Modern European Literature and Art*. Manchester: Manchester University Press, pp. 1–12.

Toh, D. (2011), 'The Heartlands at Toa Payoh'. ComeSingapore.com Your One- Stop Travel Guide to Singapore. 13 April. http://comesingapore.com/travel- guide/article/557/the-heartlands-@-toa-payoh. Accessed 26 August 2011.

Toop, D. (2000), *Rap Attack 3*. London: Serpent's Tail.

Trienekens, S. (2002), '"Colourful" Distinction: The Role of Ethnicity and Ethnic Orientation in Cultural Consumption', *Poetics*, 30 (4): 281–98.

Tuan, Y. F. (1977), *Space and Place: The Perspective of Experience*. Minneapolis: University of Minnesota Press.

— (1979), *Topophilia: A Study of Environmental Perception, Attitudes and Values*. Englewood Cliffs, NJ: Prentice-Hall.

Unfinished Modernisations (2012), www.unfinishedmodernisations.net.

Urry, J. (2002), *The Tourist Gaze* (2nd edn). London: Sage.

— (2004), 'The "System" of Automobility', *Theory, Culture & Society*, 21 (4/5): pp. 25–39.

Van Duyn, M. (2003), *Selected Poems*. New York: Alfred A. Knopf.

Vaughan, L., Griffiths, S., Haklay, M. and Jones, E. (2009), 'Do the Suburbs Exist? Discovering Complexity and Specificity in Suburban Built Form', *Transactions of the Institute of British Geographers*, 34 (4): 475–88.

Velayutham, S. (2007), *Responding to Globalization: Nation, Culture and Identity in Singapore*. Singapore: Institute of South East Asian Studies.

Verbitsky, B. (1957), *Villa Miseria También es América*. Buenos Aires: G. Kraft.

Vidler, A. (2011), *The Scenes of the Street and Other Essays*. New York: Monacelli Press.

Vincendeau, G. (2005), *La Haine (Mathieu Kassovitz, 1995)*. London and New York: I.B. Tauris.

— (2007), '*La haine* and After: Arts, Politics, and the Banlieue', www.criterion.com/current/posts/642-la-haine-and-after-arts-politics and-the-banlieue.

von Sternburg, J. (2010), 'Wurmchens Sommer. Georg Kleins neuer Roman', *Frankfurter Rundschau*, 16 March.

Waldie, D. J. (1996), *Holy Land: A Suburban Memoir*. New York: St Martin's.

— (2004), *Where We are Now: Notes from Los Angeles*. Los Angeles: Angel City Press.

— (2007), 'Ordinary Time: The Making of a Catholic Imagination', *Spiritus*, 7 (1): 58–67.

Wall, J. (1995), '"Marks of Indifference": Aspects of Photography in, or as, Conceptual Art', in A. Goldstein and A. Rorimer (eds), *Reconsidering the Object of Art: 1965–1975*. Cambridge: MIT Press, pp. 265–66.

War Memorials in Australia Database, www.msk.id.au/memorials2/pages/listvic.htm. Accessed January 2012.

Webster, R. (2001), 'Introduction: Suburbia inside out', in R. Webster (ed.), *Expanding Suburbia. Reviewing Suburban Narratives*. London: Berghahn Books, pp. 1–14.

Westgate Bridge Memorial Organisation (2012), www.westgatebridge.org/memorials. Accessed May 2012.

Whyte, W. H. (1956), *The Organization Man*. London: Pelican.

Wiese A. (2005), *Places of Their Own: African American Suburbanization in the Twentieth Century*. Chicago: Chicago University Press.

Wiese, H. (2009), 'Grammatical Innovation in Multiethnic Urban Europe: New Linguistic Practices among Adolescents', *Lingua*, 119: 782–806.

Wilbur, R. (1989), *New and Collected Poems*. London: Faber and Faber.

Williams, R. (1973), *The Country and the City*. Oxford: Oxford University Press.

— (1993 [1973]), *The Country and the City*. London: Chatto and Windus.

Wilson, E. (1992), *The Sphinx in the City: Urban Life, the Control of Disorder, and Women*. Berkeley: University of California Press.

— (1995), 'The Rhetoric of Urban Space. *New Left Review*, 209: 146–60.

Wilson, R. and Connery, C. L. (eds) (2007), *The Worlding Project: Doing Cultural Studies in the Era of Globalization*. Santa Cruz: New Pacific Press.

Wilson, S. (2005 [1955]), *The Man in the Gray Flannel Suit*. Harmondsworth: Penguin.

Wirth-Nesher, H. (1996), *City Codes: Reading the Modern Urban Novel*. Cambridge: Cambridge University Press.

Witt-Brattström, E. (2006), 'Vem äger svenskan?' *Dagens Nyheter*, 12 April.

Wittgenstein, L. (1953), *Philosophical Investigations*. Oxford: Blackwell.

Wollenberg, C. (1985), *Golden Gate Metropolis: Perspectives on Bay Area History*. Berkeley: Institute of Governmental Studies, University of California.

Wright, J. (1963), *The Branch Will Not Break*. London: Longmans, Green and Co.

Wylie, P. (1943), *Generation of Vipers*. New York: Dalkey Archive Press.

Yates, R. (2001 [1961]), *Revolutionary Road*. London: Methuen.

Young, J. E. (1993), *The Texture of Memory: Holocaust Memorials and Meaning*. New Haven: Yale University Press.

Yunovsky, O. (1984), *Claves políticas del problema habitacional argentino, 1955–1981*. Buenos Aires: Grupo Editor Latinoamericano.

Zaimoglu, F. (1995), *Kanak Sprak. 14 Mißtöne vom Rande der Gesellschaft*. Hamburg: Rotbuch.

— (1997), *Abschaum*. Hamburg: Rotbuch.

— (1998), *Koppstoff. Kanaka Sprak vom Rande der Gesellschaft*. Hamburg: Rotbuch.

Zanfi, C. (2007), 'Bill Owens: A Life in Suburbia', in A. M. Holmes, B. Owens and C. Zanfi (eds), *Bill Owens. Photographs 1967–2007*. Bologna: Damiani, pp. 211–15.

Zukin, S. (2010), *Naked City: The Death and Life of Authentic Urban Places*. Oxford: Oxford University Press.

Contributors

Hugh Bartling is Associate Professor of Public Policy at Depaul University, Chicago. His research looks at the environmental impacts of urban planning and policy and the politics of sustainability in metropolitan regions and, particularly, how these dynamics function in suburban settings in North America. He also has a long-standing interest in the historical development of planning in suburbia. He is the co-editor of *Suburban Sprawl: Culture, Theory and Politics* (2003) and *What is a City?: Rethinking the Urban after Hurricane Katrina* (2010).

Neil Campbell is Professor of American Studies and Research Manager at the University of Derby, UK. He has published widely in American Studies, including the books *American Cultural Studies* (with Alasdair Kean), and as editor, *American Youth Cultures*, co-editor of *Issues on Americanisation and Culture, Land and Identity*, and *Photocinema*. He has published articles and chapters on John Sayles, Terrence Malick, Robert Frank, J. B. Jackson, D. J. Waldie, Wim Wenders and many others. His major current research project is an interdisciplinary trilogy of books on the contemporary American West. The first two are *The Cultures of the American New West* (2000) and *The Rhizomatic West* (2008) and the final part, *Post-Westerns,* on the cinematic representation of the New West is due in 2013.

Martin Dines is Senior Lecturer in English Literature at Kingston University London and a researcher in Kingston's Centre for Suburban Studies. He is a partner of the Leverhulme Trust-funded Cultures of the Suburbs International Research Network and a founding member of the Literary London Society. He is the author of *Gay Suburban Narratives in American Literature and Culture: Homecoming Queens* (2010), and has published articles and chapters on landscape and environment in the work of various American and British writers, including John Barth, Dennis Cooper, Pam Conrad, Jeffrey Eugenides and Alan Hollinghurst.

Tim Foster has a PhD in American Literature from the University of Nottingham, UK. His doctoral research was on representations of suburbia in contemporary US novels and short stories, and was entitled 'Escaping the Split-Level Trap: Postsuburban Narratives in Recent American Fiction'. He is currently a Teacher of English and Film Studies at a school in Bedfordshire.

Jo Gill is Senior Lecturer in Twentieth-Century Literature at the University of Exeter, UK. She is the author of *Anne Sexton's Confessional Poetics* (2007), *Women's Poetry* (2007), *The Cambridge Introduction to Sylvia Plath* (2008) and *The Poetics of the American Suburbs* (2013). She is the lead partner in the Leverhulme Trust-funded Cultures of the Suburbs International Research Network.

Bridget Gilman is a PhD Candidate in the History of Art at the University of Michigan, Ann Arbor. Her research interests lie at the intersection of art history and urban studies, focusing on the ways contemporary artists have responded to shifts in the American landscape. Her dissertation, 'Re-envisioning Everyday Spaces: Photorealism in the San Francisco Bay Area', examines the evolution of hybrid media practices, networks of exchange in the visual and literary arts and representations of demographic transformations on the West Coast. Her work has been supported by the Social Science Research Council, the Smithsonian American Art Museum, the National Portrait Gallery, the Henry Luce Foundation/American Council of Learned Societies and the University of Michigan Rackham Graduate School.

Caroline Jordan is an art historian and Honorary Associate in the School of Humanities at La Trobe University, Melbourne, Australia. She writes on women artists, the history of art galleries and museums, public art and the influence of philanthropy on art in Australia.

Jarrad Keyes is an independent researcher currently preparing his doctoral thesis on representations of urban space in contemporary British literature for publication. He is particularly interested in Ballard's works and is planning to write at greater length on his representations of urban and suburban space.

Gaik Cheng Khoo is an Associate Professor in the Faculty of Arts at the University of Nottingham in Malaysia, where she lectures in transnational cinema. She has published extensively on independent filmmaking in Malaysia. She is also interested in cosmopolitan spaces that transcend ethnic boundaries such as public eating places. She has also taught gender and cultural studies, Southeast Asian cinema and on Australian multiculturalism through food and sport.

Hannah Lewi is an Associate Professor in the Faculty of Architecture, Building and Planning at the University of Melbourne, Australia. Her research interests span architecture history with a focus on Australian modernism, heritage theory and the representation of place through new digital media. She is the current vice-chair of Docomomo Australia, and is co-editor of *Community: Building Modern Australia* (2010).

Alan Mace is a Lecturer in Urban Planning Studies at the London School of Economics. He trained in planning at University College London and completed his PhD at King's College London. As a qualified planner he has worked in London and has considerable experience of community involvement in policy development and major planning applications. His research interests include shrinking cities and suburbs, community interpretation of change in suburban areas, community involvement in planning and the social impact of rural second homes. He is currently collaborating in research programmes at Hosei University, Japan (shrinking suburbs) and at the Norwegian Institute for Urban and Regional Research (planning compact cities). His most recent publications include *City-Suburbs: Placing Suburbia in a Post Suburban World* (2013).

Adriana Laura Massidda is a PhD Candidate in Architecture at the University of Cambridge. Her research focuses on the history of urban informality in Buenos Aires and the interaction between shantytowns and the State. She completed an MPhil in Architecture at Cambridge in September 2011 and obtained her architectural training from the University of Buenos Aires, where she graduated in 2006. Before embarking on her current research, Adriana worked in architectural practices in Argentina and in the United Kingdom.

Caroline Merkel is a PhD candidate at the German Department of the University of Tuebingen. Her main research interests are twentieth-century German literature, cultural theory (with a focus on spatial and urban theories) as well as the relationships between literature, space and memory. She is currently working on her doctoral thesis about representations of the suburbs in German and Scandinavian literature.

Dalibor Prančević is a research assistant in the Department of Art History at the University of Split, Croatia. He teaches on twentieth-century and contemporary art and exhibition practice. Prančević is a founding member of the curatorial-artistic collective OUR (Organization of Associated Labour). He both curates and writes about independent exhibitions of contemporary art.

Nichola Smalley is in the third year of a PhD entitled 'Contemporary Urban Vernaculars in Rap, Literature and Translation' in University College London's Department of Scandinavian Studies. Her research explores how contemporary urban vernaculars are used by rappers, poets and authors in Swedish and English, and the ways in which translators deal with these forms of language when translating texts. She is also a practising literary translator, and coordinator of New Swedish Fiction Book Club, a UCL-funded public engagement project.

Carrie Tarr is Emerita Professor of Film at Kingston University London. She has published widely on gender, sexuality, ethnicity and the transnational in relation to French and francophone cinema. Her publications include *Cinema and the Second Sex: Women's Filmmaking in France in the 1980s and 1990s* (with B. Rollet, 2001) and *Reframing Difference: Beur and Banlieue Filmmaking in France* (2005).

Timotheus Vermeulen is Assistant Professor in Cultural Theory at the Radboud University Nijmegen, Netherlands, where he also directs the Centre for New Aesthetics. He is founding editor of the leading academic arts and culture webzine *Notes on Metamodernism*. Timotheus has written on contemporary aesthetics, art, film and television for among others *The Journal of Aesthetics* and *Culture, Screen, Monu, Frieze* and various collections and catalogues. He is currently preparing two books on metamodernism as well as a monograph on suburban film.

Helen Wickstead is Archaeologist and Timelord of the Free University of Seething. She also lectures in Heritage at Kingston University, London. Her recent work explores the visual culture of Archaeology, examining aerial photography and archaeologies of drawing. Her excavation projects include Neolithic burial mounds on Cranborne Chase, the workspaces, archives and collections of H. C. Bowen F.S.A. (1919–2011) and lost gardens of the London suburbs.

Index